THE M. & E. HAND
ENGLISH LEGA

60p.

THE M. & E. HANDBOOK SERIES

ENGLISH LEGAL HISTORY

L. B. CURZON, B.Com., Dip.Ed.
Barrister-at-Law

MACDONALD & EVANS LTD
8 John Street, London W.C.1
1968

First published May 1968
Reprinted October 1970

©

MACDONALD AND EVANS LTD
1968

S.B.N.: 7121 0512 3

*Printed in Great Britain by Butler & Tanner, Ltd,
Frome and London*

GENERAL INTRODUCTION

The HANDBOOK Series of Study Notes

HANDBOOKS are a new form of printed study notes designed to help students to prepare and revise for professional and other examinations. The books are carefully programmed so as to be self-contained courses of tuition in the subjects they cover. For this purpose they comprise detailed notes, self-testing questions and hints on examination technique.

HANDBOOKS can be used on their own or in conjunction with recommended text-books. They are written by college lecturers, examiners, and others with wide experience of students' difficulties and requirements. At all stages the main objective of the authors has been to prepare students for the practical business of passing examinations.

P. W. D. REDMOND
General Editor

NOTICE TO LECTURERS

Many lecturers are now using **HANDBOOKS** as working texts to save time otherwise wasted by students in protracted note-taking. The purpose of the series is to meet practical teaching requirements as far as possible, and lecturers are cordially invited to forward comments or criticisms to the Publishers for consideration.

AUTHOR'S PREFACE

THE object of this **HANDBOOK** is the provision of a series of extended study notes and Progress Tests for those who are commencing a study of English Legal History, and for those who are revising for their first examination in that subject. In accordance with the requirements of the general syllabus for this subject, the study ranges from the Anglo-Saxon era to the end of the nineteenth century. Events after that period are covered in any text on the English legal system.

It was considered appropriate to include, as the first part of the text, a sketch of general and constitutional history. Legal history cannot be understood without some reference to its political background. Legal doctrines and institutions reflect the society of which they are a part. An understanding of the growth of land law requires some knowledge of the importance of land in a non-industrial society and of the political complexities of feudalism; the workings of the Court of Star Chamber become clearer in the context of Tudor absolutism; the climax of the struggle between equity and the common lawyers had political overtones which emerge from an awareness of Stuart pretensions. The deeper one's knowledge of general history, the surer will be one's understanding of the changing patterns of development in the law.

The **HANDBOOK** can be used as the basis of a planned course of study in the following manner:

(*a*) *The book should first be read swiftly.* Progress Tests may be omitted at this stage. The object of this initial reading is to obtain a general picture of legal history.

(*b*) *The detailed study of the text should follow.* The chapters must be read slowly, and with care. Facts and important dates must be memorised at this stage. A methodical reading of each chapter should be followed by working through the Progress Test.

(*c*) *The third reading* should be for purposes of a general revision.

(*d*) *The final reading* should concentrate on a revision of details. It is at this stage that memorisation of dates and other facts should be checked carefully. This should be followed by working through the three examination papers in Appendix IV, under examination conditions.

The student who wishes to read widely in this rich and fascinating subject is recommended to obtain a selection of the texts mentioned in the Bibliography at Appendix II.

I should like to thank the Senate of the University of London for their kind permission to reprint questions from past examination papers.

March, 1968   L. B. C.

CONTENTS

PART FIVE: THE DEVELOPMENT OF
CRIMINAL LAW AND TORT

PART ONE

A GENERAL AND CONSTITUTIONAL SURVEY

CHAPTER I

THE ANGLO-SAXON PERIOD

EARLY INVASIONS AND CONQUESTS

1. Pre-Roman Britain. Celtic culture was brought to Britain as a result of two Celtic invasions: the first, by the Goidels in the Bronze Age, the second by the Belgae and Brythons in the Iron Age. By the time of the Roman Conquests (*see* **2** below) Celtic customs and Celtic speech had spread throughout the country, with the exception of a few tribes in the north. The Celts left no identifiable legacy of either legal or political institutions.

2. Roman Conquest and Occupation. Britain was invaded in 55 B.C. and 54 B.C. by Julius Caesar and became a province of the Roman Empire, ruled by a governor. The Conquest was completed in 78 A.D. by Julius Agricola, and, for over three centuries, Roman rule was maintained. In 430, the withdrawal of Roman officials and soldiers began. A last, and vain, appeal to Rome for help was made by the *civitates* (organised communities) in Britain, following which Britain's connection with the Roman world gradually ended.

3. Roman Law. With the ending of the occupation Roman Law vanished from Britain. At a very much later date its influence was felt once more, in, for example, Canon Law, and in the studies undertaken by lawyers in the twelfth century. But the few principles of Roman Law later embodied in the English Law were in no sense derived from the period of Roman occupation.

4. Angles, Saxons and Jutes.

(*a*) The three great Teutonic tribes who conquered and settled in Britain in the late fifth and early sixth centuries were closely related.

3

(*i*) The Angles came from Angeln, in S. Denmark.

(*ii*) The Saxons inhabited the area between the Weser and the Elbe.

(*iii*) The Jutes inhabited Jutland.

(*b*) The conquest by the Teutonic tribes led to the immigration and settlement in this country of a new race of conquerors.

(*c*) The three tribes, who came to be known as the "English," conquered and held the central, south-east and east parts of Britain. Many of the Ancient Britons withdrew into Cumbria and Wales, and there followed a long period of struggle between the English and the Britons.

(*d*) The conquerors founded seven principal kingdoms—*the Heptarchy*: Kent (Jutes), Sussex, Wessex, Essex (the Saxons), Northumbria, E. Anglia, Mercia (the Angles). The struggle for supremacy was a prominent feature of the 7th–9th centuries.

5. Teutonic Institutions. The forms and institutions of Teutonic society were of particular importance in the early moulding of Anglo-Saxon society.

(*a*) From the Roman historian, Tacitus (*c*. 55–120), in his *Germania*, we have some information concerning these institutions.

(*i*) Teutonic society was tribal.

(*ii*) Groups of communities of particular tribes formed a *pagus* (= a district) and the *pagi* formed the collective *civitas* (= state).

(*iii*) Freemen, to whom the tribal lands were allocated. formed an important group, differentiated by their ranks, "Cultivators of the soil" formed a group below the freemen; they held their land under the freemen and possessed no political rights. Slaves formed the bottom layer of this social hierarchy.

(*iv*) Some of the tribes had kings.

(*v*) Primitive tribal justice was administered by an elected *princeps* and his assessors. Each *princeps* had his own body of *comites* (attendants) who had the duty of protecting his person.

(*b*) Within these tribal forms may be discerned the seeds of some of the political and legal institutions which were to grow and flourish in Anglo-Saxon and Norman Britain.

THE DANISH INVASION

6. Chronology of the Invasion and Conquest.

(a) In 835 the first recorded attack by Vikings, led by their sea-kings, took place. For thirty years these raids continued, and by 865 there was a large army of Danes in England. Northumbria, E. Anglia and Mercia were conquered by 866. Wessex alone remained unconquered, until 878, when Alfred, King of Wessex, had to flee to Athelney. In the same year Alfred defeated the Danes at Ethandun, and in 879, by the Treaty of Wedmore, Alfred ceded all England north of Watling Street (*i.e.* the Dover–Chester Roman road), and the Danish leader Guthrum abandoned Wessex.

(b) By the end of the ninth century the power of the Danish conquerors was concentrated in the kingdom of E. Anglia, York, and the area of the *Denalagu* (or Danelaw— see **7** below).

(c) The Midlands, E. Anglia and York were reconquered by the English between 911–954.

(d) A resumption of Danish attacks was recorded during the reign of the weak ruler Ethelred II (978–1016). *Danegeld* (a national tax) had to be raised and paid as the price of the cessation of these raids. (*Danegeld* was levied as an occasional war tax until 1162.) In 1013, Ethelred fled before the Danish leader, Swein. In 1017, Cnut, son of Swein, became king.

(e) The royal house of Alfred was restored after the death of Hardicanute in 1042.

7. Danelaw. Danelaw (*Danelagh, Denalagu*) was the name given to those parts of north and north-east England in which the customary law of the Danes prevailed. Its three chief divisions were: the kingdom of E. Anglia, the kingdom of Northumbria, and the five great Danish boroughs around Derby, Stamford, Lincoln, Nottingham and Leicester. Danish customary law differed significantly from that which was to be found elsewhere in England, *e.g.* land could be bought and sold freely.

THE PATTERN OF ANGLO-SAXON SOCIETY

8. General. The phrase "Anglo-Saxon" is usually applied to the general period of English history prior to the Norman Conquest. King Alfred used the title *Rex Anglorum Saxonum*, possibly following the union of the kingdoms in 886. In general, the period may be placed from *c.* 597 (the reputed date of the mission of St. Augustine, who converted Ethelbert to Christianity) to *c.* 1100.

9. Social Divisions. There were four clear class divisions within Anglo-Saxon society: the slaves; the partially freemen; the common freemen; the nobility. No special rules placed a man in any particular class and movement from one class to another was frequent.

(*a*) *The slaves* (*theowas*). Trade in slaves was common. The slave population, which possessed no rights, comprised:

(*i*) Those who had been reduced to slavery as a punishment, or by voluntary sale—children over 13 had the right to sell themselves into slavery.

(*ii*) Those who were the descendants of conquered Britons or of former freemen reduced to slavery.

(*b*) *The partially freemen, or serfs.* The serf possessed some of the rights of a freeman. Thus, he had a right of marriage and a small *wergild* (*see* XVII, **12**(*a*)). In general, the serf can be considered as a slave who had acquired some rights which he was able to protect.

(*c*) *The common freemen* (*ceorls*). The *ceorl* had complete personal freedom. His *wergild* was reckoned at about 200*s*. He was considered "foldworthy," *i.e.* entitled to fold his cattle on the common pasture—an important right. He was liable to attend the local court, to pay taxes and to perform military service. In early times his holding was a minimum of one hide (*see* **14** below), but this was later reduced. Ceorls who required protection placed themselves under a powerful lord. This process of *commendation* eventually became compulsory, and by post-Conquest times most of the ceorls had lost their personal freedom. The word "churl" survived in M.E. with pejorative overtones of "brutal" and "low."

(*d*) *The nobility* (*eorls*). The eorl was a person of noble birth, or one who had achieved his nobility by service alone.

The king's followers (who had developed from the Teutonic *comites*) became known as *gesiths* (companions) and were granted lands in return for their services. The king's personal attendants became known as *thegns* (servants). In time the possession of land tended to be equated with membership of the nobility, so that, for example, a freeman who owned five hides of land, and who performed duties at the king's court, became worthy of *thegn-right*. The *wergild* of a *gesith* was estimated at 1200*s*.

10. Territorial Divisions.

(*a*) *The township* (*tun*) *or vill*, represented the smallest territorial division. A *reeve* was the headman, and each *tun* possessed a *gemot* (assembly of the freemen).

(*b*) *The hundred* was a group of adjoining townships. It may have consisted of an area taxed at one hundred hides. Other explanations of the term "hundred" are that the unit may have consisted of one hundred households, or the area had to supply one hundred fighting men for the national defence. In the north and north-east the equivalent of the hundred was known by the Danish term *wapentake*. The chief officer of the hundred was the *hundredsealdor*, often nominated by a *thegn*. Each hundred had its *hundred-gemot*, which was held once a month.

NOTE: The term "hundred" survives today, *e.g.* in the Chiltern Hundreds—the old Buckinghamshire Hundreds of Stoke, Desborough and Burnham.

(*c*) *The shire* consisted of groups of hundreds or *wapentakes*. The *shire-moot* met regularly. In each shire the authorities had the responsibility of calling out the local militia (*fyrd*) at the king's command.

NOTE: *The borough* originated in the defended areas (*burh*) which were created at the time of the Danish invasions. They were defended by earthworks and walls and contained a market, dwelling places, and open fields used by the inhabitants among whom they were shared.

11. The king. Early and medieval society cannot be understood without reference to the powerful position occupied by the kings.

(*a*) The king (*cyning*) was the head of the nation. In early times he was its elected representative. Later he became not only the representative of his people, but their lord.

(*b*) Kingship became hereditary, but the *witan* (the assembly of the *witenagemot*—*see* **13** below) possessed the right to select a king from the males of the ruling house. Alfred, for example, was preferred to the sons of Ethelred.

(*c*) The king was commander-in-chief of the national armies and, in the final resort, was obliged to execute justice in his realm.

(*d*) He was entitled to maintenance for his person and his court in their progress throughout the country, and to chattels forfeited by outlaws (*see* XVII, **24**), to tolls, wrecks, and fines resulting from breaches of the law.

(*e*) He had very close links with the church, whose clergy had an important status in the kingdom. Thus, the king's coronation oath in the tenth century began with a promise to "this Christian people my subjects," and was taken in the name of the Holy Trinity.

12. The government officers.

(*a*) *The Ealdorman.* The administration of a shire was the responsibility of an ealdorman, usually a nobleman of high rank. His duties included maintenance of law and order in the shire, leading of the local militia, and presiding over local moots. In some shires he was entitled to the profits of manors.

(*b*) *The gerefa* (*king's reeve*). The king's reeve acted as deputy to the ealdorman.

(*c*) *The sheriff* (A.S. *scirgerefa*). The king's reeve became known as the *shire-reeve* and, as such, was nominated by the king, whose authority he represented. He was responsible for maintaining the peace, for the proclamation and enforcement of laws, for military levies, and for matters involving the royal revenue and the royal demesnes in his shire.

13. The witenagemot (= a meeting of the wise; A.S. *wite* = a wise man).
The composition of this national assembly depended on the will of the king. There was no right to sit in the assembly, and its aristocratic composition was, in no sense, representative of the nation. Its members were the king, his

thegns, bishops and abbots, ealdormen and principes. Thus, a witenagemot held at Luton, in 931, included archbishops, two Welsh princes, ealdormen, bishops, abbots and thegns—102 persons in all. It could give the king advice when he asked for it. Thus, Alfred consulted the assembly concerning the testamentary disposition of his inheritance. It did not meet at regular intervals. Its powers included:

(a) *The election of kings.* The sons of the last king could be passed over (*see* **11**(*b*) above). In 1066 the assembly passed over Edgar and chose Harold as king, thus by-passing the royal house.

(b) *The deposition of kings.* Thus, Alcred was deposed in 774.

(c) *The sanction and proclamation of laws or statements of ancient custom.*

(d) *The enactment of laws and the levying of taxes* (*in conjunction with the king*).

(e) *The raising of armed forces.*

(f) *The appointment and deposition* (*in conjunction with the king*) *of ealdormen and bishops.*

NOTE: In some cases the witenagemot acted as a supreme court of justice.

ANGLO-SAXON LAND HOLDING

14. General. During the Anglo-Saxon era land was cultivated by the inhabitants of the townships. Individual households often occupied *one hide* (= approx. 120 acres), and the basis of cultivation was the open field strip system, several strips being held by each family. Each *vill* possessed large areas of common pasture land and woodland. Transfer and inheritance of family holdings was based largely on family and village custom. Two important features of this system were:

(a) There was no general theory of tenure, *i.e.* rights in land.

(b) Property in land was classified as *bocland, folcland,* and *laenland* (*see* **15–17** below).

15. Bocland (bookland). This term was applied to land which was held by charter, handbook, or written title.

(a) Apparently such land was held only by the great noblemen and the churches, in the form of very large estates.

(b) The grant was made by the king, often with the consent of the witan.

(c) The grant carried an important privilege, by which the grantee was exempted from the incidents of service due from holders of *folcland* (*see* **16** below). But there was no freedom from the contributions known as *trimoda necessitas* (*i.e.* *fyrd-fare*, liability to military service; *brycg-bot*, contribution for the repair of bridges; *burh-bot*, contribution for the repair of fortresses).

(d) *Bocland* was devisable and alienable, and, unless entailed, did not carry family restrictions.

(e) Alienation of bocland rarely involved a written form of conveyance. It sufficed for the donor to hand to the donee the document containing the king's grant, or for the donor to endorse the document with a statement of transfer.

(f) The king and the witan heard litigation involving bocland. No oath against a charter of grant was admissible.

16. Folcland (folkland). There are very few references to folcland in Anglo-Saxon legal literature. Thus, in the will of one ealdorman Alfred, bocland is devised to his sons and daughter, but to an illegitimate son five hides of folcland are left, provided that the king grants his consent. It was generally land held by folk right, without written title, and according to customary law.

(a) The term did not refer to *ager publicus, i.e.* the so-called "land of the people."

(b) In early times the holder owed a *food-rent, i.e.* provisions to sustain the king and his retainers for one day. This was later commuted to a money rent, known as *ferm.*

(c) Folcland could not be alienated without the consent of those having some interest in it, nor, in principle, could it be bequeathed without appropriate consents. Inheritance depended on custom.

17. Laenland (loanland). Bocland and folcland could be leased to free cultivators. Land which was leased was known as laenland.

(*a*) The lease could be made without a written charter.

(*b*) Laenland often involved incidents of tenure, *e.g.* the tenants might be obliged to perform military service.

(*c*) Laenland was inheritable, but the duration seems to have been limited to three lives, *i.e.* three holders in succession (an interesting echo of an enactment by Justinian which had limited leases of church lands to three lives—*Nov. 7, iii*).

NOTE: *Anglo-Saxon feudalism.* Some of the distinctive features of later feudalism (*see* II, 5–7) may be seen in embryo in the Anglo-Saxon period. The lands of the thegns and other large landowners were often cultivated by servile labour, or by freemen who might have held part of their land in return for service. The principle of commendation to a lord (*see* 9(*c*) above); the compulsion on lordless men to find a lord (Laws of Athelstan (925–940)); the social hierarchy (*see* **9** above) in which the concept of service was all-important; the size of the large estates as compared with the shrinking size of the freemen's holdings; the growth of the manorial courts; oaths of fealty taken by a man to his lord—here are the patterns of economic feudalism, and, to a lesser extent, of political feudalism.

ANGLO-SAXON LAWS AND COURTS

18. General principles. In the body of information concerning Anglo-Saxon laws which has come down to us, particularly in the form of *dooms* (*see* **25** below), we may discern certain principles. It should be emphasised, however, that the Anglo-Saxon lawmakers were not motivated by a desire to establish a systematic and comprehensive code of laws, nor were they influenced by any coherent general theory of law. The law was made up in large part of customary rules and dooms, local rather than national in their operation, and based very often on oral tradition. Among the principles and practices can be noted:

(*a*) A purposeful transition from self-aid (*e.g.* the blood feud, *see* XVII, **11**) to public aid (*e.g.* the blood fine).

(*b*) Pre-determined penalties for many offences.

(*c*) The preservation of public order and peace (*see* king's peace, **20** below, and XVII, **14**).

(*d*) The concept of pledges, by which an individual was to answer personally in any litigation, or was to have a representative who was obliged to make answer for him (*see* 22(*d*) below).

(*e*) The growing opposition between folk-right and privilege. Folkright has been explained as those rules, often tribal in origin, formulated or not, which expressed the "judicial consciousness" of the people. The power of the king, however, often manifested itself in special grants or laws which tended to weaken, or destroy, folk-right. Thus, the privileged system of land tenure known as bocland (*see* **15** above) helped to abolish the rules concerning the succession of kinsmen, which derived from folk-right.

19. Penal law. That part of Anglo-Saxon law which was concerned with "wrongs" was characterised by certain elements: the existence of the blood feud; a tariff of compensation; the punishment of wrongs to the person and dignity of the king, which were transformed later into *Pleas of the crown*. These topics are touched on below and further details are given at XVII, **10–14.**

(*a*) *The blood feud*. In essence this was controlled vengeance, allowing the avenging of a wrong upon the wrongdoer.

(*b*) *The tariff of compensation*. A wrongdoer could atone for his crime by a money payment to the relatives of the person he had injured.

(*c*) *Pleas of the crown*. Certain serious offences were heard by the king and his court. These offences were considered to harm, in some way, the dignity of the royal person, or the good order of his realm.

20. The concept of the king's peace. In general, every freeman "had his peace," and the king's peace was attached to his royal household and to the great roads. Acts of violence at these places were breaches of that peace and were punished. The importance of this rudimentary concept in the development and maintenance of public order is obvious. For details, *see* XVII, **14.**

21. The courts. These courts are considered in detail at XII, **1–10.**

(*a*) *The Hundred Court. See* **10**(*b*) above. This court sat in early times at least once a month, and was presided over by the hundred-man, or sheriff, or his deputy. Originally judgment was passed by all the freemen in the hundred. Jurisdiction was criminal and civil.

(b) *The Shire Court. See* **10**(c) above. The shire court, or shire moot (*scir-gemot*) was convened twice a year, or more, by the sheriff. Its jurisdiction was wide, but was not available unless the hundred court had denied justice to the party seeking it. An appeal could be made to the king only where justice had been denied in the shire court.

22. Procedure and penalties. In general, procedure involved primitive processes such as *compurgation* and *ordeal*. These are noted here, and are considered in detail at VI, **9**, and XVII, **15–18**.

(a) *Compurgation.* An accused person could make a sworn denial of the accusation and could bring forward twelve relatives or close neighbours who swore on oath to the validity of his statement.

(b) *The Ordeal.* This was compulsory where a criminal had been taken in the act, or where an accused person was guilty of a previous perjury, or was not a freeman, or was unable to produce the requisite compurgators. The ordeal was considered as God's judgment, and was supervised by a priest.

(c) *Penalties.* These were varied and often disproportionately severe. Exile, outlawry, money compensation, fines, confiscation of property, mutilation and death were the main penalties. Imprisonment was rare.

(d) *Frankpledge. See* **18**(d) above. The kindred (*i.e.* agnatic and cognatic relatives) of the accused had, in early times, a collective responsibility for ensuring his attendance to answer the allegation. This responsibility passed later to the *tithing*, based on the hundred. By the time of the Conquest there had appeared the frankpledge. A freeman, aged twelve or above, had to enter an association of ten men headed by a senior man (*borhs-ealdor*). The association acted collectively as bail for any one of its members who was obliged to answer an accusation before a court. Where that person was found guilty and escaped, the members of the *friborh* (the frankpledge) had to establish their non-complicity in his escape, failing which they had to pay a monetary penalty.

SOURCES OF ANGLO-SAXON LAW

23. General. The main sources of our information concerning Anglo-Saxon law are ecclesiastical documents, wills, charters (*diplomata*) concerning grants of land, and the dooms of the Anglo-Saxon kings. Much of this material is in a fragmentary form.

24. Diplomata. These charters deal with grants of land by landowners, but it is believed that many may have been forged by the Norman Church so as to lend substance to false claims to land. Because land—its holdings, its incidents and its value—was so important in Anglo-Saxon society, documents concerning these grants are of much significance.

25. The dooms. *See* V, **9.** Dooms were royal proclamations of parts of the existing law, and announcements of new law. The dooms of the early Saxon kings were usually amendments of existing customs. At a later date (*e.g.* under Alfred and Cnut) the dooms take on the character of codes of law.

(*a*) The earliest dooms are those of Ethelbert, King of Kent (*c.* 600).

(*b*) Later collections of dooms were made by the Kentish rulers Hlothar and Eadric (*c.* 680) and Wihtraed (*c.* 700).

(*c*) Dooms of the Wessex kings include those of Ine (*c.* 690) and the celebrated *Laws of Alfred*. Alfred collected the laws of earlier kings and selected those which seemed to him to be particularly useful: "I then, Aelfred, King of the West Saxons, to all my Wise Men these showed, and they then quoth that to them it seemed good all to hold."

(*d*) The last collection is the great dooms of Cnut (*c.* 1029).

(*e*) The dooms are concerned largely with public law and contain, for example, laws dealing with the administration of justice, revenue, tariffs of fines, procedures for proof, details of punishments and compensation, and preservation of the peace.

PROGRESS TEST 1

1. What was meant by (*a*) *dangeld*, (*b*) *danelaw*? **(6, 7)**
2. How were the vills and shires organised in Anglo-Saxon times? **(10)**

3. What were the functions of (a) the *ealdorman*, (b) the *sheriff*, (c) the *witan*?   **(12, 13)**

4. Explain the meaning of (a) *bocland*, (b) *folcland*.   **(15, 16)**

5. What was *laenland*?   **(17)**

6. What was meant by "the king's peace"?   **(20)**

7. What was (a) the hundred court, (b) the shire court?   **(21)**

8. What was the meaning of *frankpledge*?   **(22)**

9. Enumerate the main sources of our knowledge of Anglo-Saxon law.   **(23)**

CHAPTER II

THE PERIOD FROM THE NORMAN CONQUEST TO THE END OF THE HOUSE OF PLANTAGENET

THE NORMANS AND THE CONQUEST

1. General political background. Following the death of Edward the Confessor in 1066, the witan gave its approval to Edward's recommendation of his brother-in-law, Earl Harold, as his successor. William, Duke of Normandy, laid claim to the throne, partly on the basis of an alleged promise by Harold to recognise his claim. With the support of the Papacy, William invaded England and, after defeating Harold at Hastings, he was crowned on Christmas Day, 1066, as "king of the English." The Conquest is considered to be one of the most decisive events in English history.

NOTE: The Normans were Northmen (and, therefore, akin to the Anglo-Saxons and Danes) who had lived in France for almost one and a half centuries, acquiring during that time their own distinctive identity.

2. Effects of the Conquest on the development of our law.

(*a*) William confirmed the English laws. (It was the usual practice in the Middle Ages for a conquered nation to keep its own legal system.) "This I will and order that all shall have and hold the law of King Edward as to lands and all other things with these additions which I have established for the good of the English people."

(*b*) William established a feudal system in England (*see* **7** below) which had a profound effect on land tenure and land law. Land was considered henceforth as being held of the king.

(*c*) A system of baronial courts was set up (*see* XII, **13–14**).

(*d*) Separate ecclesiastical courts were set up (*see* **3** below, and XII, **23–24**).

(e) The systematisation of those English customs upon which much of the existing law was built commenced. Upon this systematisation was to be constructed the massive fabric of the common law.

(f) The framework of strong centralised government, and the development of national unity, hastened the growth of a national system of law.

(g) The place of royal power in the legal system was emphasised.

3. Church and state. In Normandy there existed ecclesiastical courts which administered ecclesiastical law in matters such as marriage, legitimation, and the general affairs of the clergy. In Anglo-Saxon England, the church was bound by allegiance to Rome, but there existed no separate ecclesiastical jurisdiction. Thus, for example, the witenagemot included bishops, who sat also in the shire courts. An important effect of the Conquest was the establishment of separate ecclesiastical and non-ecclesiastical jurisdiction. As a result, a system of ecclesiastical courts was created. Bishops were to hear civil and criminal cases which involved church matters, not in the shire courts, but in their own ecclesiastical courts in which canon law, and not English law based on custom, was to be dominant. Sheriffs were not to interfere in "spiritual causes." This duality of jurisdiction was to have important consequences in the reign of Henry II (*see* **13** below). It should be noted that the papal approval of William's invasion had been conditional, in part, on his promising to set up separate ecclesiastical courts.

4. The courts.

(a) The Normans introduced few changes in the functions and procedures of the shire and hundred courts. These changes included:

(i) The introduction of proof by battle (*see* VI, **10**).

(ii) The introduction of the feudal, or baronial court, held by a lord for his vassals and his freehold tenants. *See* XII, **13–14**.

(b) At the end of the Conqueror's reign the courts were organised as follows:

(i) The *Curia Regis* (*see* XIII) was the supreme court,

combining the functions of a witenagemot and a king's advisory council.

(*ii*) The ecclesiastical courts, which had jurisdiction in spiritual causes.

(*iii*) Shire, hundred and borough courts, and manorial courts baron.

FEUDALISM

5. The concept of feudalism. (*Feodum* = a fief). In essence, feudalism was an organisation of society characterised by the following:

(*a*) A social hierarchy, dominated by a chief, or king, and great tenants-in-chief who held their lands from him.

(*b*) A relationship between the tenants-in-chief, or lords, and those who, in turn, held lands from them, based on mutual promises of protection and military service.

(*c*) Tenure of land was accompanied by private rights of jurisdiction exercised by the lord over those who held land from him.

6. Feudalism in France.

(*a*) The Normans had established a feudal system based on commendation of a vassal to his lord (*see* I, **9**(*c*)) and on grants of land by the ruler to his tenants-in-chief. A system of *sub-infeudation* had grown up, which may be illustrated thus:

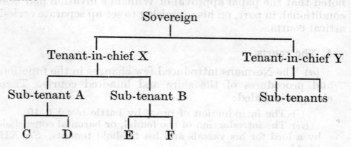

A and B owed fealty directly to X; C and D owed allegiance to A; E and F to B. This fealty was owed to the immediate lord, not to the sovereign.

(*b*) Local jurisdiction was widely prevalent.

(*c*) Most of the public law was based on feudal doctrine.

7. Feudalism in Norman England. The economic and social basis of feudal society had been maturing in Anglo-Saxon England (*see* Note to I, **17**); the political and legal superstructure was to be erected by the Conqueror and his successors.

(*a*) William confiscated the former royal lands and the lands of those who had fought against him. Some English landowners were allowed to keep their lands subject to royal regrant. Risings against William resulted in a further confiscation of lands. Eventually he possessed the ownership of all the land in the kingdom.

(*b*) Lands were granted by William to his noblemen and were held on the basis of feudal tenure, involving allegiance and homage.

(*c*) These lands were often scattered throughout England in order that concentrations of military power might be avoided.

(*d*) All those who held land were required to swear fealty to the king. *The Salisbury Oath*, 1086, exacted from all those who held land, and not merely from the king's tenants-in-chief, a promise that they "would be faithful to him against all other men." The private wars and anarchy inherent in a system based on sub-infeudation were thus largely prevented.

(*e*) Tenants-in-chief made grants of land in accordance with feudal tenure and involving incidents of service (*see* XXIII, **11**) in return for promises of protection and assistance.

(*f*) The grants of land from the king were accompanied in some cases by a partial immunity of those lands from the general jurisdiction of the king. This immunity manifested itself in the grant of a right to hold private courts and to keep some of the fines imposed in those courts.

Norman feudalism and its system of land tenure provided a basis for English law during the following centuries. The vestiges of this system are with us in the twentieth century.

DOMESDAY BOOK

8. Its purpose and importance. In the feudal economy land was the main source of wealth. Following the Conquest it became essential for William to discover the extent of his land holdings and, in particular, his fiscal rights. A Christmas Assembly in 1085 decided on a complete survey and description, from which could be established the land rights of the crown. Proceeds of crown lands and the national tax for purposes of *geld* (a war tax originating in *danegeld*) could also be determined. The importance of Domesday Book lies in:

(*a*) *Its description of society.* Land holdings, records of markets, military service, customs, make it a unique document in social and legal history.

(*b*) *Its enumeration of the various classes in society:* tenants-in-chief; sub-tenants; freeholders; villeins; serfs; and its delineation of the feudal relationships of that era.

(*c*) *Its authoritative nature.* No appeal was allowed against its contents—perhaps the name *Domesday* is derived from this fact.

9. Its compilation. Commissioners (barons, justices, *legati*) were sent into every county, and public enquiries were held based on the hundreds. The details of the return for each hundred were sworn to by 12 local jurors, of whom half were Norman, half English.

(*a*) The record of the survey sets out: the amount of arable land; the number of plough-teams; river-meadows, pastures, forests and fisheries; watermills; the number of peasants in particular groups; the past and present value of the estates.

(*b*) The annual value of the land surveyed is estimated: as it was at the time of Edward's death; at the time the new owners received their grants; at the time the survey was made. There is also an estimate of the land's potential value.

(*c*) In each county the list was headed by the king's holdings. Then followed the holdings of the church, of lay tenants-in-chief, the king's servants, and the English thegns.

(*d*) The survey omits information concerning Northumberland, Westmorland, Cumberland, Durham, and part of Lancashire.

(*e*) The findings of the commissioners were sent to the king's court at Winchester. Here the findings were checked by other commissioners, who compiled the *Liber Wintoniae* from which Domesday Book was written.

(*f*) Domesday Book consisted of two volumes: the first contained a survey of thirty-two counties; the second covered Norfolk, Suffolk and Essex.

(*g*) The survey, made in one year, contains many errors and duplications.

10. The statistics of Domesday Book. An interesting picture of eleventh century England emerges.

(*a*) Nearly 290,000 names are recorded in a population estimated at $1\frac{3}{4}$ millions. Of that number about 9000 had settled in England following the Conquest—but that group controlled almost 80 per cent of the land.

(*b*) The survey classified those who cultivated the soil into various groups, approximately thus: *freemen*, 33,000; *villeins*, 106,000; *bordars* and *cotters*, 89,000; *slaves*, 25,000.

(*i*) *The slaves*, mainly house-servants and ploughmen. Their numbers were decreasing rapidly, and by the beginning of the thirteenth century they had almost disappeared.

(*ii*) *The bordars and cotters* were peasants who held a cottage and a few acres, usually about five, of arable land, in return for customary labour servies. *Bordarii* differed from *cottarii* in the extent of their holdings, the latter holdings being based on mere cottages and crofts.

(*iii*) *The villeins*, the most numerous element in the peasantry, performed work services for their lords. They were free by birth, but could not freely dispose of their land. The legal relationships of the villein and his lord were controlled largely on the basis of custom. Some of the villein's dues and services could be commuted to rent, but his personal freedom could be gained in only a few cases, *e.g.* by manumission or by his entering the church. The status of villeinage attached to those born from villein parents, or, in the case of a mixed marriage, according to the condition (free or villein) of the tenement in which the child was born. It could also be proved in the courts by an examination of the services performed, *e.g.* weekly work on the lord's land.

DEVELOPMENT OF THE LAW UNDER HENRY I AND HENRY II

11. General. William the Conqueror was succeeded by his second son, William II (1087–1100), whose reign was notorious for oppressive rule and an extortionate taxation system administered by the Justiciar, Ralph Flambard. Following the death of William II, Henry I, the Conqueror's third son, was crowned, to be followed by Stephen (1135–1154), under whom the country drifted into anarchy and bloodshed. His successor, Henry II, a king of intense reforming energy, established himself as a great administrator and legislator.

12. Henry I (1100–1135).

(a) On his accession Henry issued a *Charter of Liberties*. Some of its important provisions promised: a relaxation of illegal exactions; fines to be assessed according to the type of offence; knights holding by military service (*see* XXIII, **9**) to have their lands free from *geld*; to the nation, a grant of the law of Edward the Confessor, together with those alterations made by William I.

(b) His governmental and legal administration was based on:

(i) *The Great Council* (*Magnum Concilium*)—a court of the king's tenants-in-chief, his archbishops and bishops.

(ii) *The King's Court*—a committee drawn from the Great Council, headed by the king, or his justiciar.

(iii) *The Court of the Exchequer*—a court which managed the financial affairs of the government.

(c) He consolidated the office of justiciar (*justiciarius* = a judge). Roger, Bishop of Salisbury, was an outstanding Chief Justiciar. Henry sent his justices on circuit to hear pleas of the crown (*i.e.* accusations of the more serious crimes).

(d) His disputes with the church, in the person of Archbishop Anselm, which resulted in a compromise by which Henry retained his claim to the oath of fealty and homage from new prelates, was of great significance in the development of theories concerned with the nature of kingship and the authority of law.

13. Henry II (1154–1189). Under this great administrator, the first Plantagenet, the power of the crown increased rapidly and decisively, the powers of the clergy and the feudal barons were curtailed, and a number of administrative reforms resulted in a centralised and efficient administration. As a result of deliberate policy, the power and importance of local tribunals declined and the common law developed. It was during this reign that one of the first books of English law, known as *Glanvill*, was written (*see* V, **19**).

(*a*) The important *Constitutions of Clarendon*, 1164, resulted from conflict between Henry and Beckett, Archbishop of Canterbury, who had been Chancellor and Chief Clerk of the *Curia Regis*. Henry insisted that all clergy charged with criminal offences should be tried, not in the bishops' courts, but in the king's courts. Beckett opposed this, but signed the Constitutions, rejecting them later. There were sixteen constitutions, the most important of which were:

(*i*) Clerks (*i.e.* clergy) accused of crime were to be summoned initially before the king's justices who would decide whether or not they were entitled to be tried in a spiritual court.

(*ii*) Laymen could be tried in the bishops' courts only if accused by lawful accusers and witnesses.

(*iii*) The excommunication of a tenant-in-chief of the king required royal consent.

(*iv*) Appeals were to be made to the bishop, and from him to the archbishop. In the last resort appeal could be made to the king, but there was to be no appeal to the pope without the king's assent.

(*b*) Henry gave royal protection to those whose *seisin* of freeholds (*i.e.* their possession, *see* XXIV, **1**) had been disturbed. They were able to seek remedies in the king's courts.

(*c*) The writ system (*see* VI, **2**) developed considerably during his reign.

(*d*) A number of important assizes (*see* Note below) were issued:

(*i*) *The Assize of Clarendon*, 1166, established trial by grand jury. Hundred-juries were to declare their opinions on matters arising out of accusations of crime.

(*ii*) *The Assize of Northampton*, 1176, divided the country into six circuits, and Justices in Eyre (*see* XIII, **21**) travelled each circuit. Forgery and arson were added to the list of offences to be dealt with by the king's justices. Severe punishments, *e.g.* mutilation and exile were decreed for some convicted criminals.

(*iii*) *The Assize of Arms*, 1181, reorganised the national *fyrd* (militia) by re-defining the non-feudal military service due to the king. As such, it acted as a counter-balance to the barons' growing feudal power. Scales of armour and weapons were laid down, and persons were sworn to bear arms in the service of the crown when required.

(*iv*) *The Assize of Woodstock*, 1184, defined, for the first time, the crown's forest rights.

NOTE: The term "assize" bears several meanings in legal history. It may mean: a *session* of a court or council; an *enactment* of such a body; the *procedure* made available by that enactment; the *court* which hears cases involving that procedure.

JOHN AND MAGNA CARTA

14. The political background. Henry II was succeeded by his son, Richard I (1189–1199) who spent most of his reign abroad in the Crusades. During his absences the realm was administered by four successive justiciars. He was succeeded by John (1199–1216), fourth son of Henry II. Mounting dissatisfaction with the tyranny of this capricious and violent monarch was brought to a peak by his excommunication and subsequent humiliation, the loss of Normandy, and the burden of taxation which affected all sections of his subjects. In 1213 the barons met and accepted the Coronation Charter of Henry I (*see* **12** above) as a basis for the demands they were to make upon John. In 1214 they met at Bury St. Edmunds and swore to compel John to grant a charter of rights, or, if he refused, to fight against him. John delayed for three months, and in 1215 was obliged by the barons assembled at Runnymede to sign the great Charter.

15. The Charter. *The Great Charter of Liberties* is dated June 15th, 1215. It is a statement, in solemn form, of those concessions made by John to the English church and to all the freemen in his kingdom. It contains a preamble and 63 clauses. The more important provisions may be grouped thus:

(*a*) *Ecclesiastical.* The church was declared free, and the election of bishops was to be free.

(b) *Feudal obligations*. Abuses concerning wardship, reliefs, marriages (*see* XXIII, **13, 16, 17**) were to end. The lands of convicted felons were to be held by the crown for only one year and a day. Aids could be collected only with the consent of the council, except in the case of ransoming the king's body, or, in the case of a mesne lord, knighting his eldest son, or marrying his eldest daughter (*see* XXIII, **15**).

(c) *Cities and boroughs*. London and other cities, boroughs, towns and ports were to have their ancient liberties and free customs. In the towns and elsewhere in the realm there was to be one standard of weights and measures.

(d) *Purveyance and royal exactions*. Immediate payment was to be made by a royal bailiff who took a man's corn or chattels. Horses and carriages of freemen were not to be taken by the king's sheriffs without the owners' consent. Land was not to be seized for debts due to the crown if the debtor's chattels sufficed.

(e) *Law and justice*. The Court of Common Pleas (*see* XIII, **11**) was to be held in one place and was not to follow the king's court. Judges were to go on circuit. Sheriffs, constables and coroners were forbidden to hold pleas of the crown. Anyone could leave the realm and return at his will, unless in time of war. A fundamental principle was enunciated: "To none will we sell, to none will we deny or delay right or justice."

(f) *Constitutional principles*. No freeman was to be taken, or imprisoned, or disseised, or outlawed, or exiled. . . . "nor will we go upon him, nor will we send upon him, unless by the lawful judgment of his peers or by the law of the land."

(g) *Enforcement of the Charter*. The barons were to elect a group of 25 representatives, charged to ensure that the provisions of the Charter were observed. A violation was to result in a demand for immediate redress and, should this not follow within 40 days, the barons and commonalty of the realm were to distrain and distress the king "in all possible ways."

16. Importance of the Charter.

(a) It is the first statement in detail of feudal law, and one of the first specific agreements between a king and his barons.

(b) It embodied a precise renunciation by the crown of several unlawful actions.

(c) It remained for several centuries as a basic statement of restrictions upon the power of the crown.

(d) While it may be mere hyperbole to suggest that "all legal history since Magna Carta is but the story of an extension of its principles," the spirit of its main constitutional principles remained as a background to much subsequent legal development.

(e) The Charter was subsequently confirmed 37 times, from the reigns of Henry III to Henry VI. It may be that these confirmations had as their objective not so much a recognition and continuation of the precise provisions of the Charter, as a pledge by the king that, to some extent, he would act in accordance with the law.

FROM HENRY III TO THE END OF RICHARD II's REIGN

17. Henry III (1216–1272). During Henry's reign, which was dominated by a rebellion of the barons—essentially a continuation of the struggles in John's reign—the common law took further shape. Judge-made law, in the form of judicial declarations concerning the law, grew swiftly. In particular, the power and importance of the king's court increased during this period. A great legal treatise, known as *Bracton*, appeared at this time (*see* V, **21**); it attempted to expound the general principles of the existing law. The following events in Henry's reign were of particular legal significance:

(a) *Provisions of Oxford,* 1258. One of the causes of baronial discontent was the flood of new writs available for suitors and issued from the *Cursitor Office.* (Clerks who issued writs were known as *cursitors.*) This invention of new writs allowed the king's court to widen its jurisdiction considerably. The barons feared this growth of royal power and it was provided that, henceforth, the chancellor would seal no writ, which was not an existing writ (known as a writ "of course"), except with the sanction of the king and council. Henry assented unwillingly to this and to the other provisions of Oxford.

(b) *Development of Parliament.* The famous Parliament of

1265 was summoned by a leading noble of the realm, Simon de Montfort. It included barons, knights from the counties, clergy, and—for the first time in national councils—representatives from the main cities and boroughs. This meeting is of great significance in the history of constitutional development.

(c) *Division of the Curia Regis.* The judicial functions of the *Curia* (*see* XIII, 6) were divided in the following manner by the end of Henry's reign:

(i) Fiscal affairs and disputes were dealt with by the *Exchequer.*

(ii) Civil disputes were heard by the *Court of Common Pleas.*

(iii) Other matters were dealt with by the *Court of King's Bench.*

NOTE: These courts are considered at XIII.

18. Edward I—"the English Justinian." The reign of Edward (1272–1307) saw an extraordinary proliferation of legislation. It was only in the nineteenth century that a similar expansion of law again took place. During this reign statute law came into its own. As a result of the growth of statute law, the growth of common law, which was nurtured by judicial decisions, was relatively slow. This era produced two celebrated law textbooks, *Fleta* and *Britton* (*see* V, **22**) and the *Year Books* (*see* V, **17**(*a*)).

(a) *The courts in the time of Edward I.*

(i) Local courts remained in existence, but their powers had declined.

(ii) Manorial courts continued to operate.

(iii) The King's Court had split into Exchequer, Common Pleas and King's Bench.

(iv) Justices in Eyre (*see* XIII, **21**), acted under commission from the king and travelled through the counties. As well as the Commission for a General Eyre, three other commissions were issued: the *Commission of Assize*, the *Commission of Oyer and Terminer*, and the *Commission of Gaol Delivery* (*see* XIII, **28**).

(b) *Legislation of Edward I.* The following matters are of importance:

(i) *Statute of Westminster*, 1275. This was a miscellaneous group of enactments including jury trial, the committing to a *prison forte et dure* of those who refused jury trial (*see* XVI, 32(*b*)), and the fixing of "legal memory," in a claim by writ of right, at 1189.

(*ii*) *Coroners Act,* 1276. Coroners (first appointed *c*. 1194) were authorised to keep records concerning treasure trove and sudden death. *See* XVI, 27–28.

(*iii*) *Statute of Gloucester,* 1278. Amendments were made to the law of land, concerning waste and dower. Actions for trespass were to be heard in the king's courts only if the goods involved had a value of more than 40 shillings.

(*iv*) *Statute of Mortmain,* 1279. The king's licence became necessary for the conveyancing of land to churches, monasteries and corporate bodies.

(*v*) *Statute of Westminster II,* 1285. In 50 Chapters, this statute dealt with land law, writs, bills of exceptions, and matters arising from *nisi prius* (*see* XIII, 27). C.1 (*De donis conditionalibus*) enacted that, on failure of a donee's heirs, the land was to revert to the donor, notwithstanding an intervening alienation. C.24 (*In consimili casu*) allowed the clerks in chancery to issue writs if the facts of the case resembled those which would justify the issue of an existing writ (*see* VI, 4(*c*)). C.30 (*Nisi prius*) extended the commissions of assize to hear civil pleas pending in King's Bench or Common Pleas. C.31 allowed a court to enrol an exception which it had overruled, so that it might be considered by a higher court.

(*vi*) *Statute of Winchester,* 1285. Freemen between 15–60 were to possess armour, according to their wealth, in order to defend the peace. The armour would be inspected twice a year by elected constables in every hundred. A regular watch and ward was introduced. (This statute remained in force until 1827.)

(*vii*) *Statute of Merchants,* 1285. A system of recording debts was introduced.

(*viii*) *Statute of Westminster III,* 1290. This statute, known as *Quia Emptores,* designed to prevent sub-infeudation, is considered at XXIII, 7.

19. Edward II (1307–1327). Edward I was succeeded by his son, Edward II. His reign included relatively few outstanding enactments concerning legal matters, with the exception of the *Statute of York,* 1322, which included the significant clause that, in future, matters concerning the estate of the king and the country were to be determined by the king in Parliament, with the assent of prelates, earls, barons, and "the commonalty of the realm as has been hitherto accustomed."

20. Edward III (1327–1377). Edward III's reign witnessed momentous social and economic changes, resulting from the Black Death, 1348–49. The manorial system, based on a free supply of labour, was disorganised. *The Statute of Labourers* attempted to control the wages paid to labourers. In 1351 the important *Statute of Treasons* defined the types of crime which were to constitute high treason (*see* XVIII, **19**).

21. Richard II (1377–1399).

(*a*) The social position of the villeins had deteriorated and, under the influence of doctrines of liberty and equality taught by the Lollards, a great revolt took place in 1381. The peasants' demands included the abolition of villeinage and free access to all markets and fairs. The revolt was put down with severity, but villein service ceased to be enforced with rigidity from that time, and eventually it died out.

(*b*) The foundations of constitutional law were further strengthened by the Commons' successful demand that money should not be levied, and no laws should be passed, without their consent, and that they should have the right to impeach ministers of the crown for misconduct, and the right to examine public accounts.

(*c*) *The Statute (Third) of Praemunire*, 1393, enacted that no bulls or excommunications were to enter the realm, nor were suits of patronage to go to Rome. A writ of *praemunire* began with the words "*Praemunire facias . . .*" (= that you cause to be forewarned . . .).

NOTE: *Praemunire*. This term was afterwards applied to other laws which created offences involving an issue of the writ. The writ was used very rarely indeed: in the time of Charles II it was used against Quakers who would not swear allegiance to the Crown—see *R. v. Crook* (1662) 6 St. Tr. 201. Praemunire offences included:

(*i*) In the time of Henry VIII, refusal of a dean and chapter to elect a royal nominee as bishop.

(*ii*) Under *Habeas Corpus Act*, 1679, the unlawful sending of a prisoner beyond the realm so as to place him outside the protection of that Act.

(*iii*) Under the *Royal Marriages Act*, 1772, to assist at a marriage forbidden by that Act.

Praemunire was punished by imprisonment for life and forfeiture of all property.

PROGRESS TEST 2

1. What were the general effects of the Conquest upon the development of English law? (2)

2. What were the characteristics of feudalism? (5)

3. Explain the term *sub-infeudation*. (6)

4. What was the purpose of Domesday Book? How was it compiled? (8, 9)

5. Outline the *Constitutions of Clarendon,* 1164. (13)

6. What were the *Assizes of Clarendon and Northampton*? (13)

7. Outline the important provisions of *Magna Carta*. (15)

8. What was the importance of *Magna Carta*? (16)

9. Explain the *Provisions of Oxford,* 1258. (17)

10. Outline the structure of the courts in the reign of Edward I. (18)

11. Enumerate some of the important legislation of Edward I. (18)

12. What was meant by *praemunire*? (21)

CHAPTER III

THE PERIOD FROM HENRY IV TO THE END OF THE PROTECTORATE

THE LANCASTRIAN AND YORKIST KINGS

1. Henry IV (1399–1413). As a result of the tyranny of Richard II, Parliament compelled him to resign the crown. The Duke of Lancaster was declared king, and he ruled as Henry IV. His reign was dominated by foreign and domestic wars—war with Scotland, insurrection in the north and west, a Welsh uprising led by Owen Glendower, and a rebellion of the earls. The following events in his reign are of interest:

(*a*) The important constitutional right of succession to the crown was reconsidered, and in 1406 a final arrangement settled the crown upon Henry and the heirs of his body.

(*b*) In 1407 there was established the authority for the parliamentary principle that a money grant must originate in the Commons, and that only when both houses were agreed should the fact be reported to the Speaker.

(*c*) In 1401 a statute, *De heretico comburendo*, forbade preaching without a licence from a bishop, and ordered public burning for a heretic who had relapsed into his heresy.

(*d*) In 1403 Henry formally recognised the privilege of members of Parliament to freedom from arrest during a session of Parliament.

2. Henry V (1413–1422). Henry's short reign saw the invasion of France and the conquest of Normandy. His chief aims were to recover the lost prestige of England in Europe and to secure peace at home. A lesser problem involved the growing schism within the English church, which resulted in a Lollard revolt in 1414. Two events of significance in the development of constitutional law were:

(*a*) In 1413 it was enacted that those who were to be elected to parliament must be actually resident within the county they represented.

(b) In 1414, the Commons presented a petition to the king (the first petition to be presented in the English language) in which they reminded him that no statute or law should be made without their assent. Henry accepted this, but added the significant clause: *"Savyng alwey to our liege lord his real prerogatif, to graunte and denye what him lust of their petitions and askynges aforesaid."*

3. Henry VI (1422–1461).

Henry was a feeble monarch and eventually became insane. Domestic strife came to a head in Cade's rebellion, 1450, a rising of the men of Kent, followed by the Wars of the Roses. Abroad, all of France, save Calais, was lost. The following enactments are of interest:

(a) In 1430 the qualification of county electors was restricted to freeholders who had lands to the value of 40s. per year. The sheriff was empowered to ascertain on oath from electors the value of their property. This, in effect, disenfranchised leaseholders and many small freeholders.

(b) In 1445 it was enacted that county representatives should be "notable knights . . . or otherwise notable esquires, gentlemen born, of the same counties as shall be able to be knights; and no man to be such knight which standeth in the degree of vadlet [*i.e.* yeoman] or under."

4. Edward IV (1461–1483).

The Lancastrians were defeated by Edward at Towton in 1461, following which he was crowned king. The alleged usurpation of the previous years was declared ended. His government was firm, and, in several ways seemed to anticipate Tudor absolutism (*see* 6–8 below). He had little need of parliaments which, during his reign, met on only seven occasions. The Court of Chancery (*see* IX, 9–13) increased in importance as a result of the growth in the number of petitions presented to the king. It was during this reign that *benevolences* made their first appearance.

(a) The benevolence was, in fact, a forced loan, which was not repayable. Its use led to much hostility from Parliament.

(b) In 1473 Edward asked the City of London, and his lords, to contribute voluntarily, as an expression of their "goodwill and benevolence," to the expenses of his French campaign.

(c) An innovation was the use of torture by Edward's Council in its judicial proceedings. The rack, and similar tortures, began to appear in procedures designed to extort confessions.

(d) Edward also legislated on matters concerning trade affairs. The rebuilding of commerce and trade became vital after an era of wars.

5. Richard III (1483–1485). Edward V reigned for two months only. The crown was then offered to, and accepted by Richard, Duke of Gloucester, as "true and undoubted king of the realm of England by divine and human right." He held one parliament, in which benevolences were declared illegal. The Court of Requests (*see* XIV, **14–16**) may have originated during his reign, when a clerk to the council was made responsible for dealing with the increasing number of petitions, requests and supplications received from poor people.

The Wars of the Roses which had bedevilled the Lancastrian–Yorkist era gave a further blow to an already weakened feudalism. From this time the royal power became supreme, and the subsequent Tudor absolutism was to bring drastic changes in our legal system, in its institutions and its underlying theories. With the end of Yorkist rule came the close of the Middle Ages.

TUDOR ABSOLUTISM

6. Henry VII (1485–1509). With the accession of Henry VII there commenced the era of the House of Tudor, an age of brilliance and of profound development in our law. Henry, characterised by Bacon as "the best lawgiver to this nation after Edward I," laid the foundations of the absolutism which was to flourish in later Tudor reigns. Submission to the monarch, an end of civil conflicts, a reduction of the power of the nobility—such were some of Henry's aims which were reflected in the development of the law during his reign. Some of the important developments were:

(a) *The Court of Star Chamber*, 1487. This great court, in which trial was by examination, without a jury, is discussed at XIV, **6–13**.

(b) *Growth in importance of the Council.* It was through the Council that the Tudors ruled. The Council reflected the king's will and, in general, was subservient to royal power.

(c) *Growth in the use of royal proclamations.* With the increased use of proclamations, Henry found that he was able to dispense with parliaments. Only seven were called during his reign.

(d) *Legislation against trusts.* The growth of the trust is outlined at X, 3–8. In 1487 Henry declared void all trusts of chattels to the use of the settlor. In 1489 relief was held due from heirs who were *cestuis que use (see* X, 4) of military tenures, and in 1504 it was held that execution could be made against lands held in use.

(e) *Growth of the common law was checked.* The great popularity of the new conciliar courts, resulted in a check to the growth of common law, and to increasing rivalry between the common law judges and those of the new courts.

(f) *Levying of taxes became unrestrained.* Henry extorted vast sums by using the techniques associated with benevolences, and penalties and fines under obsolete statutes. At his death he was said to have been "the richest prince in Christendom."

7. Henry VIII (1509–1547). The outstanding incident of this reign, and one which had lasting political, religious and legal significance, was the break with Rome which led to the Reformation. As a result of this, the church was subjected to the state, the power of the monarch was extended, and legislation, much of it designed to provide a basis in law for the changed relationship of church and state, was enacted. Among this legislation we note the following:

(a) *Changed relationship of church and state.* Appeals to Rome were forbidden in 1533. In 1534 there was passed the *Act of Supremacy*—an Act "concerning the King's Highness to be Supreme Head of the Church of England and to have authority to reform and redress all errors, heresies and abuses in the same." In 1536 there followed an Act "extinguishing the authority of the Bishop of Rome."

(b) *New courts were established.* In 1536 the Council of the North was set up, with criminal jurisdiction in Yorkshire and the northern counties. The short-lived Court of Augmentations was also set up in that year. A Council of the West was established in 1539. In 1540 a Court of Wards and Liveries was created. The Court of the Council of Wales was confirmed in its authority in 1542, and in that year there was also created the Court of General Surveyors to administer crown lands. Some of these courts are discussed at XIV and XV.

(c) *New statutory treasons were created.* It became treason, for example, to publish in writing, or orally, that the king was a heretic, an infidel or a usurper, or to assert the validity of his marriage to Anne of Cleves, or to refuse an oath abjuring the supremacy of the Pope.

(d) *Real property legislation was developed. The Statute of Uses,* 1535, attempted to put an end to the fraudulent evasion of feudal dues and sought to restrict the power to devise lands. *See* X, **9.** This restriction was very unpopular and, in the subsequent *Statute of Wills,* 1540, the power to devise was conditionally restored.

(e) *Ecclesiastical Chancellors were replaced by common lawyers.* Following the downfall of Cardinal Wolsey in 1529, Sir Thomas More was made Lord Chancellor, one of the first laymen to occupy the position. The effect on the development of Equity of Chancellors who had been trained in the common law, and who had a deep respect for precedent, was to be decisive (*see* VIII).

(f) *The power of the monarch grew.* In 1539 the growth of royal absolutism was intensified with the passing of the *Act of Proclamations* which enacted, in effect, that the king's proclamations were to be as valid as Acts of Parliament. As the royal power grew, so a series of very subservient parliaments (which, for example, had released the king from his debts in 1529, 1542 and 1544) failed to check royal pretensions.

NOTE: (*i*) *Edward VI* (1547–1553) repealed all the treason legislation of his father, Henry VIII. *The Act of Uniformity,* 1549, enforced the use of the first Book of Common Prayer.

(*ii*) *Mary* (1553–1558) re-established the Roman Catholic religion, annulled the legislation relating to religious matters passed by Edward VI, and repealed all the statutes passed against the Papacy since the twentieth year of the reign of Henry VIII.

8. Elizabeth I (1558–1603). Elizabeth, younger daughter of Henry VIII, was the last of the Tudor monarchs. Her long reign was an era of great advances in commerce and national prosperity and of victories in the face of attempted invasion and deposition. The absolutism inherited from her father was in no way diminished during her reign, and over church and state she ruled as a despot.

(*a*) *The Protestant religion was restored*, and appropriate legislation attempted to make safe the restoration. A second *Act of Supremacy*, 1559, declared that the Sovereign was the supreme head of the Church, and a second *Act of Uniformity*, 1559, enforced use of the Prayer Book of Edward VI and imposed monetary penalties on those failing to attend church. In 1571, the thirty-nine Articles of the English Church were made binding upon the clergy. From Rome, in 1570, was issued a Papal Bull, stating: "We declare her [Elizabeth] to be deprived of her pretended title to the crown and of all lordship, dignity and privilege whatsoever," and releasing the Queen's English subjects from their allegiance to her.

(*b*) *Legislation against Jesuits and Sectaries.* Royal proclamations punished the harbouring of Jesuits, and celebration of the mass was punished by fine and imprisonment. Protestant sectaries were also liable to imprisonment.

(*c*) *The High Commission Court.* *See* XII, **30.** In 1583 the High Commission Court was established and given very wide supervisory powers on matters concerning religion and church government.

(*d*) *Poor Law and Bankruptcy Statutes* were enacted for the first time.

(*e*) *The House of Commons grew in importance*, and there were many clashes with Elizabeth on matters of privilege.

(*f*) *The grant of monopolies became an instrument of financial oppression.* Royal grants of patents for exclusive dealings in *e.g.* coal, salt, iron, leather, led to very high prices and to bitter protests by the Commons. "The principalest commodities both of my town and country are ingrossed into the hands of bloodsuckers of the Commonwealth": Mr. Martin, in the House, 1601.

(*g*) The development of the charitable trust was given impetus by the important *Statute of Charitable Uses*, 1601.

At the end of the Tudor era, in which royal absolutism had bred resentment and opposition, and in which there had been reared a generation of Puritan non-conformists who were beginning to see liberty of religious thought as incompatible with the uncontrolled exercise of royal authority, could be discerned the commencement of preparations for the future Crown-Parliamentary conflict. An era which had seen a massive breach in the continuity of religious doctrine and practice was to be followed by an era of civil war and a breach in monarchical rule, with profound effects upon legal doctrine and procedure.

THE STRUGGLE BETWEEN PARLIAMENT AND JAMES I

9. The theory of the divine right of kings. "The state of monarchy is the supremest theory upon earth; for kings are not only God's lieutenants upon earth, and sit upon God's throne, but even by God himself they are called gods . . . Kings are justly called gods for that they exercise a manner or resemblance of divine power upon earth. . . . I conclude then this point touching the power of Kings with this axiom of Divinity, that as to dispute what God may do is blasphemy, but *quid vult Deus,* that divines may lawfully do and ordinarily dispute and discuss, for to dispute *a posse ad esse* is both against logic and divinity; so it is sedition in subjects to dispute what a king may do in the height of his power, but just kings will ever be willing to declare what they will do, if they will not incur the curse of God." (James I, in a speech to Parliament, March, 1610.)

10. James I and his Parliaments. In an era when Parliament's attitude to absolution was undergoing considerable modification, the arbitrary rule of a monarch who announced his divine right to rule was destined to cause conflict. The subsequent struggles answered the questions: "Where, in a realm, does political sovereignty rest, and how far may the law restrain a king in the exercise of his power?" The Parliament of 1604 reminded James of the limitations to his power when they told him: "Our privileges and liberties are our right and due inheritance no less than our very land and goods." Subsequent events were the forerunners of the coming struggle for parliamentary freedom.

(a) *Abuse of proclamations.* Parliament complained bitterly of this abuse which, they feared, could "bring a new form of arbitrary government upon the realm."

(b) *Dissolution of Parliament.* James ruled without parliaments from 1611–14, and from 1621–24.

(c) *Imprisonment of Members.* Four opponents of James were sent to the Tower in 1614.

(d) *Use of benevolences.* From 1614–20 James ruled in an arbitrary fashion and collected revenue by means of benevolences. Those who refused to pay were imprisoned.

(e) *Quarrel with Chief Justice Coke.* Coke, who had attempted to curb the growing powers of Chancery, refused to agree to the king's suggestion that legal proceedings be postponed in a case where the king considered that his "power and profit" were in question. Coke's reply was that he would do only what he felt it fitting for a judge to do. He was later removed from office. *See* IX, **18.**

(f) *The Protestation of* 1621. The Commons recorded in their Journal that: "the liberties, franchises . . . of Parliament are the ancient and undoubted birthright and inheritance of the subjects of England." James, with his own hand, tore out the page on which this was recorded from the Journal, and dissolved Parliament.

(g) *Impeachment and monopolies.* The Commons revived the practice of impeachment, and impeached Sir Francis Mitchell and Lord Bacon. In 1624 they passed a *Monopolies Act,* by which the use of monopolies was to be confined to new inventions.

THE STRUGGLE BETWEEN PARLIAMENT AND CHARLES I

11. The opposing parties. Macaulay has written of Charles I: "There is reason to believe that he was perfidious, not only from constitution and from habit, but also on principle." Tyrannical, insincere and obstinate, he had been brought up to believe, as his father had believed, in absolutism and in the divine right of kings. He was faced by a parliament which knew that a contest could not be long delayed, and which was fully aware of what was at stake. The doctrines of the common law, emphasising precedent as against arbitrary action, were to prove important weapons in the hands of parliament.

12. The First and Second Parliaments. The First Parliament was called in 1625 in order to help the financing of the war against Spain. Customs duties of tonnage and poundage were granted to the king for one year only. This he refused, and proceeded to levy the duties without the authority of Parliament. This parliament was dissolved upon its refusing to grant further supplies without the redress of its grievances. The Second Parliament was called in 1626 and was dissolved in that same year.

13. The Third Parliament and the Petition of Right. In 1628 the Third Parliament met and presented to Charles a petition which he accepted. The terms were: that no person should be compelled to pay a loan, benevolence or tax levied without the consent of Parliament; that no subject of the king should be imprisoned without cause shown; that no person should be tried by martial law; that the military forces should not be billeted in private houses.

14. Rule without Parliament. Charles ruled without a parliament from 1629–40. During that period the Star Chamber and the High Commission Court assisted him in the exercise of arbitrary power. Money was raised by means which were virtually illegal, *e.g.* fines on Catholics, the sale of monopolies. Ship money was imposed and caused great popular resentment.

15. The Fourth and Fifth Parliaments. The Fourth Parliament was called in 1640 and was dissolved after three weeks, following a refusal to grant a subsidy to the king. The Fifth Parliament (the so-called "Long Parliament") met in the same year and impeached two unpopular royal ministers, Laud and Strafford. Some victims of arbitrary proceedings in Star Chamber were released. The *Triennial Bill*, 1641, enacted that every parliament should be dissolved after three years, and that a new parliament should be summoned within three years of the dissolution. In that year the Star Chamber, High Court of Commission, and Council of the North were abolished. The Commons published a *Grand Remonstrance* which listed the unconstitutional acts of the king, and which demanded the appointment of ministers by Parliament. Charles retaliated by marching on Parliament with a large armed escort so as to arrest five members who opposed him. It has been said that this act heralded the commencement of the Civil War.

16. The Civil War (1642–48). The general causes of the conflict were the opposition of Parliament to continued arbitrary government, to illegal taxation, and to Charles' unpopular advisers. The conflict was precipitated by the king's attempted arrest of his parliamentary opponents, and by his refusal to surrender to the Commons the command of the militia. In 1648 the Parliamentary forces, under Cromwell and Fairfax, defeated the Royalist forces near Preston, and the Civil War was brought to an end. Charles, "capital and grand author of all the troubles and woes that the kingdom had endured," was brought to trial by a court whose authority he refused to recognise. He was executed in 1649.

The absolutist rule of James and Charles had bred militant opposition which passed over into civil war. There was to follow a unique interregnum in which a new type of government committed itself to an intensive programme of constitutional and legal reform.

THE COMMONWEALTH AND THE PROTECTORATE
(1649–1660)

17. The "Rump" Parliament. In 1648 members of the House who had refused to participate in judgment upon the king were dismissed. Those who remained (about 50 in all) and who had voted for the trial were known as "the Rump." In 1649 the Rump passed the following revolutionary measures:

(a) A Council of State (consisting of 41 members) was to govern the country.

(b) The office of king—"unnecessary, burdensome and dangerous to the liberty, safety and public interest of the people"—was abolished.

(c) The House of Lords was abolished.

(d) The people of England and its dominions and territories were to be constituted "a Commonwealth and Free State."

18. The Commonwealth and its enemies. Cromwell and his associates ruled as a military autocracy. Opposition came from within and without the realm. In England the extreme Republicans, the "Levellers," denounced the government's measures as half-hearted and inadequate. In Ireland the English Royalist Protestants and Irish Catholics refused to acknowledge the Commonwealth. In Scotland Prince Charles was proclaimed as king. War was waged against the Dutch who refused to ally with the Commonwealth. Cromwell saw the need for a new Parliament and, in 1653, he forcibly dissolved the Rump.

19. The Protectorate. In 1653 Cromwell summoned an Assembly of Nominees (about 140). An *Instrument of Government* was drawn up which stated that the supreme authority "shall be and reside in one person, and the people assembled in Parliament, the style of which person shall be, 'The Lord Protector of the Commonwealth of England, Scotland and Ireland'". Cromwell was to be Lord Protector. A Parliament of 400 members was to be summoned every three years and was to sit for at least five months.

(*a*) A First Parliament was summoned under the authority of the Instrument in 1654.

(*b*) In 1655 internal plots against Cromwell led to the appointment of Major-Generals, with absolute powers, who ruled the twelve military districts into which the country was divided.

(*c*) A Second Parliament was called in 1656, and the Third assembled in 1658, in which year Cromwell died.

(*d*) Cromwell's death was followed by General Monk's recall of the Long Parliament. The stage was now set for the Restoration.

20. The courts during the Interregnum. Chancery, which had been closely associated with the crown, and which had been attacked by Coke and the common lawyers, came under severe criticism, and its abolition was resolved. The Admiralty courts (*see* XV, **8–12**) were reorganised. Legal records were kept in English, and there was a revival of legal education in the Inns of Court.

21. Legal reforms. Many legal reforms—some of them far ahead of their day—were considered.

(a) "The Law as it is now constituted," said Cromwell, "serves only to maintain the lawyers and to encourage the rich to oppress the poor." "To see men lose their lives for a petty matter," he told Parliament, "is a thing God will reckon."

(b) Among the suggested reforms was a reduction and codification of English law "to the bigness of a pocket book."

(c) Acts were passed for the relief of poor prisoners; genuine bankrupts were to be released from prison; it was forbidden to carry out capital punishment which involved burning women alive; laws for civil marriages and the swift probate of wills were designed; a new High Court of Justice was to be set up; a public post-office, voting by ballot, a national bank, recording of land transfers, were also considered. The equity of redemption (*see* X, **17**) was to be restricted; entailed interests were to be barred by deed; rules of inheritance were to be modified; the name of the King's Bench was to be changed to Upper Bench.

(d) With the Restoration came a rejection and repeal of almost all the reforms made during the Interregnum.

22. General results of the Interregnum. Absolute monarchy was firmly rejected, as was the extremism manifested during the Cromwellian era. Parliament and the common law were strengthened considerably, for the struggle between Parliament and the Stuarts, and between the Lord Protector and his opponents, was, essentially, a struggle between the law and absolutism. The danger from the increased powers of the prerogative courts was almost at an end. With the passing of the Interregnum came an era in which judges were to be freed from any interference by the crown, and in which the modern law was to take shape.

PROGRESS TEST 3

1. What were benevolences? **(4)**

2. Outline the important developments in law during the reign of Henry VII. **(6)**

3. Enumerate some of the new courts established by Henry VIII. **(7)**

4. What events in the reign of Elizabeth I contributed to the development of our law? **(8)**

5. What was meant by the divine right of kings? **(9)**

6. What were the causes of the struggle between King and Parliament? (11–16)

7. Enumerate some of the legal reforms considered during the Interregnum. (21)

8. What were the general results of the Interregnum? (22)

CHAPTER IV

THE PERIOD FROM THE RESTORATION TO THE END OF THE NINETEENTH CENTURY

THE RESTORATION AND THE END OF STUART ABSOLUTISM

1. The Restoration. General Monk (*see* III, **19**) recalled the Long Parliament which summoned a Convention in 1660. The Convention recalled Charles who was restored to the throne, ruling from 1660–1685. Lands confiscated under the Commonwealth were restored to the Crown and Church, and the First Parliament of Charles II annulled all the Acts passed by Cromwell's parliaments. Non-conformists were severely discriminated against, under the *Clarendon Code* of 1661. In 1662 came the first *Declaration of Indulgence* which repealed penal laws against Catholics and non-conformists. A year later, Parliament compelled the king to withdraw it. In 1673 the *Test Act*, forbidding Catholics to hold public office, was passed.

2. The Habeas Corpus Act, 1679. "An Act for the better securing the liberty of the subject, and for prevention of imprisonment beyond the seas." Among its provisions were the following:

(*a*) That an unconvicted prisoner (except one charged with treason) could demand from a judge a writ of *Habeas Corpus* by which a gaoler was directed to produce the body of the prisoner in court and to certify "the true cause of the commitment."

(*b*) That a person must be indicted in the first term after his commitment and tried in the following term.

(*c*) That no person once delivered by *Habeas Corpus* should be recommitted for the same offence.

(*d*) That no inhabitant of England should be sent to imprisonment out of England.

44

3. Legal reform at the Restoration. During the reign of Charles II a number of important legal reforms were undertaken. Some of the most important are mentioned here:

(a) *Abolition of military tenures* (*see* XXIII). An Act of 1660 abolished fines for alienation, tenures by homage, wardships, liveries. Tenures held of the king were, with a few exceptions, turned into free and common socage.

(b) *Statute of Frauds*, 1667. This important statute had as its object the prevention of fraud, for example, by requiring the production of written evidence to support certain actions.

(c) *Statute for the Distribution of Intestates' Estates*, 1670. This allowed the wife of an intestate to take one-third of the estate, the rest to pass to the children or their representatives.

(d) *Parliamentary reforms.* The House of Lords abandoned its original jurisdiction, but established its right to hear appeals from Chancery. The Commons established its right to decide taxation measures.

(e) *Juries.* Members of juries were no longer personally liable for a verdict considered by the presiding judge to be unsatisfactory.

(f) *Developments in Equity.* (*See* IX.) Lord Nottingham, Chancellor from 1673–82, attempted to establish the importance of precedent in Equity (*see* IX, **31**). Chancery had escaped abolition during the Cromwellian era. Following the Restoration there was a development towards a systematisation of equitable principles.

4. James II (1685–1689). During his reign James had, among his main aims, the establishment of absolute rule and the restoration of Catholicism. Illegal taxation, levied in the form of customs duties voted to Charles II for life only, was a feature of his rule. *The Dispensing Power*, a prerogative right of the crown to exempt individuals from the operation of the law, was recognised by the courts and was exercised by James. In 1686 he established a Court of Commissioners for Ecclesiastical Causes, which furthered his aims by attempting to control the government of the church. In 1688 a *Declaration of Indulgence*, which suspended penal laws against Catholics and nonconformists, was followed by the trial of seven bishops who refused to read it to congregations in their churches. On the very day on which the bishops were acquitted an invitation was sent by the leaders of the Tories and Whigs to William of Orange (the recognised Head of Protestantism in Europe) and his wife Mary (daughter of James II) to come to England with an army so as to redress grievances. James fled to the Continent. Stuart absolutism was now ended.

THE GLORIOUS REVOLUTION

5. William and Mary (1689–1694) and William, alone, (1694–1702). The outstanding event of legal significance during this era was the passing of the *Bill of Rights*, 1689—"An Act declaring the rights and liberties of the subject, and settling the succession of the throne." Among its provisions were the following:

(*a*) That the pretended power of suspending or dispensing with laws, the Court of Commissioners for Ecclesiastical Causes, the levying of money without consent of Parliament, the maintenance of a standing army without consent of parliament were to be illegal.

(*b*) That subjects were to have a right to petition the king.

(*c*) The elections of members of Parliament ought to be free.

(*d*) That debates and speeches in Parliament ought to be free.

(*e*) That excessive bail ought not to be required, excessive fines ought not to be imposed "nor cruel and unusual punishment inflicted."

NOTE: Of this enactment Macaulay wrote in the nineteenth century: "It contained the germ . . . of every good law which has been passed during more than a century and a half, of every good law which may be hereafter, in the course of ages, be found necessary to promote the public weal, and to satisfy the demands of public opinion."

6. Other significant legislation.

(*a*) *The Second Treason Act*, 1696, was a landmark in the development of criminal procedure. Accused was to have the aid of counsel, two witnesses were required, a copy of the indictment and the jury list were to be given to him before the trial.

(b) *Act of Settlement*, 1701. Its important provisions included: "That whosoever shall hereafter come to the possession of the Crown shall join in communion with the Church of England as by law established," and, "That . . . judges' commissions shall be made *quamdiu se bene gesserint*" (*i.e.* as long as they conduct themselves properly). (*See* XVI, **22.**)

The "Glorious Revolution" was the beginning of a new era in our history. Absolute monarchy was dead. In the new epoch, in which society was to undergo a fundamental industrial and economic transformation, the law would reflect these changes in its institutions.

THE BEGINNINGS OF THE EIGHTEENTH CENTURY

7. Anne (1702–1714). The following matters in Anne's reign were of particular importance:

(a) In 1705 it was enacted that fraudulent disposal of goods by a bankrupt was to be a non-clergyable felony. *See* **XVII, 27.**

(b) Promissory notes were made negotiable in 1705. This reflects the growing importance of commerce in the country's life.

(c) *The Regency Act*, 1706, declared that Parliament was not to be dissolved *ipso facto* by the demise of the Sovereign.

(d) *The Aylesbury Election case.* The Commons had resolved that they had the sole right "to examine and determine all matters relating to the right of election of their own members." In *Ashby* v. *White* (1702–4), 2 Ld. Raym. 938, the Lords reminded them that: "who has a right to sit in the House of Commons may be properly cognisable there; but who has a right to choose is a matter originally established, even before there is a parliament. A man has a right to his freehold by the common law and the law having annexed the right of voting to his freehold, it is of the nature of his freehold, and must depend on it. The same law that gives him his right must defend it for him."

(e) *Act for the Union of England and Scotland*, 1707. By

this Act Scotland was to retain her own Church, her laws and her courts of justice.

(*f*) *Final exercise of the royal veto.* The Crown's loss of power was epitomised by the final royal veto of a legislative measure (the *Militia Bill*, in 1708).

THE HOUSE OF HANOVER

8. George I (1714–1727). Jacobite riots, led by supporters of the Stuart cause, resulted in the passing of the *Riot Act*, 1714, which remains on the Statute Book today. In 1716 the *Septennial Act* extended the duration of parliament to seven years. The category of crimes for which capital punishment might be imposed was extended in 1722 to cover setting fire to crops, wounding cattle, and being armed and in disguise on high roads or open heaths.

9. George II (1727–1760). This reign was dominated by wars: the War of the Austrian Succession, the Rebellion in Scotland, the Seven Years' War, and war in Canada. The Industrial Revolution, which was to transform economic and social life, may be said to have commenced in this era. Commerce, industry and agriculture developed rapidly. Land was no longer the most important source of wealth. Hence, commercial law, the law of companies, of personal property, of partnership, of bankruptcy, were to grow in importance. The law of master and servant, inseparable from the rise of industrial society, was to develop. A new class—the manufacturers —was to become as powerful as the old aristocracy.

10. George III (1760–1820). Wars in France, America and India, fear of the French Revolution, and a growing struggle for internal reform were prominent features of the second half of the eighteenth century. The French Revolution caused near-panic in England. *Habeas Corpus* (*see* 2 above) was suspended, laws against seditious meetings were passed, and press freedom was restricted. Calls for internal reform were taken as manifestations of French-inspired subversion. The following legal developments were of importance:

(*a*) *Roman Catholic Relief Act*, 1778, which repealed some of the harsh laws under which Catholics suffered.

(b) *Combination Acts*, 1799–1800. Combinations to alter hours of work and advance wages became crimes. Wilberforce regarded combinations for these purposes as "a general disease of society for which the remedy should be general." (The first trade unions grew up in this era.)

(c) *The modern tort of fraud came into existence in* 1789.

(d) *The Accumulations Act*, 1800, limited accumulations of capital at interest to 21 years.

(e) *Embezzlement* became a statutory crime in 1779.

(f) *A number of reforms in criminal law penalties were introduced.* The burning of women convicted of treason was ended in 1790; the pillory was abolished in 1816; the public whipping of women was ended in 1817.

(g) *Trial by battle was abolished in* 1819. *See* VI, **10**.

NOTE: An outstanding figure of this era was the great jurist, *Jeremy Bentham* (1748–1832). Educated at Oxford and Lincoln's Inn, and writer of *Introduction to Principles of Morals and Legislation* (1789), he believed that men were governed by the two sovereign motives of pleasure and pain, and that the object of all legislation should be "the greatest happiness of the greatest number." The codification of the law and prison reform occupied much of his life. He had a remarkable influence on reform of the law.

11. George IV (1820–1830). Reflecting the growth of the industrial working class, three Acts were passed in 1824–25 which repealed laws allowing magistrates to fix wages, repealed laws preventing workers who sought employment from travelling around the country, and permitted combinations for the sole purpose of agreeing on wages or hours of work. Catholic emancipation was furthered by the *Roman Catholic Relief Bill*, 1829. In that year Peel's *Metropolitan Police Act* created a police force in London, and abolished the old force of "watchmen." Peel brought in bills for the abolition of capital punishment for over 100 crimes.

NOTE: The number of those committed at the assizes, largely for petty larcenies, rose from 3163 in 1811, to 14,947 in 1832. The growth of a large urban population, and more efficient police methods may have been responsible.

12. William IV (1830–1837). The struggle for the *Reform Bill* was the most important development in William's reign.

The *First Reform Bill* was rejected in Committee in 1831, the *Second Bill* was rejected by the Lords, and was followed by riots at Nottingham, Derby and Bristol. In 1832 the Bill was passed. It disenfranchised 56 "rotten boroughs" (*i.e.* depopulated constituencies which, in the gift of patrons, sent members to the Commons), deprived others of members, and redistributed the seats. The franchise was given in the boroughs to all householders paying a yearly rental of £10; in the counties it was given to freeholders to the value of 30*s.*, to copyholders to the value of £10 p.a., and to leaseholders for 21 years paying an annual rent of at least £50. Other significant events were:

(*a*) *Act for the Abolition of Slavery in all British Dominions*, 1833. Twenty million pounds compensation had to be paid to slave owners.

(*b*) *The First Factory Act*, 1833, which resulted from growing anxiety concerning the exploitation of labour in factories, forbade the employment of children under 9 in factories, and limited the factory working day to eight hours for those under 13, and to twelve hours for women and for those under 18.

(*c*) *The Educational Grant Act*, 1833, granted, for the first time, an annual sum for elementary education.

(*d*) *The Poor Law Amendment Act*, 1834, abolished outdoor relief, except for the infirm and aged.

(*e*) *The Municipal Reform Act*, 1835, enforced the publication of accounts by town councils, and allowed the election of members by ratepayers.

(*f*) *The Marriage Act*, 1836, allowed the marriage of nonconformists in their own chapels, or before a district registrar.

(*g*) *Procedural reforms* were effected by the *Uniformity of Process Act*, 1832, and the *Civil Procedure Act*, 1833.

THE VICTORIAN ERA—AN AGE OF REFORM

13. Victoria (1837-1901). The reign of Victoria spans a period which ends in the present century. An intensive movement for legal reform culminated in a large number of statutes which affected the law at many points. Some of these statutes are enumerated below.

14. Land Law. *Law of Property Act*, 1845, *Vendor and Purchaser Act*, 1847, *Contingent Remainders Act*, 1877, *Settled*

Estates Act, 1877, *Settled Land Act*, 1882, *Land Transfer Act*, 1875, form important sections of our land law. A suggested codification of land law, mooted in the early days of Victoria's reign, came to nothing.

15. Law of Torts. The *Fatal Accidents Act*, 1846, modified the old common law rule that personal actions could not be brought after the death of an injured person. The *Parliamentary Papers Act*, 1840, and *Lord Campbell's Act*, 1843, modified the strict rules of defamation (*see* XX).

16. Commercial Law. The *Bills of Exchange Act*, 1882, the *Companies Acts of* 1844 and 1867, the *Bills of Lading Act*, 1855, the *Merchandise Marks Act*, 1862, the *Debtors Act*, 1869, reflect the vast commercial expansion of the Victorian era.

17. Criminal law. Reform was nowhere more in evidence than in criminal law. The number of capital offences was reduced from almost 200 in 1826 to 4 in 1861. Among the important measures were: *Treason Act*, 1842, *Indictable Offences Act*, 1848, setting up of the *Court for Crown Cases Reserved*, 1848, *Criminal Procedure Act*, 1851, *Larceny Act*, 1861, *Forgery Act*, 1861, *Offences against the Person Act*, 1861, *Forfeiture Act*, 1870.

18. Equity. Important measures were the *Court of Chancery Acts*, 1841 and 1850, *Chancery Amendment Act*, 1858. *The Judicature Acts*, 1873–75 (considered at XI, **31–38**) were a landmark in the movement towards a fusion of law and equity.

19. General social legislation. The historic *Bill for the Repeal of the Corn Laws*, 1846, which led to the adoption of free trade, was but one of many important social legislative measures of the era. In 1867 the *Parliamentary Reform Bill* was passed, enacting that the franchise was to be based on rating, and not upon rental. In 1872 the *Ballot Act* introduced secret voting. Industrial legislation included the *Apprentice and Servant Act*, 1851, the *Master and Servant Act*, 1867, the *Trade Union Act*, 1871. Reform in education was implemented by the *Elementary Education Act*, 1870. The *Adulteration of Food Act*, 1860, was a forerunner of later legislative protection of the consumer.

c

The Victorian era, with which this general survey ends, saw the recasting of much of our judicial system, and the transformation of much substantive law into patterns suitable for the new society which had grown out of the Industrial Revolution.

PROGRESS TEST 4

1. Outline the principal provisions of *Habeas Corpus Act,* 1679. **(2)**

2. Enumerate some of the legal reforms undertaken at the Restoration. **(3)**

3. What were the provisions of the *Bill of Rights,* 1689? **(5)**

4. What was the importance of the *Act of Settlement,* 1701? **(6)**

5. Mention some of the legal developments in the reign of George III. **(10)**

6. What developments in the law took place in the reign of William IV? **(12)**

7. Enumerate some of the important social legislation of Victoria's reign. **(19)**

PART TWO
THE COMMON LAW

CHAPTER V

THE MEANING, SOURCES, AND LITERATURE OF THE COMMON LAW

MEANING AND SCOPE OF THE COMMON LAW

1. General. The term "common law" has a variety of meanings, often determined by its context. It has been used to describe the unwritten, as opposed to the written, law, the law common to the realm, as distinguished from that peculiar to particular groups of persons, the temporal, as opposed to ecclesiastical, law, the body of law other than equity and statute law, and the law which originated in Anglo-Saxon and Norman times, in contrast to the civil (*i.e.* Roman) law. It has been described in general terms as: "the commonsense of the community, crystallised and formulated by our forefathers."

2. Blackstone on the common law. Blackstone (*see* **30** below) divides the law into written or statute, and unwritten or common, law.

(*a*) The unwritten law derives its binding power "by long and immemorial usage and by universal reception throughout the kingdom."

(*b*) This unwritten or common law is distinguished by Blackstone into three kinds:

(*i*) *General customs* (the universal rule of the whole kingdom, forming the common law in its stricter sense).

(*ii*) *Particular customs* (affecting only particular parts of the realm).

(*iii*) *Certain particular laws* (by custom adapted and used by particular courts).

(*c*) Blackstone speaks of: "the chief cornerstone of the laws of England which is general and immemorial custom, or common law, from time to time declared in the decisions of the courts of justice; which decisions are preserved among our public records, explained in our reports, and digested for general use in the authoritative writings of the venerable sages of the law."

(d) Hence, according to Blackstone, we must search for statements of our early common law in:

- (i) Decisions of our courts;
- (ii) Records;
- (iii) Reports;
- (iv) Books accepted as authoritative.

Some of these sources are discussed below.

3. Features of the common law. From some of the many writings on the common law may be derived the following significant features:

(a) The phrase "common law" seems to have come into use at the end of the thirteenth century, when reference is made in the Year Books (*see* **17**(*a*) below) to *"la commune ley."*

(b) The important constituents of the common law may be considered to be the rules originally based on the Anglo-Saxon concept of *folcright* (stated in the laws of Edward as bestowing equal right, law or justice on persons of all degrees) and administered by the common law courts from time immemorial, and the customary law (based on rights established by long use and consent of our ancestors), together with extensions and modifications.

(c) Judicial decisions are of great importance in the common law. Dicey refers to: "the mass of custom, tradition or judge-made maxims, known as the common law." Another writer refers to the common law as: "the body of law judicially evolved from the general custom of the realm."

(d) The common law is considered as evolving, or unfolding, as judicial decisions are made. Hence, a judge was considered not as making law, but rather as declaring or revealing that which had always been the law (*jus dicere* as opposed to *jus dare*). Precedent, therefore, is of great importance in the building of the common law. In *Mirehouse* v. *Rennell* (1833) 8 Bing. 515, Lord Wensleydale spoke of the common law as "a system which consisted in applying to new combinations of circumstances those rules which we derive from legal principles and judicial precedents."

(e) The early growth of the common law depended largely

on the journeyings of itinerant justices carrying the law to all parts of the realm, on the growth of centralised government which produced uniformity of administration, and on the increasing importance of the king's courts.

(*f*) Anglo-Saxon and Norman customs shaped the earlier common law, which was concerned particularly with land, but the growth of English feudalism with many unique features shaped the later common law.

(*g*) The development of the common law is inseparable from the development of the writ system (*see* VI). It hardened eventually into a rigid system based on fixed forms, particularly in procedural matters.

4. A working definition. We shall consider the common law as that part of the corpus of English law which, prior to 1873–75, was administered by the common law courts, which had its origin in the ancient common customs of the country, and which was largely developed and formulated by judicial decisions.

5. The importance of the common law. The common law is the ground in which English law has been nurtured and has flourished. Its development is reflected in the growth of the law of crime, contract, and torts. Its achievements were such that it withstood the rivalry of the Roman *Corpus Juris* (*see* **6** below), and its spirit permeated much of the political philosophy which helped to shatter the absolutist pretensions of the Stuarts. Common Law principles have spread to other continents and have affected many judicial systems. Coke wrote of "the fundamental rules of the common law, which in truth are the main pillars and supporters of the fabric of the commonwealth."

6. Common law and Roman law. The Renaissance saw a revival of interest in the study of Roman law. The movement for its adoption as a replacement for native law based on custom, known as "the Reception", was strong on the Continent and in Scotland. The universality and "completeness" of the *Corpus Juris Civilis* were particularly attractive, as was its authoritarian nature, which made an appeal to rulers and statesmen of many nations. In England, Henry VIII founded the Regius Professorship of Civil Law at Cambridge. (N.B. The term "civil law" is often used to mean Roman law.) But the common law stood its ground. There was a firmly-established educational system at the Inns of Court, based on common law teaching, and the obvious difficulties in replacing existing courts and the existing complicated law (particularly that which concerned the land) made the adoption of Roman law impracticable and undesirable. But in spite of the disappearance of Roman law at the ending of the Roman occupation, and the failure of the "Reception," the history of our law is not without traces of its influence. For example:

(a) The division of our law into public law and private law reflects a Roman concept.

(b) The parallels between the *praetorian formulary system* and some of the English forms of action are marked.

(c) Actions such as *Novel Disseisin* (*see* VI, **18**) may have had Roman origins.

(d) The early Christian Church in England, and the doctrines of canon law, reflected Roman teaching.

(e) Lanfranc, William's leading adviser, had taught Roman and canon law at the famous law school in Pavia. In the mid-twelfth century Vacarius came to Oxford to teach Roman law, at the invitation of Archbishop Theobald.

(f) The early judges of the *Curia Regis* (*see* XIII) were often ecclesiastics who had studied Roman law.

(g) Bracton (*see* **21** below) derived some of his views from Roman legal doctrine, and, in particular, from Azo, who taught at Bologna.

(h) Our modern law concerning waste and easements, for example, derives in some measure from Roman doctrine.

NOTE: References to Roman law and its authority have been made in a number of leading cases. See, for example, the judgment of Willes, J., in *Bechervaise* v. *Lewis* (1872) L.R.7 C.P., and the judgment of Blackburn, J., in *Taylor* v. *Caldwell* (1863) 3 B & S 826.

SOURCES OF THE COMMON LAW

7. General. The sources of common law are many. We mention the following as of particular historical significance:

(a) Custom (*see* **8** below).

(b) Anglo-Saxon dooms (*see* **9** below).

(c) Roman law and canon law (*see* **10** below).

(*d*) *Diplomata* and charters (*see* **11** below).

(*e*) Anglo-Norman compilations of the *Lex Terrae* (*see* **12** below).

(*f*) Statutes (*see* **13** below).

(*g*) Plea rolls (*see* **14** below).

(*h*) Pipe rolls (*see* **15** below).

(*i*) Other rolls and records (*see* **16** below).

(*j*) Law reports and year books (*see* **17** below).

(*k*) Legal textbooks (*see* **18–30** below).

8. Custom. During the early growth period of the common law, custom was of particular significance. The ancient communal courts acted largely on the basis of customary law, and the sanctions in use were based on custom. The feudal courts developed custom in the context of the prevailing system of feudal relationships. *Note* Blackstone's comments on custom at **2** above. The customs of towns, counties (*see* gavelkind, XXIII, **27**(*b*)), groups of people such as merchants (*see* law merchant at XV), contributed to this source of common law. Custom gave way to judicial precedent and legislation as the law developed. In order that a practice might be considered as a valid custom it must satisfy the following criteria:

(*a*) It must have been exercised so long "that the memory of man runneth not to the contrary," *i.e.* it should have been exercised "from time immemorial" (fixed at 1189, the first year of the reign of Richard I): *Simpson* v. *Wells* (1872) L.R. 7 Q.B. 214.

(*b*) It must have been exercised continuously: *Hammerton* v. *Honey* (1876) 24 W.R. 603. An interruption of the right within legal memory defeats the custom.

(*c*) It must have been observed as of right, *i.e.* the right should have been exercised *nec vi, nec clam, nec precario* (not by violence, stealth, or entreaty), and it should have been enjoyed peaceably: *Mills* v. *Mayor of Colchester* (1867) L.R. 2 C.P. 567.

(*d*) It must be reasonable, the test being: "whether it is in accordance with fundamental principles 'of right and wrong": per Brett, J., in *Robinson* v. *Mollett* (1875) L.R. 7 H.L. 802.

(*e*) It must be contrary neither to statute law nor to the fundamental principles of the common law: *Perry* v. *Barnett* (1885) 15 Q.B.D. 388.

(*f*) It must be regarded as having obligatory force.

(*g*) It should not be inconsistent with other customs.

9. Anglo-Saxon dooms. The dooms (*see* I, 25) were royal proclamations of the law. The most celebrated are:

(*a*) *The Code of Ine* (King of the West Saxons, 688–95). Only fragments of this text remain.

(*b*) *The Code of Alfred* (*see* I, 25(*c*)), also known as the *Dombok*, or *liber judicalis*. Alfred declares in his preface that he has combined his own laws with those of Ine, Offa and Aethelbert, preserving only those which were suitable. The Code is influenced by Christian thought, and begins, "The Lord spake all these words, saying, I am the Lord thy God." There follow the Ten Commandments, extracts from the Mosaic criminal law, and passages from the New Testament.

(*c*) *The Dooms of Cnut* are made up of older texts. Latin translations of this Code were made after the Conquest.

NOTE: The complete texts of these Codes have not come down to us. The first collection of extracts was published in 1568 by William Lambarde in *Archainomia sive de priscis Anglorum legibus libri*. It was printed in parallel columns, one containing the Anglo-Saxon text, the other containing a Latin translation.

10. Roman law and canon law. *See* **6** above. The influence of the canon law was important, in that some of the fundamental common law principles, such as the protection of the rights of a free man, were derived from ecclesiastical doctrine. Our laws of marriage grew from the body of canon law; the law of charitable trusts was affected by that part of church law concerned with "gifts to pious uses"; succession on death, and the control of the administration of intestates' estates were, for a long period, under the control of the church. Legitimacy, in particular, was a concern of the church. During the reign of Henry III, the clergy attempted to change the existing laws of inheritance of land so that the canon law doctrine of *legitimum per subsequens matrimonium* might prevail. The barons, enacting the *Statute of Merton*, 1236, gave their answer: "We will not change the common law of England."

11. Diplomata and charters. *See* I, 24. *Diplomata* were Anglo-Saxon records of grants of land, and from them we are able to discover some of the customs surrounding land transfers. The charters are grants of rights which, in some cases, recognise those claims of the conquered English ceded by their conquerors, *e.g.* the Charter to the City of London granted by William I.

12. Anglo-Norman compilations of the Lex Terrae (Law of the Land).

(*a*) *The Quadripartitus* (*c*. 1114). The author is unknown, but it has been conjectured that he may have been an ecclesiastic of the time of Henry I. The work is divided into four parts, of which only the first two have survived. It attempts to arrange the laws into a logical sequence. The four parts are:

    (*i*) Anglo-Saxon laws. (*Leges Anglicae in Latinum translatae*)
    (*ii*) Contemporary documents. (*Scriptae necessaria temporis nostri*)
    (*iii*) Procedure. (*De Statu et agendis causarum*)
    (*iv*) Larceny. (*De Furto et partibus ejus*)

(*b*) *Leges Henrici Primi* (*c*. 1118). The author is unknown, but may have been, according to some suggestions, a cleric responsible also for the *Quadripartitus*. The name of this compilation is taken from its opening document, the Coronation Charter of Henry I. It contains accounts of Anglo-Saxon Law, together with amendments issued by William and Henry. Legal memoranda and customs are cited, together with references to canon law, Roman law, Frankish and Salic law. Written in poor Latin, its style and meaning are often obscure.

(*c*) *Leges Willelmi* (*c*. 1090–1150). The author is unknown. The compilation is also known as the *bilingual code*, the laws being stated in Latin and Anglo-Norman. It states those usages and customs guaranteed by William to the English as having been in force during Edward's reign. Its three parts are:

    (*i*) A summary of Anglo-Saxon rules, and those laws enacted by William.
    (*ii*) General principles of the civil law.
    (*iii*) A translation of excerpts from the Code of Cnut.

(d) *Leges Edwardi Confessoris* (*c.* 1130–35). This Latin compilation may have been the result of an enquiry ordered by the Conqueror in 1070 with the object of discovering the true nature and extent of the laws of Edward. The enquiry is thought to have been entrusted to twelve sworn notable men in each county. The tone of the compilation is biased against customs with a Danish origin, and in favour of West Saxon customs. There are suggestions that the work may have been a forgery.

13. Statutes. From William to Edward I most legislation in the form of statutes had as its object the declaration of existing law, with amendments.

(a) Early statutes were often known by their first words (*e.g. Quia Emptores*). Later they were cited in accordance with the place at which the legislative body was sitting (*e.g. Statute of Westminster*, *Statute of York*). By the end of the fourteenth century they were cited by the regnal year.

(b) In general, statutes were considered void if they offended against the basic principles of common law. "When an Act of Parliament is against common right and reason, or repugnant, or impossible to be performed, the Common Law will control it, and adjudge such Act to be void": per Coke, in *Bonham's Case* (1610) 8 Rep. 114. (This doctrine was later questioned. "Are we to act as regents over what is done by Parliament with the consent of the Queen, lords and commons? I deny that any such authority exists"; per Willes, J., in *Lee* v. *Bude Railway Co.* (1871) L.R. 6 C.P. 576.)

14. Plea rolls. These early records are official documents recording facts such as appearance and plea of defendant, judgment, and, in some cases, the reasons for the judgment. *Curia Regis* pleas were recorded from the time of Henry II. In the reign of Henry III the rolls had particular names: *Exchequer rolls*—pleas heard by the Court of Exchequer; *Coram Rege rolls*—those of the King's Bench (which were later divided into civil cases and a *Rex roll* recording criminal cases); *De Banco rolls*—Court of Common Pleas. Eyre and Assize rolls were also kept.

15. Pipe rolls. The Pipe rolls (so called possibly because of their pipe-like appearance when rolled up and stacked) were the Great rolls of the Exchequer and consist of parchment skins sewn together. Roger of Salisbury, Henry I's Treasurer, had established a rudimentary national financial system and the Pipe roll recording financial details at the end of Henry's reign is in existence. A second series, started in 1156, continued until 1832. The rolls contain much information concerning royal debtors, administration, and personnel of the King's government.

16. Other records and rolls.

(a) *Memoranda rolls.* As the work of the Exchequer increased, matters reserved for detailed consideration by Exchequer officials were recorded in a series of *Memoranda rolls.* Thus, in 1220 there was drawn up a special roll concerning Jewish merchants and their transactions. Such rolls included details of appointments, minutes of proceedings and orders issued by Exchequer.

(b) *The Feet of Fines. See* XXIV, 11(a). These records (*pedes finium*) give details of compromised actions in conveyancing matters.

(c) *Rotuli Parliamentorum* (*rolls of Parliament*). Records of petitions made to Parliament, 1290–1503, and some statutes are included in this compilation.

(d) *State papers, Letters Patent, Acts of the Privy Council and the King's close rolls* (containing the king's sealed private instructions) also provide information of interest.

17. Law reports. The development of common law, the significance of precedent and the growth of case law, depended to a great extent on the availability of recorded judicial decisions. *The Year Books, the Abridgments, and the Private Reports,* played a considerable part in the establishing of the doctrine of *precedent.*

(a) *The Year Books.* This great series of reports runs from 1283–1536, spanning the reigns of Edward I and Henry VIII.

(i) *Authorship.* The authors are unknown. It has been suggested that the reports originated in the privately compiled notes of law apprentices sitting in the crib of the court. Another suggestion is that they were compiled from separate pamphlets issued by barristers for the use of their students at the end of law terms, and later published commercially. The later Year Books, which are of a high quality, may have been compiled by official reporters of the crown.

(*ii*) *Their name.* The title "Year Books" is derived from their being grouped under the regnal years of the sovereigns in whose reigns the cases reported were decided.

(*iii*) *Their content.* Facts of cases, counsel's arguments, and matters of substantive law are given. Extraneous and irrelevant matter is often included, *e.g.* the altercations and arguments of the serjeants (*see* XVI, 6), supper table discussions between serjeants and judges. Much of the material is incomplete and in summary form. By the time of Richard II, many of the cases are reported with great clarity.

(*iv*) *Their importance.* Although the Year Books were not official they were often cited in the seventeenth century as authoritative documents. Coke and Plowden referred to them in a way which might suggest that the books had been compiled officially. The Year Books reveal a growing respect by the judges for precedent, and citations of decided cases appear frequently. In the Books case law is seen in its formative stages. The importance in the common law of the procedures of pleading emerges clearly, and *Year Books 40–50* of Edward III (the so-called *Quadragesms*) were used in later times as a text book in the art of pleading.

(*b*) *The Abridgments.* Abridgments were collections of reports, condensed, arranged according to subject matter and presented in the form of digests of Year Book cases. Some may have been the work of law students who grouped the side notes in the Year Books alphabetically. The most famous of the Abridgments were:

(*i*) *Statham* (*c.* 1480), based on selections from earlier abridgments. It consists of 258 titles which record 3750 summaries and points of cases.

(*ii*) *Fitzherbert's Graunde Abridgement* (*c.* 1516). In this celebrated three-volume Abridgment written by Sir Anthony Fitzherbert, a judge of Common Pleas, many reports, including those upon which Bracton based his *Note Book* (*see* 21 below) were used. The form is based on consecutive titles which are arranged alphabetically. Some of the cases heard during Richard I's reign as recorded by Fitzherbert are not found elsewhere. (Fitzherbert was also the author of the *Tabula of the Graunde Abridgement, The Diversity of the Courts,* and the *New Natura Brevium,* a selection of writs accompanied by a commentary.)

(*iii*) *Brooke's Abridgment* (pub. 1574) and *Rolle's Abridg-*

ment (1668) present digests of cases under the headings of titles and sub-titles.

(*c*) *The private reports.* Following the end of the Year Books private law reports were compiled, one of the first compilations being by Keilway. Dyer's *Reports* (1537–82) became well known. Edmund Plowden (1518–85) published his *Reports or Commentaries*, a collection of reports in Law French of cases heard from 1549–78 in the King's Bench, the Exchequer, and Common Pleas. His reports are more extensive than those in the Year Books. Coke's celebrated *Reports* cover 1572–1616 in 13 volumes, and include the pleadings, occasionally the arguments, and subjective comments intermingled with legal history. *The Term Reports* (1785–1800) were regularly issued. Burrow's *Reports* (1756–1772) set out facts clearly, gave arguments, judgments, and reasons for decisions.

NOTE: The Incorporated Council of Law Reporting was founded in 1866.

LEGAL TEXTBOOKS

18. General. The early textbooks tell us much of the procedures, the doctrines and the principles which made up the common law in its formative years. Below are mentioned the great texts of Glanvill, Bracton, St. Germain, Coke, and others, together with some minor authors.

19. Glanvill. *The Tractatus de Legibus et Consuetudinibus Regni Angliae tempore Regis Henrici Secundus* was finished *c.* 1187–89. Its author is believed to be Ranulf de Glanvill, Justiciar of Henry II, a judge, sheriff and diplomatist. Some historians attribute it to Hubert Walter, Glanvill's secretary. The work is our first great manual of the common law.

(*a*) It gives an ordered account of the law as administered in the king's courts.

(*b*) The text, which is in Latin, consists of 14 *libri*, each containing a number of *capita*, or headings.

(*c*) The first four sections are devoted to distinguishing criminal pleas (the more serious, including breaches of the king's peace, which are pleas of the crown, and minor offences which belong to the jurisdiction of the sheriffs) and civil pleas (those determined in the royal courts and those within the jurisdiction of the sheriffs).

(d) 75 writs are enumerated and their application is discussed.

(e) Procedure involved in litigation concerning land is discussed extensively.

(f) There is some trace of the author's interest in Roman law, and the preface is founded on some passages from the *Institutes of Justinian*.

NOTE: The Scottish adaptation of Glanvill is known as *Regiam Majestatem*.

20. Dialogus de Scaccario (Dialogue of the Exchequer). This work was written in 1177–79 by Richard fitz Nigel, Bishop of London. It outlines the organisation and procedure of the Exchequer and takes the form of questions and answers between a pupil and his master.

21. Bracton (d. 1286). Henry de Bracton (also known as Bratton) was a Justice in Eyre, a Judge of the King's Bench, and Chancellor of Exeter Cathedral. His *De Legibus et Consuetudinis Angliae* was written in 1250–56. Its unfinished state may have been the result of his having to surrender court records on ceasing to be a member of the King's court. The work is in Latin and consists of 444 folios (it is almost ten times the size of Glanvill's treatise of the same name).

(a) It is modelled in form on the *Summa* of Azo of Bologna. It cites over 5000 decisions of the king's judges, notably Martin of Pateshull and William Raleigh, drawn from the Plea Rolls (*see* **14** above). A large notebook (discovered by Vinogradoff in the British Museum in 1884) shows 2000 of the cases prepared by Bracton; this notebook was used by Fitzherbert in his *Abridgment* (*see* **17**(b) (ii) above).

(b) *De Legibus* is Roman in style and, in parts, follows the *Institutes* closely. The section dealing with property and persons, for example, has close parallels with certain titles in the *Institutes*.

(c) *The Liber Primus* (first 106 folios) deals with general principles; *the Liber Secundus* is concerned with commentaries on procedure of writs.

(d) The work, which may have been written as a manual

of common law for the instruction of Justices in Eyre, achieved great influence when used by Coke in his writings.

22. Other law books of the thirteenth and fourteenth centuries.

(a) *Britton* (c. 1290) was written by an unknown author (perhaps John le Breton, Bishop of Hertford) in the reign of Edward I. It takes the form of a code said to have been promulgated by Edward, which begins with a prologue addressed by the king "*a toux ses feaus et sugez de Engleterre et de Hyreland*" (to all his lieges and subjects of England and Ireland). The work is divided into six books, the last is unfinished. The first book consists of 32 chapters concerned mainly with criminal law; the other books discuss real actions and matters pertaining to them. The treatise is based upon Bracton and Fleta (*see* (b) below).

(b) *Fleta* (c. 1290–92) is a treatise written in Latin and based upon Bracton. Its author is unknown, but may have been Matthew Cheker. It has been suggested that it may have been written during the author's imprisonment in the Fleet prison. Part of the treatise is a description of the workings of the courts of law.

(c) *Summa Magna and Summa Parva* give accounts of procedure in real actions and were compiled by Sir Ralph de Hengham (d. 1311).

(d) *Mirror of Justices* (author unknown, but perhaps Andrew Horn) purports to discuss the law in the thirteenth century. It was used by Coke in his *Institutes*, but its reliability is limited—it has been described as "a mixture of sense and nonsense."

(e) *Natura Brevium* is an anonymous treatise on procedure, written in Law French, and includes writs and a commentary. When Fitzherbert published his *Natura Brevium* (*see* 17(b)(ii) above) this work became known as the *Old Natura Brevium*.

23. Sir John Fortescue (c. 1395–1479). Fortescue, Chief Justice of the King's Bench, wrote *De Laudibus Legum Angliae* (In praise of the Laws of England) in 1470, apparently as a manual of instruction for Prince Edward in the general laws of England. It takes the form of a dialogue between the author and the Prince and discusses common and civil law, and absolute and limited monarchy. In his *Governance of England* (the first book written in English about our law), Sir John discusses constitutional government and absolute monarchy.

24. Sir Thomas Littleton (c. 1407–81). Littleton, a Reader of the Inner Temple and Judge of the Court of Common Pleas, wrote a celebrated treatise (printed in 1481) on the law of real property, known as *New Tenures*.

(*a*) The work, written in Law French, was compiled for the writer's son, Richard.

(*b*) It consists of 749 sections (about 90,000 words), which deal with the common law of land tenures and estates as they existed at the end of the Middle Ages.

(*c*) The first book covers estates, the second deals with the various incidents of tenure, and the third discusses particular doctrines concerning real property.

(*d*) Coke referred to the work as "the most perfect and absolute work that was ever written in any human science." He based his *First Institute* (*see* **26** below) on it.

25. Christopher St. Germain (1460–1540). St. Germain, barrister of the Inner Temple, wrote two *Dialogues between a Doctor of Divinity and a Student of the Common Law*. The Dialogues consider problems of canon law, legal philosophy and equity. The first dialogue is general; the second is concerned with rules of law. On the common law he writes: "And because the said customs be neither against the law of God, nor the law of reason, and have always been taken to be good and necessary for the commonwealth of all the realm; therefore they have obtained the strength of a law, insomuch that he that doth against them doth against justice: and these be the customs that properly be called the common law."

26. Sir Edward Coke (1552–1634). Coke became Attorney-General in 1594, Chief Justice of Common Pleas in 1606, and Chief Justice of the King's Bench in 1613. In 1603 he prosecuted Raleigh, and, in 1605, the Gunpowder Plot conspirators. As one devoted to the common law, which he called "the perfection of reason," he quarrelled with James I and was dismissed by him in 1616 (*see* **IX, 18**). Known as "the greatest common lawyer of all time," his outstanding works were the

Reports (*see* **17**(*c*) above), and the *Institutes*, based on his mastery of the *Year Books* (*see* **17**(*a*) above).

(*a*) *The First Institute* (pub. 1628) is a translation of, and an extended commentary on Littleton's *Tenures* (*see* **24** above). This became a standard textbook on land law and is usually cited as *Co. Litt.*

(*b*) *The Second Institute* (published, after Coke's death, in 1642–44) is a commentary upon 39 statutes concerning public law, particularly from the reign of Edward I, and *Magna Carta*.

(*c*) *The Third Institute* (pub. 1642–44) discusses the criminal law.

(*d*) *The Fourth Institute* (pub. 1642–44) describes the jurisdiction and the history of the courts.

27. Bacon (1561–1626). (*See* IX, 30). Bacon was made Solicitor-General in 1607, Attorney-General in 1613, and Lord Chancellor in 1618. He was impeached and removed from office in 1621. His writings on the law include:

(*a*) *Readings on the Statute of Uses* (1600).

(*b*) *Maxims of the Law* (1596), in which he comments upon 25 maxims selected from a collection of 300 which he had made.

(*c*) *Legal Aphorisms* (97 in number) which forms a part of his *De Dignitate et Augmentis Scientiarum*.

28. Other law books of the sixteenth and seventeenth centuries.

(*a*) *John Rastell* (d. 1536), who had married the sister of Sir Thomas More, compiled the first law dictionary, the *Expositiones terminorum legum Anglorum*. The 16th edition is known as *Les termes de la Ley*.

(*b*) *Sir Thomas Smith* (1513–77), wrote, in 1565, *De Republica Anglorum*, which deals with the issues of constitutional law and procedure in the courts of law. The object of the treatise was to show "how England standeth and is governed at this day."

(*c*) *Gerald Malynes* (d. 1641), wrote *Lex Mercatoria* (1622), which outlines the legal basis of the bill of exchange, with reference to continental doctrines of mercantile law.

(*d*) *Richard Zouche* (1589–1661,) Professor of Civil Law at

Oxford, wrote a two-volume treatise on feudal law, entitled *Elementa Jurisprudentiae.*

(e) *John Selden* (1584–1654) edited *Fleta* (*see* 22(b) above) and wrote *Janus Anglorum* (1610), and a *History of Tithes* (1618). *Table Talk* consists of notes of his conversation, recorded by his secretary, Richard Milward.

29. Sir Matthew Hale (1609–76). Hale, Chief Justice of the King's Bench, wrote *Jurisdiction of the Lord's House*, which discussed the position of the House of Lords, an incomplete *History of the Common Law*, and the celebrated work on criminal law, *Pleas of the Crown.*

30. Sir William Blackstone (1723–80). Blackstone was the first Vinerian Professor of English Law at Oxford, M.P. for Westbury, and a Judge of Common Pleas. He wrote the famous *Commentaries on the Laws of England* (pub. 1765). The work gives a detailed picture of the English legal system and appeared in four volumes—*The Rights of Persons*; *The Rights of Things*; *Private Wrongs*; *Public Wrongs.* In Blackstone's view laws are rules of civil conduct prescribed by the supreme power in a state, commanding that which is right and forbidding that which is wrong. Such laws are valid only if they conform to the law of nature or of God. "No human laws are of any validity if contrary to this."

PROGRESS TEST 5

1. What is meant by the phrase "the common law"? **(1)**

2. What is the importance of judicial decisions in the common law? **(3)**

3. Is there any connection between the early common law and Roman law? **(6)**

4. Enumerate the main sources of the common law. **(7)**

5. What criteria must be satisfied before a practice might be considered as a valid custom? **(8)**

6. What were (a) *the Quadripartitus,* (b) *Leges Willelmi,* (c) *Leges Henrici Primi*? **(12)**

7. What were the Pipe rolls? **(15)**

8. What were the Abridgments? **(17)**

9. Give an account of Glanvill's *Tractatus.* **(19)**

10. What was the importance of the work of Bracton? **(21)**

11. What were the contributions to legal literature of (a) Littleton, (b) Coke? **(24, 26)**

CHAPTER VI

FORMS OF ACTION AND PROCEDURE UNDER THE COMMON LAW—1

THE FORMS OF ACTION

1. General. "So great is the ascendency of the Law of Actions in the infancy of Courts of Justice, that substantive law has at first the look of being gradually secreted in the interstices of procedure." (Maine: *Early Law and Custom*). "The system of Forms of Action or the Writ system is the most important characteristic of English medieval law. . . . The Forms of Action we have buried, but they still rule us from their graves." (Maitland: *The Forms of Action at Common Law*). In the development of our common law, forms of action and their appropriate procedures played a vital part.

(*a*) The term "forms of action" includes the *writs* by which proceedings were started, the events leading to judgment, and, in some cases, the execution of the judgment. The writ system was at the basis of the forms of action.

(*b*) Each form of action had its appropriate procedure.

(*c*) The system of forms of action as outlined below lasted, in general, until the nineteenth century.

2. Writs. A writ (A. S. *gewrit*) was primarily an administrative document, authenticated by a seal, in the form of a letter. It was used for administrative and judicial purposes and when issued by the king it took the form of a command, often to the sheriff. An example of a writ: "The King to the Sheriff of Essex, Greeting. We command thee to execute justice without delay against X so that he shall justly and swiftly render to Y the twenty shillings which he owes him, as it has been said, and as Y may reasonably show he ought, that we may hear no more clamour for default of justice thereof."

The following matters are important:

(*a*) An action began with a writ, obtainable only from the *officina brevium* controlled by the king's chancellor.

71

(b) The writ chosen would result in a particular form of action and appropriate procedure.

(c) Procedure was all-important; it became more significant than the right itself. Faulty procedure, even an error in mere formalities, led to a loss of remedy.

(d) For some time the rule was: "*Ubi remedium, ibi jus*" (where there is a remedy there is a right) *i.e.* unless there is an appropriate writ there is no cause of action.

3. Classification of actions. Actions came to be considered under three headings:

(a) *Real actions*. These concerned real property and were used to determine questions concerning title to land.

(b) *Personal actions*. These concerned debt and satisfaction in damages for injury done to a plaintiff's person or property.

(c) *Mixed actions*. These were in the nature of (a) and (b).

4. Early development of the writ system. By the thirteenth century there had been a considerable growth in the number of writs issued. The limitation on available writs (*see* 2(d) above) had made it impossible to obtain justice in many cases and, as a result, there had been a successful demand for the invention of new writs.

(a) Bracton (*see* V, 21) was able to say that in his day: "*Tot erunt formulae brevium quot sunt genera actionum*" (there are as many forms of action as there are causes of action). Thus, where a wrong was complained of and there was no remedy in existence, one would be created.

(b) This great expansion of the writ system aroused the hostility of the barons. The growing number of writs (50 in the time of Henry III; 500 in the time of Edward I) had led to a great extension of the jurisdiction of the king's courts, and, hence, to an increase in royal power. Following the success of the Barons under de Montfort in the reign of Henry III, the *Provisions of Oxford*, 1258, ruled that the Chancellor should seal no "new writs" without the permission of the king and the Great Council (which was under baronial control). Thus, the issue of writs was limited to *brevia formata* (recognised writs), known also as writs *de cursu* (writs issued as of course); the issue of *brevia magistralia* (writs which might be varied in accordance with the complainant's particular circumstances) was forbidden. The situation was now: *"Tot erunt actiones quot sunt formulae brevium"* (there are only as many causes of action as there are forms of action), or, *"Ubi remedium, ibi jus"* (*see* 2(*d*) above).

(*c*) *The Statute of Westminster II*, 1285, enacted that the clerks in Chancery could vary writs *in consimili casu* (in like case), *i.e.* where plaintiff's case was based on facts which would have allowed the issue of a *brevium formatum*. The Statute allowed the variation of existing writs, but not the creation of new rights or remedies: "And whensoever from henceforth it shall fortune in the Chancery that in one case a writ is found, and in like case falling under like law, and requiring like remedy, is found none, the clerks of the Chancery shall agree in making the writ."

5. Writs and the king's courts. In the early communal and feudal courts (*see* XII), the common modes of proof were often by oath and ordeal (*see* **9** below, and XVII, **15**–**18**). The king's courts used a more advanced procedure: there might be an inquest by a jury, there were professional judges, and there was power to enforce judgments. Hence the importance of these courts increased. Under Henry II it was established that the king's writ was essential to the commencement in any court of litigation concerning freehold land. As a result, side by side with the growth in the importance of the king's courts, there was a considerable growth in the significance of writs, particularly in connection with land—the most important form of wealth in that era.

PROCEDURE IN ACTIONS BEFORE THE FEUDAL AND COMMUNAL COURTS

6. Summons and preliminary proceedings. Failure to obey a summons could result in outlawry, by which the protection of the law was withdrawn from the outlaw (*see* XVII, **24**). Plaintiff's claim had to be voiced before the court according to a strict pattern, deviation from which could result in termination of the proceedings. Defendant replied in formal terms and was then required to provide some security, which was evidence of his guaranteeing to accept the decision of the court. Plaintiff's assertions were supported by a body of witnesses who swore to the genuineness of his complaint.

7. Proof. The court would then allot the responsibility of proof. In general the onus of proof was on the defendant. Three important modes of proof were in use: witnesses; compurgation, or wager of law; battle. They are considered at **8–10** below.

8. Witnesses. Witnesses swore on oath to the truth, or lack of truth, concerning the facts on which the claim was based. The number of witnesses produced by a party was often taken into account when considering the credibility of his case.

9. Compurgation, or wager of law. In this mode of proof plaintiff or defendant took an oath, and was supported by a group of oath-helpers (compurgators) who swore that his oath was "clean and without perjury."

(a) When a party was adjudged so that he had to provide proof of his case in this mode, he was obliged to provide security that he would produce compurgators; this was known as "waging one's law" (vadiare legem).

(b) When he performed successfully in this mode it was known as "making one's law" (facere legem).

(c) Twelve compurgators were required, but more could be called, usually in multiples of three, in the case of a very serious allegation.

(d) The oath was taken in a highly formal manner. If one wrong word were used, the oath was said to have "burst" and the case was lost.

(e) In some cases the party could choose between compurgation and the ordeal (see XVII, **15**).

(f) The solemnity of the oath reflected the medieval religious fear of the consequences of perjury.

(g) The mode was gradually discredited as courts came to prefer impartial testimony. (The last case involving a wager of law was King v. Williams (1824) 2 B. & C. 538.)

10. Battle. Trial by battle was a Norman institution. It was, in essence, an appeal to the God of Battles to bring victory to the rightful party.

(*a*) It was used in Norman times in disputes concerning title to land and in appeals of felony (*see* XX, 7).

(*b*) The party concerned was generally required to do battle, but hired champions were used where the appellant was an infant, a woman, a priest, blind or disabled, or over sixty.

(*c*) The parties, each armed with a leather shield and a staff one ell long, took an oath as to the righteousness of their cause, and then, at the place of battle, took another oath.

(*d*) Plaintiff, or his champion, was placed at the east end of the battle list, the defendant at the west end. (If either failed to appear a non-suit was recorded.) The fight continued until nightfall (in which case plaintiff was considered as having lost) or until one side gave in.

(*e*) The outcome of the battle was considered as a divine judgment.

(*f*) In *Ashford* v. *Thornton* (1818) 1 B. & Ald. 405, an attempt was made to claim the procedure, which had been obsolescent for a long period. It was abolished in 1819.

EARLY PROCEDURE IN THE KING'S COURTS

11. Use of writs. The rule was *"Non potest quis sine brevi agere"*—there could be no action in the king's common law courts without a writ from the king. The writs were issued from the Chancery and commanded defendant to appear to answer the claim stated therein. To fail to appear was to incur a penalty for contempt of the writ.

12. The "original writ." Proceedings started with the issue of an *original writ*, under the seal of the Chancellor. Such a writ was essential to appearance in the king's courts.

13. The "judicial writ." During the proceedings (*i.e.* bringing parties to court, obtaining and executing judgment—known collectively as the *mesne process*) a *judicial writ* could be issued (*e.g.* in order to bring a witness to court). Such a writ was issued by the judges and was sealed in the Chancery.

14. The trial. Proceedings were very formal, and culminated in an order to a party to prove his case by an established mode of proof. Jury trial was later introduced. From such trials there emerged, of particular significance in the growth of common law procedure:

 (a) The use and development of fictions (*see* VII, **12–15**);

 (b) The development of oral and written forms of pleadings (*see* VII, **16**).

WRIT OF RIGHT AND THE POSSESSORY ASSIZES

15. Writ of right. In the time of Henry II it was ruled that a man need not answer a claim concerning the land he held by free tenure *unless a royal writ had been obtained*. The writ was known as a writ of right (*breve de recto tenendo*).

 (a) Where the dispute was between two tenants-in-chief the writ was known as a *praecipe*. It was addressed to the sheriff, commanding him to order defendant to surrender the land to plaintiff, or to answer in the king's court for failure to do so.

 (b) Where the dispute involved a tenant holding from a mesne lord (*i.e.* one who held, in turn, from a superior lord), the writ (known as a *writ of right close*) ordered the lord to do full right in his court, otherwise the matter would be removed, by the process of *tolt* into the county court. A further precept to the sheriff, known as *pone*, could remove the case into the king's court.

 (c) The procedure was very slow and could involve considerable delay. Thus, defendant could delay proceedings by *essoins*, *i.e.* excuses made for non-appearance. Bracton tells of such an excuse, arising from defendant's "taking to his bed for one year and one day," such *languor* to be verified by a visiting committee of four knights.

16. The Grand Assize. Trial by battle was the recognised mode of determining questions concerning title to land. In 1179 Henry allowed the defendant to a writ of right a choice between trial by battle and decision by inquest in the king's court. This ordinance became known as *the Grand Assize*, and where a party took advantage of it, he was considered as having "put himself upon the Grand Assize." Glanvill says of the Grand Assize: "It is a royal boon conceded to the people by the clemency of the prince. . . . It proceeds from the highest equity; for the right which after many and long delays can hardly be said to be proved by battle is more rapidly and more fitly demonstrated by this beneficent ordinance."

(a) Where defendant put himself upon the Grand Assize, a royal writ was issued directing the sheriff to summon four knights of his shire. They, in turn, chose another twelve knights, who were to decide by sworn verdict which party had the greater right to the land. Here is a significant step along the road to jury trial.

(b) The right was available only to defendant; plaintiff might be offered only trial by battle. It is doubtful whether it was available to a purchaser.

(c) The right could be exercised only in the king's court.

17. The Possessory (or Petty) Assizes. Under this procedure, which has overtones of the Roman Praetorian interdict *unde vi*, Henry II gave summary remedies to those who claimed that they had been dispossessed of freehold land. A successful demandant was put back in possession, even though defendant might have had a better right—which could be maintained by a writ of right (*see* **15** above). The Assizes of *Novel Disseisin*, *Mort d'Ancestor*, *Darrein Presentment* are discussed at **18-20** below.

18. Novel Disseisin. The concept of *seisin* is discussed at XXIV. It was, in general terms, a phrase used to indicate *possession* of an estate of freehold in land. The essence of the *Novel Disseisin* was a complaint by P to the King that D had, without judgment, unjustly disseised P of his freehold tenement. The complaint was followed by a request that the king's court should give judgment so that P might be put back into seisin.

(a) Immediately P lodged his complaint, a writ was issued to the sheriff ordering him to empanel twelve freemen of the neighbourhood to view the disputed land and to report to the king's judge on his next visit to the county as to whether P had been disseised by D unjustly and without judgment. Where the answer was "yes," P was put back into seisin.

(b) P was allowed a few days (usually four) following the disseisin to recover the seisin himself, where that was possible.

(c) The assize was available only for a disseisee against a disseisor; it was not available to heirs.

(*d*) It did not decide proprietary rights—the writ of right was available for this.

(*e*) It had to be brought within a limited time, as fixed by royal ordinance, usually in relation to a recent event, *e.g.* the king's last visit to France.

(*f*) No *essoins* (*see* **15**(*c*) above) were allowed.

(*g*) The procedure was available only in the king's court.

19. Mort d'Ancestor (Assisa de Morte Antecessoris). Where X died seised as of an estate in fee, and his heir, P, should have been seised of that estate, then if any person obtained seisin before P, that person was to be turned out and seisin restored to P.

(*a*) The procedure resembled that of *Novel Disseisin*.

(*b*) The remedy was not available to those claiming through the disseisor.

(*c*) The assize was available only in the case of the death of a father, mother, brother, sister, uncle or aunt. It was extended in 1237 in the Actions of *Aiel* (a grandfather), *Besaiel* (great-grandfather), *Cosinage* (all other relations).

20. Darrein Presentment, or last presentation (de ultima presentatione). In the Middle Ages the advowsons of churches (*i.e.* the rights of patronage involving presentation of a parson to a church or benefice) were of importance. The principle of the assize of *Darrein Presentment* was that where a benefice was vacant, the right to present belonged to the person who last presented, or to his heir. The panel of freemen (*see* **18**(*a*) above) would decide who last presented. The act of presenting was considered as possession of the advowson, or *seisin*.

NOTE: *The Assize of Utrum* also concerned church property. Where land was dedicated to the use of a church in *frankalmoin* (free alms—*see* XXIII, **23**), the church had a right to decide disputes relating to that land. But if a question arose as to whether the land was held in *frankalmoin* or in lay tenure, twelve freemen were empanelled to decide whether (*utrum*) the tenement was held in one mode or the other. Procedure was laid down in the *Constitutions of Clarendon*, 1164, *c*. 9.

THE WRIT OF ENTRY

21. Basis of the writ. Writs of entry were invented in the thirteenth century. Actions on a writ of entry were brought by those from whom land had been wrongfully withheld. In the writ was stated an alleged flaw in defendant's title, which would justify the hearing of such an action in the king's court. The writ might have run thus: "To the sheriff of Surrey, Greeting. Command A that he render justly and without delay to B the manor house at High Wykehurst which B claims to be his by right and inheritance and into which A had no entry save through C who had demised it to A and who unjustly and without judgment disseised D, the father of B since the voyage of our Lord the King into Normandy." (A's refusal to surrender the property would result in his answering in the king's court.)

22. Types of writ of entry. Such writs could be:

(a) *Writs of entry sur disseisin* (as in the example at **21** above); or

(b) *Writs of entry not sur disseisin,* as where the alleged defect in defendant's title did not arise as the result of disseisin, *e.g.* as in the writ *Cui in Vita* (involving the granting away of land by a husband during marriage).

23. Development of the writ. Originally the writ of entry was confined to relatively recent flaws in defendant's title. By the *Statute of Marlborough,* 1267, defendant's title could be traced back without any limitation as to time. Writs of entry were abolished under the *Real Property Limitation Act,* 1833.

NOTE: *The querela.* Procedure without writ, by direct complaint to the king's itinerant justices was possible after *c.* 1170. By use of the *querela,* a plaintiff in the time of Henry III could make a statement of claim which was heard by the justices if the alleged wrong had been committed while the Eyre (*see* XIII, **21**) was actually in session. With the exception of the duration of the Eyre's sessions, the *querela* was limited to a period of one year.

PROGRESS TEST 6

1. What was a writ? **(2)**
2. How were actions classified? **(3)**

3. Explain (a) *brevia formata*, (b) *brevia magistralia*. **(4)**
4. Explain *in consimili casu*. **(4)**
5. What was the procedure of compurgation? **(9)**
6. Outline the main features of trial by battle. **(10)**
7. Explain the rule *non potest quis sine brevi agere*. **(11)**
8. What was a writ of right? **(15)**
9. Explain the importance of the Grand Assize. **(16)**
10. What were the Possessory Assizes? **(18–20)**
11. What was (a) *the Assize of Utrum*, (b) *the querela*? **(20, 23)**

CHAPTER VII

FORMS OF ACTION AND PROCEDURE UNDER THE COMMON LAW—2

TRESPASS—"THE FERTILE MOTHER OF ACTIONS"

1. General. One of the most important writs was the writ of trespass. From trespass developed a number of personal actions, some of which are considered in this chapter.

(*a*) The writ of trespass was issued in the case of a wrong committed with force and arms against the king's peace—*vi et armis contra pacem domini regis*. From the time of Edward I the main varieties of trespass came to be:

(*i*) *Trespass vi et armis, i.e.* an injury to plaintiff accompanied by force and violence.

(*ii*) *Trespass quare clausum fregit* ("because he broke into the close"), *i.e.* unlawful entry on plaintiff's land.

(*iii*) *Trespass de bonis asportatis, i.e.* the wrongful taking of chattels.

(*b*) It was sometimes possible to vary the writ to suit the circumstances of other types of case.

(*c*) "With force of arms" and "against the king's peace" were essential factors for a successful action in trespass. Absence of one of these factors led to a failure of the action.

(*d*) A successful action led to damages and was thus in the nature of civil proceedings. But a breach of the peace as alleged in the writ was semi-criminal in nature, since it could lead to fine and imprisonment by the king's court.

2. Origin of trespass. A number of suggestions have been put forward:

(*a*) The writ of trespass to goods may have originated in the appeal of felony (*appellum de felonia—see* XX, **7**). The appellant alleged of the appellee a felony committed *vi et armis et contra pacem domini regis*. Trespass is thus considered in the nature of an appeal based on alleged violence.

(*b*) Trespass to land may have originated in the *Assize of Novel Disseisin* (*see* VI, **18**). That remedy led to the recovery of land, but there may have been no remedy for chattels on the land (*e.g.* crops) which may have been destroyed. The assize was modified so that damages could be awarded in such a case. From this may have stemmed damages in trespass.

(*c*) The writ may have developed as a response to the general disorders in the realm following the baronial wars in the reign of Henry III.

(*d*) The writ may have originated in the desire of the crown to increase its jurisdiction and revenues. Defendants were liable to the payment of a fine to the king, and a breach of peace alleged in the writ was considered as a *plea of the crown*.

NOTE: Trespass is considered further at XX.

3. Writ of ejectment. An important variety of the action of trespass was the *action of ejectment*, which was used for the recovery of land. The two main types of the writ were:

(*a*) *Quare ejecit infra terminum*. This writ could be brought by a leaseholder against his landlord.

(*b*) *Ejectio firmae*. A possessor of a term of years was able to recover damages if ejected from his land. At the end of the fifteenth century, however, not only damages but possession of the land could be recovered by the use of the writ. This development enabled the writ to be used in place of the old forms of *real actions*, and it became possible to recover freehold land by bringing an action in the name of a tenant. The procedure was as follows:

(*i*) Plaintiff entered the land and handed a lease to A.

(*ii*) A then entered under the lease and was ejected by defendant.

(*iii*) A brought an action against defendant.

(*iv*) The validity of A's lease was decided by judgment in his favour. If A received judgment the lease was considered valid, and, as a result, plaintiff who had handed the lease to A was considered as having a good title.

From this developed the fictitious action which is considered at **15** below.

The *action of ejectment* was abolished by the *Common Law Procedure Act*, 1852.

4. The personal actions. The important personal actions other than trespass were: *detinue, debt, account, covenant replevin, case, trover, assumpsit.* Some are considered below or at appropriate points in other chapters.

5. Detinue. *See* XX, **13**. This action may have grown out of the *action of debt* (*see* **6** below). It lay where D was unlawfully detaining a chattel the possession of which was claimed by P.

(*a*) D was ordered to deliver the chattels *quae ei injuste detinet* (which he unjustly withholds) to P.

(*b*) Originally the action was limited to a claim arising out of bailment; but by 1400 it was available generally in the case of a wrongful detention.

(*c*) D might be allowed to keep the chattel and pay its value, if he so wished.

(*d*) The defence of wager of law (*see* VI, **9**) was available to plaintiff.

6. Debt. *See* XXI, **10**. A writ of debt lay for the recovery of a liquidated sum. Plaintiff was required to show that defendant had obtained a benefit which had a money value. This *quid pro quo* was essential to the action. Thus, where D agreed to sell P a chattel, P could not recover damages if D repudiated the agreement before delivering the chattel to P. In this case D had received nothing and there was no *quid pro quo*. It was necessary to prove the exact amount of the debt. In the case of a debt on a contract, wager of law was allowed. The action was used *e.g* to recover statutory penalties, arrears of rent, and price of goods sold.

7. Account. *See* XXI, **14–16**. This action seems to have originated in the thirteenth century. In its origin it may have been available to the lord of a manor so as to order his bailiff to account for the profits of the manor. Later it became available to any plaintiff who wished to compel a defendant to provide details of the debts owed by him (to plaintiff). The action was not based on contract, but rested on a *duty* by D to account to P. Wager of law was available to a defendant. The procedure was very lengthy and technical.

D

8. Replevin. *See* XX, **14.** Replevin lay originally to determine the legality of an allegedly wrongful distress. The distrainee had to provide security that he would contest the distrainor's right, and, at that point, the distrainor was obliged to surrender the goods. If he failed to do so, the sheriff could retake them with the assistance of the *posse comitatus* (power of the county), a group of able-bodied men of the county.

(*a*) Defendant was allowed to wage his law.

(*b*) Where defendant obtained a judgment for the re-delivery of goods and the sheriff returned *elongata* (*i.e.* that the goods had been taken to a place unknown), a writ of *capias* commanded the sheriff to seize plaintiff's goods to the value of those replevied, and to deliver them to defendant, who was to keep them until the goods taken were returned.

(*c*) By the *Statute of Marlborough*, 1267, a simpler form of replevin was allowed, by which a complaint to a sheriff, without a royal writ, sufficed.

TRESPASS UPON THE CASE

9. General. As society developed in the fifteenth and sixteenth centuries, so the rigidities and deficiencies of the writ system began to be burdensome. The growth of commerce and trade led to demands for a modification of that system. The procedure known as *action on the case* extended the viability of the forms of action and provided the foundations of the modern law of contract and torts. The action avoided the restrictive formulae of the older writs and was based upon a form of writ which stated plaintiff's particular case. According to Coke, action on the case originated in the procedure of *in consimili casu*, 1285 (*see* VI, **4**(*c*)). As special writs of trespass upon the case developed they were given special names, *e.g. trover*. Innominate actions were referred to as "actions upon the special case." Two particularly important actions of trespass on the case were *trover* and *assumpsit*.

10. Trover. *See* XX, **15.** Trover lay for conversion of property to the defendant's use. It appeared *c.* 1480 and was later developed by the procedural incorporation of a fictitious loss and finding by defendant.

(*a*) P alleged that he possessed the goods in question until he had casually lost them. He alleged, further, that D then found them and converted them to his (D's) use.

(*b*) D was not allowed to dispute the allegation of loss and finding, but had to answer the allegation of having converted the goods.

(*c*) Trover was not available if there was merely interference with the goods.

(*d*) The action eventually covered cases of unlawful taking (trespass) and unlawful detention (detinue).

11. Assumpsit. *See* XXI, **22.** This action, which grew out of trespass on the case was one of the foundations of the law of contract. It applied originally only to a *misfeasance, i.e.* where D had caused damage to P by his mode of carrying out something *he had undertaken to do*, as where D promised to cure P's horse and the horse later died as a result of D's negligence. There could be no action for trespass here because D had not wrongfully interfered with P's possession.

(*a*) In the early fifteenth century, the action covered the case of *malfeasance, i.e.* performance involving fraud or guile.

(*b*) In the early sixteenth century *assumpsit* was allowed as a remedy for *non-feasance, i.e.* failure to carry out a promise.

(*c*) In *Slade's Case* (1602)—*see* XXI, **24**—it was decided that "every executory contract imports in itself an assumpsit." As a result *assumpsit* superseded *debt.*

LEGAL FICTIONS IN THE DEVELOPMENT OF THE FORMS OF ACTION

12. The meaning and purpose of fictions. A legal fiction is based on a supposition which is known to be untrue, but which is not allowed to be denied. Fictions were used in the development of the forms of action for the following purposes:

(*a*) To extend the jurisdiction of the courts;
(*b*) To extend the scope of available remedies;
(*c*) To by-pass some of the more ancient forms of action.

Examples of these fictions are given below.

13. Fictions which extended jurisdiction. Two such fictions are considered here:

(a) *Bill of Middlesex.* The bill was issued so as to cover the case of a defendant who was somewhere other than in Middlesex. It alleged that defendant had committed a trespass *vi et armis* and that he was resident in Middlesex. The sheriff then made a return to the writ of *non est inventus* (he is not found). A writ of *latitat (latitat et discurrit =* he lurks and runs about) was then issued to the sheriff of the county in which defendant was to be found. The alleged trespass became, in time, a fiction, and, at a later date, proceedings began with *latitat.* In the reign of Charles II, the real cause of the action had to be stated in an additional clause, known as *ac etiam* (= and also). This fiction was abolished by the *Uniformity of Process Act,* 1832.

(b) *Writ of quominus.* See XIII, **10**(a). This Exchequer writ, issued *c.* 1300, alleged that P had lent D a sum of money and that P was unable to repay a debt of similar amount to the crown because of D's debt. P's debt to the crown was fictitious. Because the Exchequer was concerned with crown revenues its jurisdiction was extended as a result of the employment of this fiction.

14. Fictions which extended the scope of available remedies. In *trover (see* **10** above) it was alleged fictitiously that D had found P's goods and had converted them to his (D's) own use. In this way the writ was extended so as to cover a case of unlawful detention and unlawful taking.

15. Fictions which by-passed the more ancient forms of action. The writ of ejectment *(see* **3** above) originated to protect a leaseholder. By a fictitious process it was made available to a freeholder. The process was as follows:

(a) The nominal plaintiff was a fictitious person, known as John Doe. It was declared that the real plaintiff had granted a lease to Doe, and that he had entered under that lease. It was alleged further that Richard Roe, another fictitious character, had ejected him.

(b) The action commenced under the title of *Doe* v. *Roe.*

(c) The real plaintiff served the real defendant who was in

possession of the land with a notice stating that Roe had been served but had declined to defend the action.

(d) The real defendant could then defend, if he agreed to the prior fictitious steps in the process.

(e) The action was renamed *Doe on the demise* [*i.e. lease*] of *A.* v. *B,* or, *Doe d. A.* v. *B.*

This fiction disappeared under the *Common Law Procedure Act,* 1852.

NOTE: *See* also the fictitious procedure in *Quare Clausum fregit,* at XIII, **12**(*f*).

SOME PROCEDURAL DEVELOPMENTS

16. Pleadings. The very early pleadings were oral, and consisted of sworn statements which declared the matter in issue. In later times the pleadings were addressed to the court, which was called upon to settle the issue. "Pleading to the issue" involved plaintiff's asserting through his counsel the factual matters which entitled him to the judgment demanded in the writ. Defendant replied by suggesting alternative facts. This oral pleading took place before the judges, but no jury was present. The judges then accepted a plea which was recorded in the plea rolls.

17. Written pleadings. In the fifteenth and sixteenth centuries a change in procedure took place. Plaintiff and defendant now made their allegations of fact in written documents. This helped to define the issue clearly before it came to court. It also resulted in the growth of technicalities peculiar to the consideration of written pleadings. If the pleadings were accepted they were recorded in the court roll. Thus the skill of the pleader became of great importance. It became his task to express points of law in the particular terms of the selected form of action, and to reduce questions of fact to an issue which the jury could accept or reject.

18. Issue of the writ. In time procedure was altered so that it became unnecessary to issue the original writ. The issue of the writ was presumed when defendant came before the court as a result of the use of other procedures.

DECLINE OF THE FORMS OF ACTION

19. Rigours and complexities of the forms of action. In its origin and early stages the common law was not hampered by technicalities. But in the era of its development associated with the writ system it acquired a complexity and a rigidity which often combined to produce injustice. This led to a search for new remedies, provided eventually by the Chancellors, which resulted ultimately in the establishment of the system of equity (*see* Part Three). Writs were expensive and, hence, not available to all who required them. They were available only in certain cases and, for a long period, were incapable of extension to embrace new circumstances. An added difficulty was that joinder of actions was severely restricted.

20. Procedural technicalities. Procedure came to dominate the writ system so that it acquired more importance than the rights in issue. The correct writ had to be chosen, and an incorrect choice often left plaintiff without a remedy. A slight error in the writ, or in the pleadings, could rob plaintiff of his remedy. The dominance of technicalities was epitomised by the rules of the action in debt.

(*a*) Such an action was not available to recover a sum which was neither certain nor fixed. A claim on a *quantum meruit* was not recognised. Brian, C. J., declared in 1473: "If I bring cloth to a tailor to have a cloak made, if the price be not determined beforehand that I shall pay for the making, he shall not have an action of debt against me."

(*b*) If plaintiff obtained a verdict for more or less than the precise sum claimed, he recovered nothing.

(*c*) The inflexibility and growing irrelevance of the restrictive technical rules is epitomised in *Denom* v. *Scot* (1343) 17 Ed. III (R.S.) 298. X sued Y on a debt of £20. Y pleaded truthfully that X had recovered judgment on the very same debt in a previous action and had received payment. (In fact, Y was being asked to pay again.) The deed which recorded the debt had not been cancelled after the payment. The court's judgment was that Y had to pay X again. The judgment of Shardelowe, J., stated: "The court adjudges that he [X] do recover his debt and damages assessed by the Court. And see now that the deed be cancelled."

21. Abolition of the forms of action. Equity, which had been called into existence to modify the harshness of the writ-dominated forms of action, itself almost succumbed to technicalities which produced inflexibility. The nineteenth century witnessed attempts to overcome the rigidity of both equity and the common law.

(*a*) *Uniformity of Process Act*, 1832, abolished many of the fictions employed in the actions (*see* **13–15** above). Personal actions were to be commenced by a common writ which would state the nature of the action.

(*b*) *Real Property Limitation Act*, 1833, abolished sixty of the real actions and left three only.

(*c*) *Common Law Procedure Acts*, 1852–60, abolished the remaining real actions.

(*d*) *The Judicature Act*, 1873, which is discussed in XI, completed the abolition of the forms of action. Rules of pleading were to be governed by rules of the court, and proceedings could be commenced henceforth in a variety of ways.

PROGRESS TEST 7

1. What were the main varieties of trespass?   **(1)**
2. What was the origin of trespass?   **(2)**
3. Explain *ejectio firmae*.   **(3)**
4. Enumerate the important personal actions.   **(4)**
5. Explain *posse comitatus*.   **(8)**
6. Give an outline of *assumpsit*.   **(11)**
7. What was meant by a fiction?   **(12)**
8. Explain the procedure of the *Bill of Middlesex*.   **(13)**
9. Why did the forms of action decline?   **(19, 20)**

PART THREE
EQUITY

CHAPTER VIII

THE MEANING AND GENERAL SCOPE OF EQUITY

ITS MEANING

1. The popular meaning. Equity is defined in the dictionary as "the quality of being equal or fair; impartiality; even-handed dealing," and its derivation is indicated as *aequus* (= even, fair). In popular usage the term denotes ideas of that which is just or right, or that which is derived from the exercise of the conscience or from the doctrines of so-called natural justice.

2. The technical meaning. Maine speaks of equity as "any body of rules existing by the side of the original civil law, founded on distinct principles and claiming incidentally to supersede the civil law in virtue of a superior sanctity inherent in these principles." In general, doctrines of an equitable character tend to appear in the development of legal systems when the working of those systems no longer corresponds to the needs of society, and when the rigid application of the rules of those systems not only ceases to develop the law but, instead, fetters that development. When this situation has arisen there has usually emerged a body of supplementary rules, designed to make good the deficiencies of the system, and, in particular, to modify the injustices produced by an inflexible application of that system's rules.

3. A working definition of equity. We shall consider equity as, in its essence, a system of legal doctrines and procedures which developed side by side with the common law and statute law, having originated in the doctrines and procedures evolved by the Court of Chancery in its attempts to remedy some of the defects of the common law.

EQUITY IN THE ANCIENT LAW

4. The Greeks. Greek thinkers had attempted to analyse the contradictory elements of a system of law which, on the one hand, necessitated the universal application of its rules in the community, but which, on the other hand, demanded some modification of those rules in certain individual cases. Judicial discretion was of great importance.

(a) *Plato* (c. 428 B.C.–348 B.C.). In the *Statesman* Plato explains: "The differences of men and their actions do not allow any universal or simple rule. No art can lay down any rule which will be eternal. . . . But this the law seeks to do. . . . A perfectly simple principle cannot be applied to a state of things which is the opposite of simple."

(b) *Aristotle* (384 B.C.–322 B.C.). In the *Ethics* Aristotle states· "That which is equitable is just, not legally just, simply a correction of legal justice. This is so because the law is universal, but it is not possible to make statements about some things. When the law makes a universal statement and a case arises out of it which is not embraced in that statement, it becomes right, when the law maker falls into error by oversimplifying, to correct such an omission . . . this is the nature of the equitable, to correct the law where, because of its universality, it is defective."

5. The Romans. *Jus est ars boni et aequi* (Law is the art of what is good and fair)—*The Digest*. Roman law developed from an elaborate and rigid code, partly based originally on the semi-legendary *Twelve Tables*, into a flexible system—the *jus gentium*—in which doctrines based on concepts of fairness played an important part. In this development a type of equity grew out of the work of the Roman jurists, whose task it was to interpret the written law, and out of the decrees of the praetors, who supplemented some inadequacies of the law by providing remedies where none had existed.

EQUITY IN ENGLISH LAW

6. General. Equity did not develop in any sense as a self-contained body of doctrine. Its origins were in the common law; it has never had an existence independent of the common law.

(a) Equity developed as a modification of, and supplement to the common law. "Equity came to fulfil the law, not to destroy it."

(b) In some circumstances it has apparently rivalled the common law. Its growing might was a cause of strife with common law judges. (See IX, **15.**)

(c) Largely as a result of the *Judicature Acts* (1873–75), which are discussed in XI, there is now a fusion of the administration of law and equity. They stand today not as rivals, but as integral parts of a unified system.

7. Conscience and equity. The ecclesiastical background of the early chancellors and their training in canon law tended to the dissemination of concepts of natural justice based on the laws of God and the doctrines of Conscience. Some chancellors considered themselves as "Keepers of the King's Conscience." In the fifteenth century it was possible for a chancellor to state that "any law is or of right ought to be according to the law of God." Equitable relief was at the discretion of the chancellor and this discretion was to be exercised in accordance with conscience. Selden, in his *Table Talk* (see V, **28**), reflected: "Equity is according to the conscience of him that is Chancellor." Sir Thomas Smith (see V, **28**) writes of chancery: "And for so much as in this case he is without remedy in the common law, therefore he requireth the Chancellor according to equity and reason to provide for him and to take such order as to good conscience shall appertain. And the Court of Chancery is called of the common people the court of conscience, because that the Chancellor is not strained by rigour of forms of law to judge but *ex aequo* and *bono* according to conscience. . . ."

8. St. Germain. In his *Dialogues* (see V, **25**), St. Germain discusses conscience as a basis of equity. No law, he states, should operate against the law of reason and the law of God. It might be necessary, therefore, to modify the rigour of the law: "Extreme righteousness is an extreme wrong . . . if thou take all that the words of the law give thee, thou shalt sometimes do against the law."

9. The major contribution of equity to English law. Equity contributed largely to the development of English law by its provision of:

(a) *Concurrent jurisdiction*—the provision of *new remedies* where common law remedies were inadequate, *e.g.* specific performance (*see* X, **22**).

(b) *Auxiliary jurisdiction*—the provision of *new procedures*, *e.g.* discovery of documents.

(c) *Exclusive jurisdiction*—the *enforcing of rights* which were not recognised by the common law, *e.g.* the trust (*see* X, **3–12**).

THE MAXIMS OF EQUITY

10. Their background. Maxims of this type were collected and used for purposes of legal training. They provide, in summary form, epitomes of doctrines and procedures in the old Court of Chancery.

(a) In 1728, Richard Francis, a barrister of Middle Temple, published *Maxims of Equity*. Little had been published on the basic principles of equity since St. Germain (*see* **8** above). Francis set out his maxims after studying the cases.

(b) The maxims do not embody nor do they state, the doctrines of equity; they merely suggest certain principles derived from rules and practice.

(c) The growth of a body of maxims, which presupposes relatively settled procedures, may have contributed to the introduction of some stability into the uncertainties of equitable jurisdiction in the eighteenth century.

11. The maxims enumerated. The following are some of the better-known maxims of equity.

(a) Equity follows the law.
(b) Equity acts *in personam*.
(c) Equality is equity.
(d) He who seeks equity must do equity.
(e) Equity looks to the intent rather than to the form.
(f) Where there are equal equities the law prevails.
(g) Equity will not suffer a wrong to be without a remedy.
(h) Equitable remedies are discretionary.
(i) Equity acts on the conscience.

(*j*) Delay defeats equities.

(*k*) Equity imputes an intent to fulfil an obligation.

SOME ASPECTS OF THE DEVELOPMENT OF EQUITY

12. General historical development.

(*a*) The king's residuary jurisdiction to "do right" allowed some equitable principles to be applied in common law courts (*see* IX).

(*b*) The growth of the Court of Chancery produced a corpus of equitable doctrines.

(*c*) From 1485–1615 common law and chancery were engaged in rivalry and struggle, which ended, for a time, with the victory of chancery.

(*d*) Under the Commonwealth and Protectorate proposals for the abolition of chancery were discussed, but they were not made effective.

(*e*) In the eighteenth century there was a great expansion in the development of equitable remedies, *e.g.* taking of accounts, equity of redemption. In this century equity came to be looked upon in its own right as a complementary system to the common law.

(*f*) By the nineteenth century the doctrines and procedures of equity had become rigid, and that century saw extensive legislative reforms designed to improve the procedure in chancery.

13. The chancellors. The title of *chancellor* may have come from the *cancelli* (screen) which marked the place in which the royal clerks worked. The chancellor was the most important of these clerks. The office of chancellor originated in the reign of Edward the Confessor. The chancellor's duties involved acting as the king's secretary, keeper of the royal seal, and chaplain to the king (in which capacity he was considered to be the "keeper of the royal conscience"). John of Salisbury (*c.* 1180) described the chancellor as "he who cancels (*cancellat*) the evil laws of the realm and makes equitable the commands of a pious prince." The growth of the chancellor's judicial duties may have resulted from his dealing with petitions to the king (*see* IX, 11).

(*a*) The early chancellors were, by the nature of their office and duties, almost always ecclesiastics.

(b) The practice of appointing ecclesiastics to the office drew to an end after the appointment of Cardinal Wolsey (1475–1530). After his fall from office he was succeeded by Sir Thomas More, a common lawyer. Succeeding chancellors were almost invariably laymen.

NOTE: Sir Robert Bourchier (1340) was the first lay chancellor; Bishop Williams (1621–25), who succeeded Bacon, was the last ecclesiastical chancellor.

(c) In a few cases non-lawyers were appointed as chancellors, e.g. Sir Christopher Hatton, Lord Clarendon, and Lord Shaftesbury.

(d) The great chancellors had a profound influence upon the development of equity and its consolidation. (See IX, 25–33.)

14. Development of equitable remedies and procedures. The growth of procedures and practices in the Court of Chancery resulted in the development of new forms of procedure, new rights protected exclusively by equity (e.g. the trust) and new remedies which were, at first, unique to equity.

15. Reform in the nineteenth century. The growing rigidity in equity (which was as productive of delay and injustice as had been the old common law) led to the scandalous delays associated with chancery in Eldon's day. An urgent demand for reform followed, and in the nineteenth century a number of enactments (considered in XI) produced some of the desired reform.

16. Equity today.

(a) The Judicature Acts have fused the administration and the jurisdiction of the old common law courts and the Court of Chancery. But there has been no fusion of the substantive law.

(b) Equity is highly systematised, with a mass of case law and precedents. The importance of conscience in equity may have diminished. Thus, Jessel, M. R., stated in *Re National Funds Assurance Co.* (1878) 10 Ch.D.118: "This court is not, as I have often said a Court of Conscience, but a Court of Law." Lord Denning stated in 1952: "The Courts of Chancery are no longer courts of equity. . . . They are as fixed and immutable as the courts of law ever were."

(c) It is now doubtful whether new equitable interests can be created. "If a claim in equity exists it must be shown to have an ancestry founded in history and in the practice and precedents of the courts administering equity jurisdiction. It is not sufficient that because we think that the 'justice' of the present case requires it, we should invent such a jurisdiction for the first time": Court of Appeal in *Re Diplock* [1948] Ch.465.

PROGRESS TEST 8

1. What is the technical meaning of equity? (2)
2. What was the importance of doctrines of conscience in the early development of equity? (7, 8)
3. Enumerate some of the maxims of equity. (11)
4. What was the role of the Chancellors in the development of equity? (13)

THE ORIGINS AND DEVELOPMENT OF EQUITY

EQUITY WITHIN THE COMMON LAW

1. General. The fact that equity grew out of the common law was noted in VIII, 6. In a sense, some of the later features of equitable jurisdiction were anticipated in the exercise of the royal residuary jurisdiction and in the procedures concerning Bills in Eyre. These and other equitable features of the early common law are considered at 2–8 below.

2. The residuary jurisdiction of the king. One of the functions of the king was to act as a "fountain of justice"; he had a residuary jurisdiction to ensure that justice was done to his subjects. Men might appeal to him when justice had been denied elsewhere, or when the remedies for which they sought did not exist. This jurisdiction could be exercised through the issue of writs.

(*a*) *Brevia magistralia* (*see* VI, **4**) were available to meet circumstances which were not met by the *brevia de cursu* (*see* VI, **4**). The issue of these writs, based on an awareness that existing practice did not cover all the circumstances in which a plaintiff might demand justice, illustrates a type of equitable procedure.

(*b*) Although the *Provisions of Oxford*, 1258 (*see* VI, **4**) temporarily checked the issuing of *brevia magistralia*, the *Statute of Westminster II*, 1285, (*see* VI, **4**) allowed for the issuing of writs *in consimili casu*—an extension of the writ system deriving in part from an awareness of the rigidity of its procedures.

NOTE: *The Statute of Westminster I*, 1275, c. 17, refers to the king, "who is Sovereign Lord" and who "shall do right unto all such as will complain."

3. The king's council. The king's council (*see* XIV) exercised a general discretionary right to give relief on the basis of petitions received. Such petitions resembled those received in chancery, and were heard by the council, which included the chancellor and other royal judges.

4. The writ of audita querela (= quarrel having been heard). This writ, introduced during the time of Edward III, was available to re-open a judgment in certain circumstances. It was issued as a remedy to defendant where an important matter concerning his case had arisen since the judgment. Its issue was based on equitable, rather than common law principles.

5. The Bill in Eyre. In the thirteenth and fourteenth centuries there existed an equitable jurisdiction exercised by the itinerant common law justices of the General Eyre. The Eyre took place when the king sent his judges from his central court through the country to hear pleas (*see* XIII, **21–22**). Bills in Eyre seem to have been parchment documents recording the petitioner's complaint to "the justices of our Lord the King," and pleading, often in the name of charity and of God, for justice. In some cases the petitioner gave his poverty as the reason for his petition. The Bills covered complaints of a variety of types, *e.g.* trespass, debts owing, unlawful detention of chattels, for which common law writs often existed. Here, within the framework of common law institutions such as the Eyre, are signs of the growth of equitable procedures.

6. Common law actions of an equitable nature. In some few cases common law actions resembled the equitable remedies of later eras.

(*a*) *The common law action of covenant* applied to land could result in defendant's being ordered to perform his obligations—a clear anticipation of the equitable remedy of specific performance (*see* X, **22**).

(*b*) *Writs of prohibition,* by which defendant could be restrained from committing waste, were an early type of injunction (*see* X, **18–20**).

(*c*) *Suit of mill,* an ancient action which obliged some tenants to grind their corn only at the mill of their lord, resembled the perpetual injunction (*see* X, **18**).

(*d*) *The writ of quia timet* (= because he fears) appeared in a later form in the equitable remedy of injunction.

(e) *A delay allowed by the king's court in the repayment of a mortgage debt*, in the time of Henry II, seems to have had something in common with the later equity of redemption (*see* X, **13–17**).

7. Common law procedures used in equity. Bills and petitions, which characterised the equitable procedure of the Court of Chancery, had their origins in requests to the king and his Council for their intervention in administrative matters. The *subpoena*, which was to become an important aspect of Chancery procedure, was used on some occasions by the common law judges, as in 1302, when a party to an action was ordered to bring a child to court "under pain" of a monetary penalty.

8. Equitable jurisdiction exercised locally. Certain seignorial courts (*see* XII), such as the manorial courts, appeared to have councils, in the time of Richard II, which adjudicated on matters, such as succession to tenants' lands, on the basis of civilian doctrines and canon law, in contrast to common law.

NOTE: In some cases Parliament gave relief of an equitable nature in actions involving a powerful nobleman, *e.g.* as in 1421 in an action involving the performance of a use. The Court of Exchequer also granted relief of an equitable nature in some actions brought before it.

Some of the doctrines and procedures of equity existed in outline form in the common law. Their later development led to the growth of a body of doctrine which was to supplement the common law at many points.

EQUITY AND THE COURT OF CHANCERY

9. The office of chancellor. *See* VIII, **7, 13.** An important function of the chancellor was as secretary to the king. In this capacity he would draw up documents for the king to which the royal seal was affixed as a sign of authenticity. In time he was given custody of the seal. (Edward the Confessor, the first English king to use a seal, was the first to use the services of a chancellor.) As the jurisdiction of the royal courts grew, so the importance of the chancellor's office grew.

(a) The growth in jurisdiction of the royal courts involved an increase in the number and types of writ available.

(*b*) These writs were issued, under warrant of the Royal Seal, from the chancery. Hence the chancellor and his staff of clerks were concerned directly with the form of writs and their substance.

(*c*) By the end of the twelfth century chancery had become a separate state department.

10. The chancellor in the thirteenth and fourteenth centuries.
During this period the common law courts increased in stature and became virtually independent of the central government in many respects. Chancery stood apart from the king's council, on the one hand, and from the common law courts, on the other hand. But the chancellor himself was linked to both: he sat in the council as an adviser to the king; he was involved in the functioning of the common law courts by virtue of his responsibility for the issuing of writs. He had also a certain measure of common law jurisdiction: chancery officials enjoyed the privilege of suing and being sued in personal actions before the chancellor and not in the common law courts; proceedings against the crown and petitions of right were heard by the chancellor. In these matters common law procedure was employed.

NOTE: The common law jurisdiction exercised by the chancellor was referred to as *the Latin jurisdiction;* his equitable jurisdiction was referred to as *the English jurisdiction*. The reason was: records in the common law courts were in Latin, those concerning equitable jurisdiction were in English.

11. Growth of the chancellor's equitable jurisdiction in the fifteenth century.
The rigidity of the common law became particularly marked in the fourteenth and fifteenth centuries. As a result those who sought justice often found their road barred by procedural technicalities which seemed increasingly to dominate the system so as to render it incapable of real expansion.

(*a*) Where a complainant was unable to obtain a writ he could, in many cases, present to the king's court a petition (*see* **13** below) which stated the facts of his complaint and which begged for relief.

(*b*) These petitions would pass to the king and his council.

(*c*) In the fifteenth century a practice grew whereby

petitions based on allegations of defects in the common law were allocated to the chancellor.

(*d*) The chancellor and his advisers would hear the petition and the resulting decree would be issued in the name of the council. (In some cases, however, the case might be sent by the chancellor for hearing by a common law court. The opinion of that court would be sent to the chancellor and he would then punish the guilty party.)

(*e*) At a later date petitions were presented *directly to the chancellor*. In 1474 the first decree made by the chancellor's own authority was issued. *It is at this point that we discern the commencement of the equitable jurisdiction of chancery.*

NOTE: The chancellor would also hear petitions which concerned matters outside the common law, *e.g.* cases involving foreign merchants who pleaded the law merchant (*see* XV, **1**).

12. Conscience, morality and discretion. The chancellors were, in most cases, ecclesiastics and petitions were often presented based on an appeal for charity in God's name. Remedies were sought in the name of reason, right and conscience. Hence the chancellors sought, *by personal examination of defendant*, to examine the principles and moral standards underlying the act complained of.

(*a*) Where the chancellor considered that the workings of a law had proved contrary to the law of God (*see* VIII, **8**) he would assume the right to prevent its operation where plaintiff's hardship could be attributed to that law.

(*b*) The issuing of a decree was at the discretion of the chancellor. Even today equitable remedies are issued at the discretion of the court.

(*c*) Equity acted *in personam*, and proceeded not against defendant's goods, but against the person and conscience of the defendant.

13. Procedure in chancery. At this stage in its growth chancery had developed its own procedural rules.

(*a*) Proceedings commenced not by writ, as in the common law courts, but by the presentation of a bill (*i.e.* a petition). The petition was usually written in Anglo-French. Petitions drawn up in English were used after the reign of

Henry V. There was no prescribed form. The petitioner set out his grounds for complaint and humbly begged for relief *"pur dieu et en oeuvre de charité."* An oral petition had to be transformed into written terms in court. The bill included a pledge by plaintiff to prosecute.

(*b*) The petition was presented so that proceedings could be commenced by ordering defendant to attend court. A writ of *subpoena* (essential to the exercise of the chancellor's powers) was issued and was served on defendant. It ordered him, on pain of penalty, to answer the writ. The writ did not specify the grounds of complaint. A defendant who ignored the writ might be arrested on a *commission of rebellion* issued by the chancellor, committed to prison and suffer sequestration of his property.

NOTE: The *subpoena* was first issued by the chancellor *c.* 1330, and developed from the writ *quibusdam certis de causis.*

(*c*) Defendant appeared at the chancery and answered the petition orally on oath. From the mid-fifteenth century written depositions were allowed. The chancellor would conduct an interrogation designed to discover the state of defendant's conscience and to "purge" that conscience where necessary. The examination of defendant under oath, by which he was compelled to reveal his case, was a novel procedure—it had no parallel in the common law of the time.

(*d*) The chancellor decided questions of fact. There was no jury.

(*e*) Relief was given, not as a right, but as a matter of grace. The chancellor, in his discretion, issued a decree in the form of a declaration of rights, or in the form of an order to defendant to do or abstain from doing something.

NOTE: (i) *Witnesses* were brought to court in the fifteenth century by *subpoena* and were subject to oral examination on oath.
(ii) *Counsel* were appearing in Chancery by the beginning of the fifteenth century.

14. The basis of chancery's special relief. At this period chancery gave relief in the following matters:

(*a*) *Matters arising out of lack of common law remedies.* For example, failure of the common law to recognise the *use* led to chancery's recognition and protection of the *use* and to the growth of equitable rights (*see* X).

(*b*) *Matters arising out of the rigid common law rules of evidence.* The chancellor adjudicated essentially according to the so-called rules of conscience. Hence, faulty pleadings, which could destroy a case at common law did not necessarily have this effect in chancery. A report in the time of Edward IV states: "In the Chancery a man shall not be prejudiced by mispleading or by any defect in form, but he shall be judged according to the truth of his case, and we must judge according to conscience and not according to things alleged by the parties."

(*c*) *Matters arising out of the inadequacy of damages at common law.* A successful plaintiff at common law was usually awarded damages. Chancery intervened by granting *specific relief*, such as the performance of an obligation, or the return of goods which had been lent to defendant.

(*d*) *Matters arising out of mutual agreement.* Under common law a successful action on a contract demanded, as a pre-requisite, a sealed document, or the performance by one party of his part of the agreement. The chancellor, who was concerned with the *good faith* underlying such obligations, was prepared to enforce some agreements even in the absence of common law requirements, and to compel specific performance.

(*e*) *Matters arising out of fraud.* The chancellor would grant relief to a plaintiff who had been induced to enter an agreement as a result of defendant's fraud or duress. He could also prevent the enforcing of a common law judgment in favour of a party whose conduct had been fraudulent.

(*f*) *Matters arising out of the transfer of debts.* The common law did not recognise assignment of a *chose in action, e.g.* a debt. Relief could be obtained in chancery in matters of this nature.

At this stage equity was not considered as a rival system to the common law. Discussions on points of law and principles of equitable relief between the chancellors and the common law judges were frequent. But by the end of the fifteenth century jealousy and hostility were beginning to dominate the attitude of the common lawyers to a system which was seen to be emerging as a powerful rival. The succeeding era witnessed the climax of the resulting struggle.

THE STRUGGLE BETWEEN EQUITY
AND THE COMMON LAW

15. Background. The sixteenth and seventeenth centuries saw a mounting struggle between chancery and the common lawyers.

(*a*) Cardinal Wolsey, chancellor under Henry VIII, created new courts of equity which, together with his arrogant behaviour towards the common law judges, aroused the hostility of the common lawyers.

(*b*) The use of injunctions by chancery angered the common lawyers. Injunctions were issued so as to prohibit a plaintiff at law from bringing an action or enforcing a judgment which was thought by the chancellor to be offensive to conscience. In 1354 it had been enacted that the impeding of an action in the royal courts was a *praemunire* offence. This had not halted the use of chancery injunctions. In practice, an issue of a so-called *common injunction* meant that a plaintiff who had obtained judgment at law would be prohibited by chancery from proceeding with that judgment.

NOTE: The misuse of injunctions by Wolsey was one of the counts in his proposed impeachment.

(*c*) *The Statute of Uses*, 1535, (*see* X, **9**) was supported by the common lawyers. It should have dealt a serious blow at the Court of Chancery, which was concerned with the enforcing of uses. As it happened, however, the statute was not really effective and chancery went on to acquire other areas of jurisdiction, *e.g.* mercantile cases.

(*d*) The amount of legal business available to the common lawyers diminished as competition from Chancery, Star Chamber and the Admiralty Courts increased.

(*e*) Attacks on the Court of Requests (*see* XIV, **14**) increased in intensity. Coke writes in his *Fourth Institute*: "Those which in former times would have this Court to be a court of judicature took their aim from a court in France. . . . But others, taking the jurisdiction to be too narrow, contend to have it extended to all cases in equity equal with the Chancery and their decrees to be absolute and uncontrollable. But neither of these are warranted by law. . . ." In *Stepney* v. *Flood* (1599), the Court of Common Pleas declared that the Court of Requests "had no power of judicature."

But the Court continued to flourish until its disappearance in 1643.

(f) Writs of *habeas corpus* were issued by the common law courts so as to release some of those imprisoned by the chancellor for failing to obey his injunctions.

16. The disputes between Coke and Ellesmere.

The continuing conflict between chancery and the common law culminated in a series of disputes between Lord Chancellor Ellesmere and Lord Chief Justice Coke.

(a) Coke bitterly attacked the Court of High Commission in *Chancey's Case* (1611) 12 Co.Rep.82.

(b) *Courtney* v. *Glanvil* (1615) Cro.Jac.343. X sold Y jewels worth £150, but misrepresented their value as £600. X had then taken a bond from Y for £600 which Y failed to honour. X was given judgment for £600 and this was upheld by the Court of Exchequer Chamber. Y then filed a bill in equity for relief, as a result of which it was decreed that Y should pay X £150 and that thereupon X should release Y. X refused and was at once committed for contempt. He was released upon a grant of *habeas corpus* by the common law judges. Coke declared the decree in equity and X's imprisonment to be illegal.

(c) *The Earl of Oxford's Case* (1615) 1 Ch.Rep.6. Merton College had the grant of a lease of Covent Garden for seventy-two years at £9 p.a. Half a century later the college sold the fee to the Earl of Oxford's predecessor for £15 p.a. Declaring that the conveyance was void under a Statute of Elizabeth forbidding the alienation of college lands, the college took possession of part of the land. An action of ejectment was brought by the Earl against the college, and judgment was given by the common law judges for the college.

The Earl then brought a bill in equity seeking relief. His bill was granted by Ellesmere on the ground that the claim of the college was against conscience. His judgment contains the following classical exposition of the role of chancery: "The cause why there is a chancery is, for that men's actions are so divers and infinite, that it is impossible to make any general law which may aptly meet with every particular act, and not fail in some circumstances. The office of chancellor is to correct men's consciences for frauds, breach of trust wrongs and oppressions, of what nature soever they be, and to soften and mollify the extremity of the law, which is called *summum jus*."

(*d*) On another occasion a plaintiff had been given judgment in a court of common law following his having enticed defendant's witnesses into an alehouse during the hearing of the action. The defendant brought a bill in equity seeking relief, as a result of which the plaintiff was prohibited from proceeding upon the judgment. Plaintiff's counsel was advised by Coke to prosecute defendant under *27 Edw. 3*, which prohibited the impeachment of a judgment of the royal court in another court. Coke made other attempts to use this statute for the indictment of those who sought relief in chancery against common law judgments.

(*e*) Coke declared eventually that he would give no hearing to any counsel who had participated in the presentation of a bill in equity seeking relief against the judgments of the common law courts.

(*f*) Lord Chancellor Ellesmere appealed to James I.

17. Resolution of the dispute. James I referred the dispute to Bacon, his Attorney-General, and a group of lawyers. (The dispute had been exacerbated by Coke's personal dislike of Ellesmere, and by Bacon's personal hostility to Coke.) *Bacon and the lawyers decided in favour of chancery.* They declared that the issue of injunctions, about which Coke had complained, was based on strong precedent, and that there were cases of common law judges having advised parties to an action to make application to chancery for such an injunction. James I (always anxious to support those who looked favourably on his claims to exercise the royal prerogative) ordered, on July 14th, 1616, that the chancellor had no need to refrain from giving relief in equity.

18. Result of the decision. Coke was humbled, and dismissed later in 1616. Chancery continued to exist and to flourish. Equity "followed the law," but did not hesitate to correct the defects of the common law and to supplement its remedies.

PROCEDURE AND EQUITABLE JURISDICTION DURING THE SIXTEENTH AND SEVENTEENTH CENTURIES

19. Procedure. General procedure was as follows:

(*a*) A bill signed by counsel for plaintiff commenced proceedings. A *subpoena* ordered defendant to attend court. Interrogations were administered to defendant and witnesses. Defendant had three courses of action open to him:

(*i*) *He could demur to the bill, i.e.* he could state that plaintiff's allegations, even if true, did not warrant the intervention of the chancellor.

(*ii*) *He could submit a plea, i.e.* he could question the jurisdiction.

(*iii*) *He could submit an answer, i.e.* he could deny plaintiff's allegation.

(*b*) Witnesses were examined after the answer. Written statements by witnesses on oath were also used.

(*c*) A decree was issued and signed by the chancellor, but until it was signed it was considered as an interlocutory judgment which could be reconsidered.

20. Jurisdiction. In this era equity had extended its jurisdiction in the following ways:

(*a*) Relief against penalties was extended, *e.g.* the development of the equity of redemption (*see* X, **13–16**).

(*b*) Relief against fraud, accident and mistake was extended. (It should be observed that the expansion of commerce in this era had led to a great increase in the use of documents, with a corresponding increase in demands for relief where documents had been signed as the result of fraud, or the exertion of undue influence, or by mistake.)

(*c*) The assignment of *choses in action* was further developed by the Court of Chancery.

(*d*) Administration of assets of a deceased person depended in part on equity's consideration of the personal representative as standing in a fiduciary relationship to the beneficiary, and on chancery's rules for the order in which legacies and debts were to be paid.

LATER DEVELOPMENTS IN EQUITY

21. Chancery and the Protectorate. Chancery was clearly associated with the prerogative government of the Stuarts—Bacon and Ellesmere, for example, had upheld the royal prerogative. During the Commonwealth and the Protectorate demands were made for the abolition of chancery ("that mystery of wickedness and a standing cheat"). It was written of chancery at this time that "for dilatoriness, chargeableness and a faculty for bleeding people in the purse vein even to their utter perishing and undoing, the court might compare with, if not surpass, any court in the world." A resolution was passed that "the High Court of Chancery of England shall be forthwith taken away." The Restoration ended these schemes for the abolition of chancery.

22. The eighteenth century. Equitable jurisdiction in the eighteenth century differed from that of the sixteenth and seventeenth centuries. Systematised rules and a mass of reported cases had contributed to the transformation of the discretionary jurisdiction of the sixteenth century ecclesiastics into "a kind of ruled justice." Equity was now a recognised supplement to the common law. It became concerned increasingly with:

(a) Those forms of property unique to equity, e.g. the trust, and the appropriate equitable rights of the beneficiary, and the property rights of married women.

(b) Administration of estates.

(c) Decrees of specific performance and the issue of injunctions to restrain unlawful acts.

(d) Matters such as the guardianship of infants, care of lunatics, supervisory jurisdiction in cases of bankruptcy.

23. Bills in this era. The bill which commenced proceedings in chancery now included:

(a) A "stating part," which gave the facts.

(b) A "charging part," which enumerated defendant's statements on the alleged facts.

(c) An "interrogating part," a series of questions which plaintiff requested defendant to answer on oath, and which it was hoped would result in the collapse of the defence as set out in the charging part.

24. The nineteenth century. The systematisation of equity was not without its accompanying difficulties. As the principles of equity began to be developed in terms of precedent, as the so-called laws of conscience and the demands of morality disappeared in a welter of archaic procedural technicalities, so the delays in chancery reached scandalous proportions in the time of Eldon. Dickens, in *Bleak House*, written in 1852–53, is bitter: "Equity sends questions to Law, Law sends questions back to Equity; Law finds it can't do this, Equity finds it can't do that; neither can so much as say it can't do anything, without this solicitor instructing and this counsel appearing. . . . Jarndyce and Jarndyce drones on. Innumerable children have been born into the cause; innumerable young people have married into it; innumerable old people have died out of it." The same century saw also a crucial period of reform in equity, culminating in the *Judicature Acts*, 1873–75 (*see* XI).

THE WORK OF THE GREAT CHANCELLORS

25. The importance of the chancellor's office. The chancellors played a dominant role in the development of equity. Their position as great churchmen, politicians and judges, enabled them to mould, often in a decisive way, the form equity was to take. The story of the development of equity is in large measure the story of chancery and of the great chancellors, some of whom are discussed below.

26. Robert Burnell (d. 1292). Burnell was chancellor under Edward I and, for a period of 18 years, he exerted a great influence on that king's extensive legislation. *Quia Emptores* (*see* XXIII, **7**) may have been prepared under his guidance.

27. Cardinal Wolsey (1475–1530). Wolsey was chancellor from 1515–29. The separation of chancery from the council was urged by him, and it was under his chancellorship that the role of chancery as a court of conscience was frequently asserted. He was one of the last ecclesiastical chancellors.

28. Sir Thomas More (1478–1535). More was a common

lawyer who, as chancellor, attempted a policy of conciliation with the common law judges. He was chancellor from 1529–32 and his tenure of office was characterised by fairness, *e.g.* in the granting of a *subpoena* only after he was really convinced that the interests of justice would be served by this.

29. Lord Ellesmere (1540–1617). Sir Thomas Egerton, later Baron Ellesmere, was chancellor from 1596–1617. He had a great knowledge of the technical detail of chancery procedure, and was responsible for compiling new rules of procedure aimed at preventing excessive delay. His triumph over Coke (*see* **16** above) ensured the continuation of the equitable jurisdiction of the Court of Chancery. Ellesmere was one of the first chancellors to enforce the application of principles based on precedent.

30. Lord Bacon (1561–1626). *See* V, 27. Bacon was chancellor from 1618 until his impeachment in 1621. He had been a great common lawyer with a profound mastery of real property law. He was aware of the defects of common law, which he sought to remedy by proposals for a type of codification in the form of digests of case law and statute law. Some of the orders issued in chancery by Bacon remained part of practice there until the nineteenth century. During his period as chancellor he attempted a reconciliation between the Court of Chancery and its common law opponents.

31. Lord Nottingham (1621–82). Sir Heneage Finch, later Lord Finch and Earl of Nottingham, "the father of modern equity," was chancellor from 1673–82. He drafted the *Statute of Frauds*, 1677, wrote a treatise on equity, and compiled and circulated his own reports. His particular contributions to the development of equity included the following:

(*a*) He developed the idea of the discretion of the chancellor being exercised, not in an arbitrary fashion, but on the basis of established precedent. In the absence of precedent the chancellor's conscience should act as his guide. He gave reasons for all his judgments.

(*b*) He commenced the systematisation of rules and procedures in equity.

(*c*) He classified trusts in a logical fashion in *Cook* v.

Fountain (1672) 3 Swanst.585: "It is infinitely better for the public that a trust, security or agreement which is wholly secret should miscarry, than that men should lose their estates by the mere fancy and imagination of a chancellor."

(*d*) He reformulated the rules concerning notice, in *Salisbury* v. *Bagott* (1677) 2 Swanst.603.

(*e*) He evolved the rule against perpetuities in the *Duke of Norfolk's Case* (1682) 2 Swanst.454. "Pray let us so resolve cases here, that they may stand with the reason of mankind when they are debated abroad."

NOTE: It was during his period of office that the right of appeal from the chancellor to the House of Lords was established in *Shirley* v. *Fagg* (1675) 6 S.T.1122.

32. Lord Hardwicke (1690–1764).

Sir Philip Yorke, later Earl of Hardwicke, was solicitor-general in 1720, and attorney-general in 1724. He was chancellor from 1736–56. In a series of outstanding judgments he emphasised the rule that a judge in a court of equity was bound by precedent. Under Hardwicke Equity came to be considered as a complementary system to that of the common law. He affirmed and developed many of the principles of equity, *e.g.*:

(*a*) In *Casborne* v. *Scarfe* (1737) 1 Atk.603, he established the principles allowing a husband curtesy out of the equitable estate.

(*b*) In *Underwood* v. *Hitchcox* (1749) 1 Ves.Sen.279, he developed the principles on which specific performance might be granted.

(*c*) In *Penn* v. *Baltimore* (1750) 1 Ves.444, he affirmed that equity acts *in personam*.

33. Lord Eldon (1751–1838).

John Scott, later Lord Eldon, was created Attorney-General in 1793, and Lord Chancellor in 1801. He was Chancellor from 1801–06, and from 1807–27. He was an ultra-conservative (*see* XI, 2), who resisted, whenever possible, political and legal reforms. During his term of office the Court of Chancery became notorious for its delays (*see* 24 above). During that time his numerous judgments helped to establish many principles of equity (particularly those involving the granting of injunctions), and to establish finally the doctrine of binding precedent. "The doctrines of this court ought to be as well settled, and made as uniform, almost, as those of the common law, laying down fixed principles, but taking care that they are to be applied according to the circumstances of each case": *Gee* v. *Pritchard* (1818) 2 Swanst.402.

NOTE: Eldon's period as chancellor was followed by the great era of reform in equity, which is considered in XI.

PROGRESS TEST 9

1. What was the importance of the royal residuary jurisdiction in the early development of equity? **(2)**

2. Explain (a) bill in Eyre, (b) suit of mill. **(5, 6)**

3. What was *the Latin jurisdiction*? **(10)**

4. Explain the growth of the chancellor's jurisdiction in the fifteenth century. **(11)**

5. Outline the procedure in chancery in the fifteenth century. **(13)**

6. On what basis was equitable relief granted in the fifteenth century? **(14)**

7. What was the general background to the struggle in the sixteenth and seventeenth centuries between equity and the common law? **(15)**

8. Outline the facts and importance of (a) *Courtney* v. *Glanvil* (1615), (b) *Earl of Oxford's Case* (1615). **(16)**

9. How was the conflict between Coke and Ellesmere resolved? **(17)**

10. Outline the jurisdiction of equity in the sixteenth and seventeenth centuries. **(20)**

11. What were the characteristics of equitable jurisdiction in the eighteenth century? **(22)**

12. Outline the work of (a) Nottingham, (b) Eldon. **(31, 33)**

CHAPTER X

THE DEVELOPMENT OF EQUITABLE DOCTRINES AND REMEDIES

EQUITABLE JURISDICTION

1. General. As the jurisdiction of the Court of Chancery developed and extended in scope, so its doctrines became more explicit and its remedies more far-reaching. Just as the common law in its origin was concerned primarily with matters arising from the ownership, possession and transfer of land, so equitable doctrines grew up around these same matters. And because the common law significantly failed to provide, in most actions concerning land, a remedy other than damages, equity produced its own particular remedies. Because these new doctrines and remedies corresponded to the changing needs of a changing society, chancery grew in significance; because they enabled justice to be done where hitherto it could not be done, equity grew in importance and stature.

2. Doctrines and remedies. We deal in this chapter with four examples of the many doctrines and remedies created by the Court of Chancery.

(a) The use and trust (*see* **3-12** below).
(b) The equity of redemption (*see* **13-17** below).
(c) The injunction (*see* **18-21** below).
(d) Specific performance (*see* **22-24** below).

THE ORIGIN OF THE USE AND THE TRUST

3. Derivation of the term "use." The word *use* is derived possibly from the word *opus*—part of a phrase *ad opus*—and perhaps transformed from that into *oes*, and then *use*. At the time of Domesday Book we hear of lands being seized by the sheriff *ad opus domini regis* (on behalf of our lord and king).

4. Putting lands "in use." The process of putting lands into use took the following form:

(*a*) A tenant (A) transferred his land by common law conveyance to the transferee (B). B undertook to hold that land *to the use of* (*i.e.* on behalf of) A, or a third person, C.

(*b*) In this case A, or C, was known as the *cestui que use*, B was known as the *feoffee to uses, i.e.* the party to whom the feoffment of land had been made.

NOTE: The earliest example of land being held permanently to the use of others may have been *c.* 1230, when land was conveyed to the use of a Franciscan community of friars whose rules forbade their owning any property. (A Papal Bull half a century later stated that a use was not considered to be property.)

5. The effect at common law of the use. The *cestui que use* had no rights at common law over the land. The land had been conveyed to another (the *feoffee*) and no common law action was available to protect the *cestui que use* against, for example, a *feoffee* who refused to carry out instructions of the *cestui que use*.

6. The chancellor's protection of the cestui que use. By the beginning of the fifteenth century the chancellor was intervening to protect the *cestui que use*. His intervention was not considered as an interference in the processes of the common law—it was recognised that the conveyance to the *feoffee* vested title in him. But where the *feoffee* acted towards the *cestui que use* in a way which suggested *bad faith or lack of morality*, the chancellor would intervene and enforce the conditions upon which the conveyance had been made. Hence, there came into existence a "dual ownership of land"; *the feoffee had legal ownership*, protected by the common law courts, while *the cestui que use had equitable ownership*, protected by the chancellor.

7. The advantages of the use. This matter is considered at XXIV, **7.** In general, the main advantages of putting land into use were:

(*a*) It became possible to devise lands—forbidden at common law.

(*b*) Settlements of land and conveyances became easier.

8. Royal opposition to the use. As the popularity of the use increased, and as it became utilised widely by tenants, it aroused the opposition of the king. The revenue from feudal dues declined and Henry VIII, whose requests to Parliament for a permanent income had been refused, turned his attention to the cause of the decline. He decided to suppress the employment of the use by removing its advantages. In 1529 a draft bill was outlined which proposed, *inter alia*, that there was to be one estate in land (the fee simple), that uses would have to be publicised and registered in the Court of Common Pleas, that land belonging to peers of the realm would be capable of alienation by royal licence only. Landowners who feared these proposals, and the common lawyers who had a stake in the continuation of the profitable transactions surrounding uses, defeated the bill in the Commons.

9. The Statute of Uses, 1535. Further bills were presented, and Henry assured himself of the support of the common lawyers by threatening to set up an enquiry into the abuses of common law procedure. In 1535 the *Statute of Uses* was enacted. The Statute—referred to by Bacon as "the most perfectly and exactly conceived and penned of any law in the book"—attempted to restore the overt and public transfer of land which was considered desirable, and which was avoided by the creation of the use. The Statute had the following effects:

(*a*) Suppose that Oswald granted Blackacre to Ralph to the use of Geoffrey, *i.e.* Ralph is the *feoffee*, Geoffrey is the *cestui que use*.

(*b*) The Statute "executed the use" and turned Geoffrey's equitable estate into a legal estate. Hence:

(*i*) *Before the Statute* Ralph would have had the legal estate, Geoffrey would have had the equitable estate.
(*ii*) *After the Statute* Geoffrey had the legal estate.

(*c*) The Statute took away common law *seisin* (*see* XXIV) from the *feoffee*. Hence:

(*i*) *Before the Statute* common law *seisin* of Blackacre would have vested in Ralph.
(*ii*) *After the Statute* the *seisin* vested in Geoffrey.

(*d*) The result of the legislation of 1535 was that the *feoffee* became a nonentity, and there was little point in conveying "to A to the use of B" rather than to B directly by common law conveyance, since the legal estate vested in B in both of these cases.

10. Failure of the Statute of Uses. The Statute was very unpopular and was followed, in 1540, by the *Statute of Wills*, which allowed a tenant to devise all his socage lands and up to two-thirds of land held by him in Knight service (*see* XXIII, **9**). Certain loopholes were discovered in the workings of the *Statute of Uses*:

(*a*) The Statute was held to have no application to an "active use," *i.e.* where a *feoffee* had to perform active duties, such as the collecting of rents and paying them to the *cestui que use*.

(*b*) The Statute had no application to the case of uses of copyholds and leaseholds and pure personalty, *i.e.* property to which the concept of *seisin* did not apply. But in such cases the use would continue to be upheld in equity.

(*c*) The Statute was considered to have application only where a *seisinee* held to the use of another person and not himself.

(*d*) The Statute had no application in the case of a grant made to a corporation on the terms that it was to hold to the use of another party.

11. Emergence o the trust. In *Tyrrel's Case* (1558) Dyer 155, it was held by the common law judges that *in the case of a use upon a use the Statute of Uses did not operate to execute the latter use*. Thus, the Statute would execute the first use and the legal estate vested, therefore, in the first *cestui que use*. The first *cestui que use* held on behalf of the second, in whom an equitable estate was vested. *This second use became known as a "trust" and was protected by the chancellor*.

12. Development of the trust. As a result of the protection extended by the chancellor, the trust developed and it became the practice to create equitable estates by conveying Blackacre "unto and to the use of X and his heirs in trust for Y and his heirs." In this case, X (the so-called trustee) obtained the legal estate and the use.

(a) In *Sambach* v. *Dalston* (1635) Toth.188, the chancellor acted so as to enforce a second use as a trust.

(b) In *Cook* v. *Fountain* (1676) 3 Swanst.591, Lord Nottingham classified trusts in a declaration which remains the basis of the modern law of trusts: "All trusts are either, first, express trusts which are raised and created by acts of parties, or implied trusts which are raised and created by act or construction of law."

(c) *The Statute of Frauds* (1677) enacted that a trust of land must be evidenced by some writing. Equity refused, however, to allow the Statute to be used as a "cloak for fraud."

(d) Equity, which followed the law, evolved rules concerning equitable interests which paralleled those concerning legal interests.

(e) When a conveyance was taken in the name of another, it had raised a presumption of a resulting trust. Nottingham ruled that such a presumption might be rebutted where the conveyance had been taken in the name of the real purchaser's child.

(f) Formal words were not considered essential in order to create a trust. In the eighteenth century precatory words (*i.e.* words of hope or wishes accompanying a gift) were considered as constituting a trust. (For the modern law, however, see *Re Adams and the Kensington Vestry* (1884) 27 Ch.D.934.)

(g) Equity evolved rules for regulating the conduct of trustees towards the beneficiaries. Nottingham ruled that trustees could receive no remuneration, other than in the form of an express gift. In *Morley* v. *Morley* (1678) 2 Ch.Cas.2, a trustee was robbed by his servant of trust money; he was held not liable for the loss, since he had shown no negligence in the matter.

THE MORTGAGE AND THE EQUITY
OF REDEMPTION

13. Terminology. A *mortgage* is a transfer of property for the purpose of securing the repayment of a debt or the discharge of some other obligation. Assume that A borrows money from B and conveys property to B as security for the repayment of the debt. A is the *mortgagor*, B is the *mortgagee*.

14. Early forms of mortgage. Pledges of land were known as early as Anglo-Saxon times. In the time of Glanvill (*see* V, **19**), two forms of mortgage seem to have been in use:

(*a*) *The Vivum Vadium* (= a living pledge). The mortgagee (lender) could take possession of the land, rents and profits being taken in discharge of principal and interest.

(*b*) *The Mortuum Vadium* (= a dead pledge). The mortgagee took rents and profits in discharge of the interest only.

NOTE: The mortgage in the thirteenth–fifteenth centuries was often made by the mortgagor's leasing his property *for a term of years* to the mortgagee. The mortgagee had possession of the land. If the mortgagor failed to repay the debt by the end of the period of the lease, the term of years was enlarged into a fee simple and was vested in the mortgagee.

15. Mortgages in the fifteenth century. The typical method of creating a mortgage in this era was by a conveyance of land in fee simple by the mortgagor to the mortgagee. The condition under which it was made was that the conveyance would be defeated, and the mortgagor could re-enter, if the loan was paid on an agreed date. But where repayment was not made on that date the mortgagor forfeited his interest in the land and the mortgagee's estate was transformed into one of an absolute nature.

16. Intervention of equity. In the mid-fifteenth century the chancellor afforded protection to mortgagors whose failure to redeem the mortgage (*i.e.* to repay on the promised date) resulted in the forfeiture of their lands. Where such a failure was the result of fraud or misfortune, for example, the chancellor would intervene.

17. Development of the equity of redemption. The chancellor proceeded on the basis of the principle, "Once a mortgage, always a mortgage." (*See Harris* v. *Harris* (1681) 1 Vern.33.) The object of a mortgage was to give security to a lender, and, hence, if that security remained in existence, a mortgagor should not be deprived of his land because of his failure to make repayment on an agreed date. (It should be noted that the forfeiture of a mortgagor's land could be followed by an action for the recovery of the unpaid debt.) Equity did not consider time to be of the essence of a mortgage transaction.

(a) In 1600 a mortgagor was given relief where the mortgagee had, with fraudulent intent, avoided receiving payment on the date fixed for this: *Courtman* v. *Conyers* (1600) Act.Canc.764.

(b) In *Thornborough* v. *Baker* (1675) 3 Swanst.628, Lord Nottingham stated: "In natural justice and equity the principal right of the mortgagee is to the money, and his right to the land is only as security for the money."

(c) Even after the date for repayment had passed, a mortgagor who had failed to repay remained entitled in equity to an interest in the land. His equitable interest was known as *the equity of redemption*. In *Casborne* v. *Scarfe* (1737) Lord Hardwicke declared that the equity of redemption was to be considered "as an estate in land."

(d) Although a mortgagee had the right to enter into possession of the land, this was discouraged by the judgment in *Fulthorpe* v. *Foster* (1687) 1 Vern.476, which declared that a mortgagee who entered would be liable to account for any advantage which accrued over and above the interest due on his loan.

(e) Thus, as a result of the intervention of equity, the position was as follows:

(i) The mortgagor had a contractual right to redeem on the agreed date for repayment.

(ii) Should that date pass without repayment, he had, nevertheless, an equity to redeem his land.

(iii) The land belonged in equity to the mortgagor, and at common law to the mortgagee.

(iv) The equitable interest was created when the mortgage was created, not as in the case of the equity of redemption, which came into existence only after the date for repayment.

THE INJUNCTION

18. Terminology. An injunction is an order of the court directing a party to refrain from doing or continuing to do an act complained of, or restraining that party from continuing some omission. The following types of injunction may be granted:

(a) *Prohibitory injunctions*, forbidding the commission or continuation of a wrongful act.

(b) *Mandatory injunctions*, restraining the continuation of an omission by directing the performance of a positive act.

(c) *Perpetual injunctions*, granted after the hearing of an action.

(d) *Interlocutory injunctions*, temporary injunctions granted on interlocutory application and intended to maintain the *status quo* until the action has been heard.

(e) *Quia timet injunctions* (*quia timet* = because he fears), granted so as to restrain a threatened action where, as yet, the rights of the plaintiff have not been infringed.

NOTE: The award of an injunction is at the discretion of the court, having regard not only to the rights of the parties to the action, "but also to the surrounding circumstances, to the rights and interests of other persons which may more or less be involved": per Kindersley, V. C., in *Wood* v. *Sutcliffe* (1851) 21 L.J.Ch.253.

19. Common law injunctions. The common law writ of prohibition was available to prevent the court exceeding its jurisdiction, and in the case of waste (an act by a tenant which permanently injures a reversioner's interest by altering the nature of the property). In the reign of Edward II an injunction was granted forbidding any interference with the holding of a market.

20. The chancellor's intervention. As early as the fourteenth century, the chancellor had granted injunctions. Later came the so-called *common injunctions* granted by the chancellor to the plaintiff personally, and not, as at common law, to the court. Such injunctions forbade a plaintiff to pursue an action considered by the chancellor to be against the dictates of good conscience. These common injunctions were, initially, not recognised at common law, and their continued employment led to hostility and dispute between chancery and the common law judges. Following the resolution of the dispute in favour of chancery (*see* IX, **16-18**) common law injunctions continued to be issued until 1873.

21. Lord Cairns' Act, 1858. Equity could not award damages in lieu of an injunction even though the nature of plaintiff's case required such an award. In 1858 it was enacted that chancery might award damages in lieu of, or in addition to, an injunction. Although this Act was repealed later by the *Statute Law Revision Act*, 1883, *s*.3, the jurisdiction remains with the High Court in all its divisions. *See* XI, **29**.

SPECIFIC PERFORMANCE

22. Nature of the remedy. A decree of specific performance is an order of the court instructing a party to a contract to perform his obligations according to the terms of that contract. The grant of the decree is at the discretion of the court and is made only where the appropriate remedy at law is inadequate. "This court does not profess to decree a specific performance of contracts of every description. It is only where the legal remedy is inadequate or defective that it becomes necessary for Courts of Equity to interfere": *Flint* v. *Brandon* (1803) 8 Ves.159.

23. Specific performance and the common law. In the twelfth century the common law courts made decrees for the specific performance of certain covenants. The ancient action of covenant admitted of a grant of specific restitution in the case of a lessee where the lessor had failed to carry out the agreement. But, in general, the common law granted no remedy in the case of a breach of contract except money damages.

24. Intervention of equity. Where money damages would not afford adequate compensation (as, for example, in the case of a breach of contract to convey land) equity would oblige a defendant to perform specifically his part of the agreement. Later, in the fifteenth century, specific performance of a contract to build was granted.

(*a*) In *Pusey* v. *Pusey* (1684) 1 Vern.273, the remedy was made available in the case of a very rare chattel.

(*b*) In *Lester* v. *Foxcroft* (1701) 2 W & T, 410, it was held that although a contract concerning land had to be in writing, equity could grant specific performance of such a contract even in the absence of writing where plaintiff had performed the contract in part—the doctrine of part performance.

The formulation and elaboration of these doctrines and remedies (and many others, such as election, conversion) resulted in the firm establishment of equity as a system complementary to the common law.

PROGRESS TEST 10

1. What was the derivation of the term *use*? **(3)**
2. What was the process of putting lands in *use*? **(4)**
3. How did the Chancellor seek to protect the *cestui que use*? **(6)**
4. Why was there opposition by the king to the use? **(8)**
5. Outline the effects of the *Statute of Uses*, 1535. Why was it not successful? **(9, 10)**
6. Explain (*a*) *vivum vadium*, (*b*) *mortuum vadium*. **(14)**
7. What was the typical method of creating a mortgage in the fifteenth century? **(15)**
8. What was the importance of the equitable maxim "once a mortgage, always a mortgage"? **(17)**
9. What was the common injunction? **(20)**
10. Under what circumstances did equity intervene in order to grant specific performance? **(22, 24)**

CHAPTER XI

THE ERA OF REFORM IN EQUITY

EQUITY IN THE FIRST HALF OF THE NINETEENTH CENTURY

1. General. The Court of Chancery in the first half of the nineteenth century was noted for its delay and inefficiency. The most marked feature of this condition was the dilatory procedure, associated in particular with Lord Eldon (*see* IX, **24, 33,** and **2** below). This, however, was a symptom rather than a cause of the inadequacies of chancery. Equity had grown up in response to the rigidity and resultant injustices of some common law procedures; but by the first half of the nineteenth century its own technicalities and complexity had given it much of the appearance of the very system it had been created to modify. The principal causes of this state of affairs were:

(*a*) The uncertainties of equity (*see* **3–4** below);
(*b*) Obsolete and inadequate procedures (*see* **5–8** below);
(*c*) Inadequacies of the court's judicial staff (*see* **9** below);
(*d*) Abuses in court administration (*see* **10–11** below);

NOTE: This malaise affected not only the Court of Chancery but was in evidence elsewhere. Thus, it was estimated that in 1847 King's Bench had a backlog of over 300 cases.

2. Eldon and Chancery. *See* IX, **33.** Attention has been drawn to the positive role played by Lord Eldon, particularly in the establishing of the doctrine of precedent in equity. But his chancellorship was notorious for his excessive procrastination in arriving at decisions, and for his steadfast opposition to reform of chancery. This attitude stemmed from his general conservative principles; thus, he vociferously opposed Catholic emancipation and the abolition of capital punishment for petty larceny. (There were 160 capital crimes in 1800.) Eldon's attitude to the suggestions for reform of his court intensified, in the minds of the law reformers, the urgency of a radical change in chancery procedures.

UNCERTAINTIES OF EQUITY

3. Lack of predictability. A large mass of decisions, some often irreconcilable with one another, meant that lawyers found it increasingly difficult to advise clients as to the possible outcome of an action in *Chancery*. Selden had commented on this matter in his *Table Talk* (*see* V, **28**(*e*)): "Equity is a roguish thing; for law we have a measure, know what to trust to; equity is according to the conscience of him that is chancellor, and as that is larger or narrower, so is equity. 'Tis all one as if they should make the standard for the measure we call a foot a chancellor's foot; what an uncertain measure would this be! One chancellor has a long foot, another a short foot, a third an indifferent foot. 'Tis the same thing in the chancellor's conscience."

(*a*) The dominant role played by the chancellors in the development of equity continued into the nineteenth century. (While Selden's hyperbole was not entirely justified, there is much evidence to suggest that, as in Eldon's case, the personal influence of a chancellor did affect in great measure the general pattern of chancery administration and jurisdiction.)

(*b*) The poor reports of decisions in previous eras made the establishing of a system based on precedent very difficult. In the absence of reliable reports predictability became almost impossible in many cases.

(*c*) The confused technicalities of the common law, with which equity was linked, and, in particular, the law of real property—feudal in its concept and often scholastic in its development—were responsible in large measure for the many imprecise decisions in chancery.

4. Delay in court procedure. *See* IX, **24.** The gibes hurled at chancery, which implied that its jurisdiction was exercised in a highly personal fashion, had led to a determination on the part of some chancellors that their decisions would be impeccable and would be rooted firmly in precedent.

(*a*) Some chancellors (Eldon in particular) tended to take

an inordinate amount of time in arriving at decisions. Eldon often announced decisions after intervals of many months. In his preface to *Bleak House* Dickens tells of "a suit before the Court which was commenced nearly twenty years ago; in which from thirty to forty counsel have been known to appear at one time; in which costs have been incurred to the amount of seventy thousand pounds; which is a friendly suit; and which is (I am assured) no nearer to its termination now than when it was begun."

(*b*) Archaic preliminary procedures, pleadings, and methods of taking evidence (*see* **5-8** below) also played a part in prolonging actions.

INADEQUATE PROCEDURES

5. Archaic survivals. The medieval nature of many aspects of chancery jurisdiction—obscure patterns of pleading, technicalities of procedure which had developed over the centuries and which now hindered the course of an action, the anomalous position and powers of the *Masters in Chancery*, time-consuming and anachronistic methods of taking evidence – all these contributed to the general inadequacy of the Court of Chancery in the early part of the nineteenth century.

6. Pleadings. These tended to be long, very detailed, and often couched in a pattern of terminology which made neither for ease of comprehension, nor for swiftness in the determination of an action.

7. Evidence. *Evidence by commission* was the form employed in obtaining evidence from witnesses. A commissioner (out of court) presented witness with a list of questions (interrogatories). The parties to the action were not present. Cross-examination was allowed only on questions previously prepared, and not on matters arising at the examination.

(*a*) This procedure was tedious, often expensive, and rarely satisfactory.

(*b*) The demeanour of witnesses under cross examination —an important matter in the assessing of evidence—could not be considered by the court, since this examination was held out of court.

(*c*) The practice had emerged whereby issues of fact were

remitted to the common law courts for jury trial—an additional source of expense and delay.

8. Lack of procedure for deciding minor points. A relatively minor point, *e.g.* concerning the administration of a trust by a trustee, and raised by him before the court, demanded a full-scale procedure. Accounts had to be taken, presented and considered, and this could involve great expense and delay, as a result of which the trust funds might be reduced disproportionately.

INADEQUACIES OF THE COURT'S JUDICIAL STAFF

9. Size of the judicial staff. Until 1813, when a *vice-chancellor* was appointed, the judges of the court were the *Chancellor* and the *Master of the Rolls*. They found it almost impossible to cope adequately with the large and growing number of actions in chancery, and it was taken for granted that many months or years might elapse between the date of a case having been entered for hearing and the date on which it was actually heard.

(*a*) The chancellor was often concerned in extra-judicial activities resulting from his political tasks, and he had an added duty of participating in those appeals heard in the House of Lords.

(*b*) The Master of the Rolls had a limited jurisdiction only. Appeals from his decisions to the chancellor threw an added burden on the latter.

(*c*) The appointment of a vice-chancellor eased the chancellor's burden only slightly, since appeals could be made to him from the vice-chancellor's decisions.

ABUSES IN COURT ADMINISTRATION

10. Background. The administrative aspects of procedure in equity occupied a much more important place than similar matters at common law. Hence the number of administrative officers of the court occupied in these matters had grown considerably.

(a) Close control of the administrative officers by the judges was essential, but impossible because of the small number of judges in chancery.

(b) Many officials were paid by fees, and received no fixed salaries; hence they had an interest in increasing, rather than in helping to diminish, the expensive administrative work which accompanied the preparation and the hearing of an action.

11. Abuses. Exploitation of litigants and peculation were commonly attributed to the masters and their subordinate clerks. Traditionally they had not been under any obligation to account for interest received on monies paid into the court by litigants. In the eighteenth century they had speculated with these funds and in 1725 (the year of the South Sea Bubble) this type of speculation had cost the funds £100,000. As a result of this, the chancellor, Lord Macclesfield, was removed, impeached and fined. Although litigants' money was henceforth deposited in the Bank of England, control over the masters remained somewhat loose.

(a) Litigants were often made to pay a double fee: one to the clerk in lieu of fees which he would have earned had he performed the work of the litigant's solicitor, and another to his solicitor as a fee for work performed.

(b) Some clerks made charges for services which were fictitious or of no value.

(c) Appeal to the chancellor from the masters was possible, but involved added expenses, and delayed a final decision.

THE NECESSITY FOR REFORM

12. Urgency of the situation. The muddle and delay of chancery, and the mounting anger of litigants should have sufficed, in the early nineteenth century, to produce an irresistible demand for immediate reform. (Even the Duke of Wellington, who could not be classed as a social reformer in any sense, referred impatiently to chancery as "that damned court.") Although reformers such as Bentham (*see* IV, **10,** *Note*) had suggested schemes which were by no means extreme in concept, reform of chancery was almost entirely held back during the chancellorship of Eldon. The extent of the reform required necessitated the intervention of Parliament. Following Eldon, and the victory of the Whigs in 1830, reform came in great measure, culminating in the great *Judicature Acts,* 1873–75, which are considered at **31–38** below. It has been said that this short era of reform accomplished more than had been done in the two preceding centuries.

13. The type of reform needed. Basically, the constitution of the Court of Chancery and its procedures had to be changed so that they might approximate more closely to the needs of a rapidly growing population and a society in which commerce now played a very important part. Chancery jurisdiction had to be more certain, more comprehensible, swifter in procedure, and free from unnecessary expense. This necessitated the following reforms:

(*a*) An increase in the judicial staff in chancery.

(*b*) More effective control of administrative staff.

(*c*) An end to delays in procedure.

(*d*) A bringing closer together, with a view to ultimate fusion, of law and equity.

THE REFORM OF EQUITY

14. Nature of the reform. The constitution of chancery and its procedures figured in the main schemes of reform. Until 1873 the reform tended to be piecemeal. In 1873 (*see* **31** below) came a major attempt at basic reform and at a fusion of law and equity.

15. Characteristics of the reform. The process of reform was undertaken in three ways:

(*a*) *Commissions of Enquiry* were set up.

(*b*) *Acts were passed aiming at the reform of particular aspects of chancery jurisdiction.*

(*c*) *Acts of a comprehensive nature, designed for general reform,* featured in the legislation of 1873–75.

NOTE: Commissions were not a novel feature of the era of reform. Eldon himself had presided over a Commission of Enquiry set up in 1825 to investigate abuses and to recommend reforms. Predictably, it suggested no basic reforms, but two results of its deliberations are worthy of note:

(*i*) The taking of evidence (*see* **7** above) was henceforth to be a matter for solicitors only, who were to act as commissioners.

(*ii*) In 1830 an Act was passed based on the Commission's report, which helped to do away with some of the scandals resulting from committals for contempt. Chancery could commit in a case of neglect of a *subpoena* or in a case of defiance of its orders. Imprisonment, so as to purge the contempt, could be for very long periods. The Act obliged a Master in Chancery to visit the Fleet Prison (where such offenders were held) at regular intervals and to examine the facts in the case of each prisoner. Where he decided that continued imprisonment was pointless, the prisoner could be discharged on payment made out of a reserve of unclaimed funds held by the court.

THE REFORMING ACTS

16. General. The following types of Act are considered chronologically below:

(*a*) Those which were designed specifically to reform chancery.

(*b*) Those which were not so designed, but which had an indirect effect upon chancery jurisdiction.

17. Bankruptcy Act, 1831. This Act transferred jurisdiction in bankruptcy (which had become the work of chancery following the Restoration) from chancery to a Chief Judge in Tankruptcy. There resulted some reduction in the work of chancery, although there remained a right of appeal in these matters to the chancellor.

18. Chancery Act, 1833. "An Act for the regulation of the proceedings and practices of certain offices of the High Court of Chancery in England."

(*a*) *Certain offices were abolished,* e.g. Master of the Report Office, Entering Clerks, and Entering Registrars.

(*b*) *Six registrars were appointed,* also clerks to registrars and assistant registrars.

(*c*) *A Master of Reports and Entries was appointed.*

(d) *Officers and clerks were to hold office "during good behaviour."*

(e) *Officers and clerks were not to take gratuities.*

(f) *Examiners were authorised to administer oaths to witnesses.*

(g) *The Lord Chancellor was empowered to make rules for simplifying and settling the practice of the court.*

19. Fines and Recoveries Act, 1833; Real Property Limitation Act, 1833; Inheritance Act, 1833. Chancery was concerned to a large measure with actions arising out of the ownership and conveyance of real property. English land law, rooted in feudal practices, was, by the nineteenth century, complicated by many anachronisms, the interpretation of which contributed to the difficulties of chancery jurisdiction. Somewhat surprisingly, the *First Report* of the Real Property Commission (1829) stated: "We have the satisfaction to report that the Law of Real Property seems to us to require very few essential alterations. . . . The Law of England [concerning Real Property] except in a few comparatively unimportant particulars, appears to come almost as near to perfection as can be expected in any human institutions." But the Report went on to recommend changes in the modes of transfer of land. The three Acts of 1833 had a revolutionary effect upon the rules concerning conveyancing, and resulted in their simplification. Indirectly, therefore, the task of equity in matters concerning real property became easier.

20. Chancery Act, 1841. "An Act to make further provisions for the administration of justice." The equitable jurisdiction exercised by the Court of Exchequer was transferred to the Court of Chancery. Two additional vice-chancellors were appointed, the first having been appointed in 1813. There were now four full-time chancery judges and the chancellor. This enabled the chancellor to give his attention to appellate hearings.

21. Chancery Act, 1842. The office of the Six Clerks and their deputies was completely abolished. Bills of costs (the abuse of which had resulted in great expense to suitors) were henceforth to be taxed by newly-created Taxing Masters.

22. Court of Chancery Act, 1850 (also known as Sir George Turner's Act). "An Act to diminish the delay and expense of proceedings." The Court was given power to make a declaratory judgment (*i.e.* a declaration of a party's rights) without the granting of any consequential relief. (This was later made more general by the *Chancery Procedure Act,* 1852, *s.* 50.) Minor points concerning the construction of deeds or wills could now be determined by the stating of a special case on originating summons.

23. Court of Chancery Act, 1851. A Court of Appeal in Chancery was set up.

(*a*) The court would hear appeals from the vice-chancellors and the Master of the Rolls, and the Chief Judge in Bankruptcy.

(*b*) It consisted of the chancellor and two Lords Justices in Chancery.

(*c*) The chancellor was empowered to sit alone to hear appeals, if he so wished.

(*d*) The Lords Justices could sit without the chancellor.

(*e*) The Master of the Rolls or a vice-chancellor could be asked by the chancellor to sit.

(*f*) There was a further right of appeal from the court to the House of Lords.

24. Master in Chancery Abolition Act, 1852. "An Act to abolish the office of Master in Ordinary of the High Court of Chancery and to make provision for the more speedy and efficient despatch of business in the said court." The office of Masters in Ordinary in Chancery was abolished and their administrative business became the responsibility of Chief Clerks who were paid a fixed salary. They and their staff were responsible to the four judges for any business transacted by them in chambers. Litigants could appeal from the decisions of a Chief Clerk to the judge.

25. Common Law Procedure Act, 1852. This Act may be said to have anticipated the spirit of the 1873 Act, in that it began to bring in line the procedures of common law and equity. Common law courts were empowered to grant relief in the case of a lease being forfeited for non-payment of rent—a power hitherto confined to chancery.

26. Court of Chancery Procedure Act, 1852. "An Act to amend the practice and course of proceeding in the High Court of Chancery." This was a very important measure.

(a) The writ of *subpoena* was abolished. In its place there was a printed copy of plaintiff's bill, which was served on defendant. The bill was to contain those facts on which plaintiff rested his case. They were to be stated concisely and were to be set out in numbered paragraphs. A concluding section would set out plaintiff's request for relief.

(b) Plaintiff's interrogatories were to be set out and filed separately.

(c) Defendant's answer would include the facts of his case.

(d) Evidence could be given orally if either party wished this. Such evidence was to be given before an examiner out of court, and his records were to be made available for the judge.

(e) In the case of affidavit evidence a party could cross-examine the other party's witnesses before the examiner on matters contained in the affidavit.

(f) The Court of Chancery was given the power to decide any matter of law which arose in a hearing; the procedure of stating a case for an opinion by a common law court was abolished.

27. Oaths in Chancery Act, 1853. The office of Master Extraordinary was abolished, and such officials were to be designated Commissioners. The Lord Chancellor could appoint solicitors to administer oaths and take declarations in Chancery.

28. Common Law Procedure Act, 1854. Fusion of law and equity was advanced by this enactment.

(a) A defendant at law was allowed to employ any equitable defence in a case in which he might have obtained relief on equitable principles. This course was at the discretion of the court.

(b) Common law courts could order discovery of documents and administer interrogatories, hitherto confined almost entirely to chancery.

(c) Common law courts could issue prohibitory injunctions.

29. Chancery Amendment Act, 1858 (also known as Lord Cairns' Act). "An Act to amend the course of procedure in the High Court of Chancery." Under this Act, the Court of Chancery was empowered to award damages in addition to, or in lieu of, specific performance or injunction.

(a) Prior to this, chancery had lacked the power to award damages to a plaintiff who had been refused specific performances of a contract. In such a case plaintiff would have been obliged to bring another action, this time at common law, for the recovery of damages.

(b) The work of chancery was increased almost three-fold following this Act.

(c) The Act was repealed by the *Statute Law Revision Act*, 1883, *s*. 3, but the jurisdiction continues to exist: *Leeds Industrial Co-op. Society* v. *Slack* [1924] A.C.851, H.L.

> NOTE: In 1860 a set of Consolidated Orders, setting out the reformed Chancery Procedure, was published.

30. Bankruptcy Act, 1869. Appeals were to be made from the London Bankruptcy Court to the Lords Justices in Chancery.

THE JUDICATURE ACTS, 1873–75

31. Nomenclature and Dates. *The Supreme Court of Judicature Acts*, 1873 and 1875 (usually referred to as the *Judicature Acts*), came into operation on November 1st, 1875, by virtue of the *Supreme Court of Judicature (Commencement) Act*, 1874, *s*. 2. The operation of the Act had been intended to take effect on November 2nd, 1874, but the large number of amendments needed for the effective implementation of the new system necessitated a postponement of the date. The Acts were later repealed and replaced by the *Supreme Court of Judicature (Consolidation) Act*, 1925.

32. Background. The reforms mentioned at **17–30** above were very important, but, in a sense, piecemeal. Equity and common law had moved together, but fusion remained incomplete.

(a) A Royal Commission was established in 1867 to report on the administration of justice.

(b) Two Reports were published, in 1869 and 1872. The Reports considered the effect of the separation of courts of law and equity.

(c) *The Judicature Act*, 1875, was based in large measure on the *First Report* of the Commission.

(d) The Act was introduced into Parliament by Lord Chancellor Selborne who had played a prominent part in the drafting of the general rules. Of this Act Selborne wrote: "If I leave any monument behind me which will bear the test of time, it may be this."

33. General objects of the Act. The Act was described as "An Act for the constitution of a supreme court, and for other purposes relating to the better administration of justice in England. . . ." It was intended:

(a) To establish one Supreme Court of Judicature which would embrace the jurisdiction of existing superior courts;

(b) To effect a concurrent administration in the Supreme Court of the rules of law and equity;

(c) To establish procedures which would be common in the Supreme Court.

THE SUPREME COURT OF JUDICATURE

34. Consolidation and unification of the courts. Under the Act:

(a) *The following courts were consolidated and united into one Supreme Court of Judicature:* Queen's Bench, Common Pleas, Exchequer, Chancery, Probate, Divorce and Matrimonial Causes, Admiralty (and, from 1883, London Court of Bankruptcy).

(b) *The Supreme Court was to consist of two parts:*

(i) The High Court of Justice,
(ii) The Court of Appeal.

(c) *The High Court of Justice.*

(i) This would exercise the former jurisdiction of Queen's Bench and Common Pleas, Exchequer (common law and revenue jurisdiction), Chancery, Probate, Divorce and Matrimonial Causes, Admiralty, London Court of Bankruptcy, and those courts existing by virtue of commissions of *oyer and terminer*, gaol delivery and assize (*see* XIII, 28).

(*ii*) It would consist of the Lord Chancellor, the Master of the Rolls, the Vice-Chancellors, the Chief Justices of Queen's Bench and Common Pleas, the judges of the common law courts, the Courts of Probate, Divorce and Matrimonial Causes, and Admiralty.

(*iii*) It would sit in five divisions: Chancery; Common Pleas; Queen's Bench; Exchequer; Probate, Divorce and Admiralty. The number of divisions could be increased or reduced by order in council.

(*iv*) The divisions were not separate courts of jurisdiction, and the Chancellor was empowered to order judges in a particular division to sit in another division.

(*d*) *The Court of Appeal.*

(*i*) This would exercise the former jurisdiction of the Lord Chancellor and Court of Appeal in Chancery, the Exchequer Chamber, the Privy Council (concerning appeals in lunacy matters from the Chancellor), the Court of Appeal from the Chancery Court of Lancaster.

(*ii*) It would consist of Lords Justices of Appeal and any High Court judge requested by the Chancellor to sit.

(*iii*) The 1873 Act ended the appellate jurisdiction of Parliament, but in 1875 an amending Act restored this (*see* XV, 18(*b*)).

(*e*) *Restraint and prohibition of proceedings.* No injunction or prohibition could be issued by one part of the Supreme Court intended to restrain or prohibit proceedings in another part.

(*f*) *The business of the Court's divisions.* In general, the rule was that where a court had exercised an exclusive jurisdiction in particular matters, business arising from those matters would be assigned to the division of the High Court into which that court had been absorbed. But where particular business has not been assigned to a division, actions could be brought in any division. Actions brought in an inappropriate division could be transferred.

(*g*) *The work of the Chancery Division.* S. 34 of the Act specifically assigned the following matters to the Chancery Division in addition to those matters in which any other Act had given exclusive jurisdiction to the Court of Chancery:

(*i*) Administration of estates of deceased persons.

(*ii*) Dissolution of partnerships and the taking of partnership or other accounts.

(*iii*) Redemption or foreclosure of mortgages.

(*iv*) Raising of portions or other charges on land.

(*v*) Sale of property subject to a lien or charge.

(*vi*) Execution of charitable and private trusts.

(*vii*) Partition and sale of real estates.

(*viii*) Wardship of infants and control of their estates.

(*ix*) Rectification and cancellation of deeds and other written instruments.

(*x*) Specific performance of contracts between a vendor and a purchaser of land.

CONCURRENT ADMINISTRATION OF LAW AND EQUITY

35. The effect of sections 24 and 25 of the 1873 Act. Where a plaintiff brought an action in the High Court and claimed any right or relief in equity, or where defendant raised an equitable defence, such defence or claim was to be given effect as if it had been raised prior to the Act in the Court of Chancery. The High Court would also note, as would the Court of Chancery prior to the Act, the incidental appearance during an action of any equitable right or liability.

36. Section 25, sub-section 11. "Generally in all matters not hereinbefore particularly mentioned in which there is any conflict or variance between the rules of equity and the rules of the common law with reference to the same matter the rules of equity shall prevail."

NOTE: The Acts did not result in a total fusion of equity and law. Matters concerning administration, rather than principles, were fused by their being vested in one tribunal. But distinctions between equity and law remained, e.g. as in the general distinction between equitable and legal rights.

COMMON PROCEDURES

37. Section 17 of the Act. The judges of the Supreme Court were empowered to create new rules of procedure which would be placed before Parliament.

38. Effect of the Act. A single code of procedure which covered most of the proceedings in the newly-created Supreme Court was drawn up. This code was based on a schedule to the 1875 Act which enumerated, in 63 Orders, a number of rules of procedure. (These rules were later increased in number and a revised set was issued in 1883.)

PROGRESS TEST 11

1. Enumerate the general uncertainties in equity jurisdiction during the nineteenth century. **(3, 4)**

2. Why was the court's judicial staff the object of complaint in the nineteenth century? **(9)**

3. What type of reform was needed in chancery in the nineteenth century? **(13)**

4. What were the characteristics of these reforms? **(15)**

5. Outline the importance of the *Chancery Act*, 1833. **(18)**

6. What was the significance of *Sir George Turner's Act*, 1850? **(22)**

7. Give an account of the *Court of Chancery Procedure Act*, 1852. **(26)**

8. What were the general objects of the *Judicature Acts*, 1873–75? **(33)**

9. How did the 1873 Act consolidate and unify the courts? **(34)**

10. Give an account of the work of the Chancery Division following the *Judicature Acts*. **(34)**

PART FOUR

THE COURTS AND THE LEGAL PROFESSION

CHAPTER XII

COMMUNAL, SEIGNORIAL AND ECCLESIASTICAL COURTS

THE COMMUNAL COURTS

1. Background. *See* I, 21–22 and II, 4. These courts were Saxon in origin, and flourished in the early Middle Ages. In general, the law they applied:

  (*a*) Was based on custom;
  (*b*) Often varied according to the locality of the court;
  (*c*) Included some legislative rules enunciated by the kings.

2. The communal courts enumerated. In the Anglo-Saxon era, the country was divided into hundreds, shires and towns (*vills*)—*see* I, **10**. Vills had no courts. The great communal courts were:

  (*a*) The Shire, or County, Courts (*see* **3–6** below);
  (*b*) The Hundred Courts (*see* **7–10** below).

THE SHIRE COURTS

3. Background. The general background of the shires is mentioned at I, **10**(*c*).

  (*a*) In the Anglo-Saxon era a *shire-moot* would assemble at regular intervals to discuss all matters arising from its administrative duties. Judicial functions were of particular importance. The presiding officer was an *ealdorman* appointed by the king, and, at one time, he received "the third penny of the country," *i.e.* one-third of any profits resulting from the shire-moot.

  (*b*) In Norman times the title of the shire was changed to *comitatus* (county), subject to a *comes* (count). The presidency passed to the sheriff (*vice comes*).

4. The jurisdiction of the county court. There were three types of jurisdiction: that based on custom; that exercised by the sheriffs; that exercised by the king's itinerant justices.

(a) *The customary jurisdiction.* During the Anglo-Saxon era this jurisdiction was without limit, but, following the Conquest, matters concerning land were transferred to the feudal courts, matters arising out of church affairs were transferred to the ecclesiastical courts, and *pleas of the crown* became the concern of the king's itinerant justices. In the reign of Edward I, the county court's jurisdiction in civil matters was confined to actions which involved a maximum claim of 40*s*. Customary jurisdiction included the unique right of declaration of outlawry (*see* XVII, **24**(*d*)). There was a right of appeal to *common pleas*, on a writ of *Recordari Facias Loquelam*.

(b) *The sheriff's jurisdiction.* The sheriff was responsible to the king for the general administration of his county. The county court provided an important medium for the exercise of many of the sheriff's functions, and he presided over it as one of the king's judges. He could hear pleas on a royal writ of *justicies* ("do justice upon" defendant). He was empowered to transfer a plea concerning land to the Court of Common Pleas by a writ of *pone*, and to transfer such an action from the manorial court to the county court by a writ of *tolt*.

(c) *The jurisdiction of the king's justices.* Following the Conquest agents were sent by the king to act as his representatives in the counties in matters of administration and justice. By the end of the thirteenth century they acted as judges in the county courts.

5. The constitution of the county courts. The court consisted of a president and a number of *suitors*. The term "suitor" was derived from *sequere* (= to follow) and may have originated in the rights and privileges of those who followed and attended the king's travelling court. Suitors were obliged to attend at the county town in order to hear the cases brought before the county court.

(a) The qualification of a suitor was ownership of land.
(b) Suit of court, *i.e.* the duty of attending, became

onerous, and, in time, emerged as one of the incidents attached to the ownership of land (*see* XXIII, **14**).

(*c*) *The Statute of Merton*, 1236, *c*. 10, allowed freemen to discharge suit of court by attorney.

(*d*) In some cases, tenants of a lord who was himself obliged to perform suit of court carried out this duty on his behalf, as an incident to their tenancy.

(*e*) Since the suitors were laymen, unlearned in the law, they were at a disadvantage when actions in the county courts became more technical and complex.

(*f*) Their task was to decide whether defendant or plaintiff should prove his case, and by which mode of proof. In theory the president merely announced the decision of the suitors.

6. The weakening of the jurisdiction of the county courts. The jurisdiction of the county courts declined for the following reasons:

(*a*) Procedure became obscure, obsolescent and archaic.

(*b*) As the administration of justice became more centralised, the sheriffs' jurisdiction declined. Writs of *Justicies* (*see* **4**(*b*) above) were abolished.

(*c*) *The Statute of Gloucester*, 1278, was interpreted as limiting the jurisdiction of the county courts to claims with a maximum value of 40*s*.

(*d*) Suitors found it increasingly difficult to pronounce on technical matters of law.

(*e*) As the king's itinerant justices came to dominate the county courts, these courts became closely identified with the king's courts, and the case for their continued independence weakened.

NOTE: The old county Courts were eventually abolished by the *County Courts Act*, 1846, which set up new county Courts.

THE HUNDRED COURTS

7. Background. The general background of the hundreds was considered at I, **10**(*b*).

(*a*) The judicial functions of the hundred had their origin in early Anglo-Saxon times. Edgar had ordered regular monthly meetings of the hundreds and had empowered them to pursue and execute judgment on thieves (including the confiscation of one-half of their property). The *Dooms of Cnut, cc.* 17–20, ordered the enrolment in the hundreds of all freemen over twelve years of age, and forbade appeals to the king unless justice was unobtainable in the hundreds.

(*b*) Many of the hundreds (one half, by the time of Edward I) passed into private hands, by purchase, grant or usurpation.

8. The jurisdiction of the hundred courts. The jurisdiction of the court was customary in nature and confined to relatively minor matters arising in the hundred. In the twelfth century the hundreds met once every two weeks, a century later the meetings were held once every three weeks. The development of frankpledge (*see* I, 22) had resulted in a decline in the hundreds' criminal jurisdiction. After the early part of the thirteenth century actions concerning land were removed from the jurisdiction of the hundred.

9. The constitution of the hundred court. The court was similar in constitution to the county court (*see* 5 above).

(*a*) Suitors seem to have been drawn from a less important class than that which provided the suitors in county courts.

(*b*) The president was often the *hundred reeve*.

(*c*) The county court could review the decisions of the hundred court.

(*d*) A writ of false judgment lay to the Court of Common Pleas.

10. The weakening of the jurisdiction of the hundred court. In general, those matters which caused the decline of the county courts (*see* 6 above) had a similar effect upon the hundred courts. Vestiges of their jurisdiction survived in the following procedures:

(*a*) *Frankpledge. See* I, 22. Frankpledge grew in importance under the Normans when tithings (groups of ten families) were given a collective responsibility for their members, and when *murdrum* and *presentment of Englishry* were introduced (*see* XVIII, 3(*a*)). Sheriffs held meetings twice a year in the hundred courts in order to ensure that the tithings were properly formed, a procedure known as *view of frankpledge*.

(*b*) *The sheriff's tourn.* These twice-yearly meetings of the hundred court, combined with the presentment of offences under the *Assize of Clarendon*, 1166, grew into the *sheriff's tourn* (tour of duty).

> (*i*) The sheriff drew up his *Articles of the Tourn*, comprising questions touching matters affecting the king's peace, to which he required answers.
>
> (*ii*) The meeting, held twice a year in each hundred, was between the sheriff and his deputy and the hundred reeve and representatives of every vill in the hundred. They were obliged to declare on oath that they would neither accuse any innocent person, nor conceal any guilty one. They then presented to the sheriff any suspicions concerning the conduct of inhabitants of the hundred. (Such presentments had been considered initially by twelve freeholders in each vill.)
>
> (*iii*) The sheriff dealt with minor offences, the more serious matters were reserved for the king's judges.
>
> (*iv*) The *tourn* declined rapidly after 1461, when it was enacted that all presentments for crime (*i.e.* indictments) were to be the subject of examination by the Justices of the Peace.

THE SEIGNORIAL COURTS

11. Background. The continental concept of feudalism (*see* II, 5) included the tenure of land accompanied by private rights of jurisdiction which could be exercised by a landowner over those of his tenants who held from him by free service. By the twelfth and thirteenth centuries this right and its corresponding duties were widespread. The courts set up in this way were known as *seignorial courts*.

12. The seignorial courts enumerated. The seignorial courts may be classified as follows:

> (*a*) The baronial courts (*see* **13–14** below).
> (*b*) The franchise courts (*see* **15–17** below).
> (*c*) The manorial courts, which gave rise to:
>> (*i*) The courts baron,
>> (*ii*) The courts customary (see **18–20** below).

F

THE BARONIAL COURTS

13. Constitution. Baronial courts were set up by the owners
of very extensive lands, which were held from the king under
military tenure. The properties so held were considered as a
barony (or *honour*). The court was often known as a *court of the
honour*. It was attended by those tenants who held immediately from the lord. Such suitors (*see* **5** above) often found
the duty to be burdensome, since the barony might be scattered in various parts of the kingdom (*see* II, **7**(*c*)).

14. Jurisdiction. The principal concern of the baronial
courts had been the administration of the barony's component
estates. Jurisdiction included the right to hear disputes concerning land held of the lord and the allocation of those incidents of knight service (*see* XXIII) which had to be shared
among the tenants.

THE FRANCHISE COURTS

15. Their origin. During the twelfth century the hundred
courts had exercised a criminal jurisdiction. Gradually many
of these courts had become privately owned and their owners
exercised the privilege, or franchise, of jurisdiction. Addi-
tionally, before and after the Norman Conquest, privileged
rights of jurisdiction, such as *view of frankpledge* (*see* **10**(*a*)
above) had been granted to some landowners. Usurpation of
such rights of jurisdiction also took place. It should be noted
that:

(*a*) Such jurisdiction was usually concerned with petty
crime, but rarely with that of a more serious nature.

(*b*) Where it was exercised, the court was known as a
court leet (the term probably derives from *lathe*—land, or an
administrative district).

16. The Quo Warranto Inquiry, 1274. Henry III had started
an inquiry into the franchises in private hands. Edward I
pursued this inquiry vigorously and sent commissions throughout the country to examine in each area the private franchises
and to establish how far they interfered with the administration
of public justice. The inquiry (known as *Quo Warranto*—the

title of a writ which asked, "By what authority . . .?") sought to discover:

(a) The extent of the royal manors;

(b) The warrants by which estates and rights of jurisdiction once possessed by the king had passed to corporations or to private individuals.

17. The Statute of Gloucester, 1290. The returns to the inquiry were recorded in the Hundred Rolls. *The Statute of Gloucester*, 1290, enacted that, where proof of title to the franchise was otherwise inadequate, a claim might be accepted as valid *where there was evidence of continuous use for a century* (*i.e.* from the coronation of Richard I, in 1189). The Statute had the effect of checking the usurpation of franchises.

THE MANORIAL COURTS

18. Background. The manorial court, constituted by those who had the duty of suit of court, existed in the single manors. The manor was essentially an economic unit, which, in medieval times, comprised:

(a) The lord's land—his demesne;

(b) The waste land, which was used for the pasturing of tenants' cattle;

(c) The land held by the lord's free tenants;

(d) The land held by the lord's villein tenants.

19. Jurisdiction of the manorial courts. Manorial rights included rights of jurisdiction to be exercised over the lord's villeins and free tenants. Such jurisdiction was exercised in the following matters:

(a) Disputes concerning the ownership of tenants' holdings;

(b) The enforcing of customary rules, *e.g.* concerning waste;

NOTE (*i*) Criminal matters were reserved for the hundred or county court.

(*ii*) *The Statute of Marlborough*, 1267, enacted that a free tenant need not carry out a duty of suit of court at his lord's court unless that duty had been specifically stated in the grant of land, or had been carried out before 1230.

20. Courts baron, and courts customary. After the four-teenth century there grew a system comprising two types of manorial court:

(a) *The court baron* (the term was used here in the sense of its Norman derivation, *baro*—a man). The court concerned itself with freeholders. Suitors and parties to the action were free tenants; the president was the lord's steward.

(b) *The court customary.* This court was held for the villein tenants. The lord's steward ("Chancellor in his manor," according to Coke) acted not as president, but as judge. (It should be observed that no action concerning a copyhold by which a villein held his land could be brought at common law until the end of the fifteenth century.)

NOTE: A court baron could not be held unless there were at least two freeholders of the manor (not including the parties to the hearing) who could try the action.

DECLINE OF THE SEIGNORIAL COURTS

21. General. The jurisdiction exercised by the medieval courts declined when the social circumstances which surrounded the appearance of those courts changed and eventually ceased to exist. When feudalism faded, the seignorial courts declined.

22. Reasons for the decline. Among the general reasons for the decay and disappearance of the seignorial courts may be discerned the following:

(a) As the administration of justice became centralised, and as the royal courts extended their jurisdiction, which involved an efficient procedure and reasonable remedies, the need for localised seignorial jurisdiction began to disappear.

(b) The use of *fictions* was extended in an endeavour to remove actions concerning land from the seignorial to the king's courts. Such fictions included:

(i) *Quia dominus remisit curiam* ("because the lord has waived his court")—a fictitious assertion that the lord had waived his right to exert jurisdiction.

(ii) *The writ of Pone*—based on the fictitious allegation that justice had been denied in the seignorial court.

(c) *Scutage* (*see* XXIII, **10**), which allowed personal

service, such as suit of court, to be rendered as a money payment, affected the attendance of suitors at the courts.

(d) *The Statute of Marlborough*, 1267, gave some relief from the burden of suit of court.

(e) *The Statute Quia Emptores*, 1290 (*see* XXIII, 7) led to an increase in the number of tenancies held directly of the king; hence the number of those liable for suit of court declined.

NOTE: (*i*) Manorial rights continued for several centuries after the decline of the courts. Manchester affords an interesting example. The manorial rights in Manchester were sold in 1579 by the family of Sir Reynold West to John Lacy. He sold them in 1596 to Sir Nicholas Mosley. They were bought in 1845 from Sir Oswald Mosley by the municipality for £200,000.

(*ii*) The borough court was a manor court of local jurisdiction, often enjoying the right, conferred by charter, of hearing civil actions to any amount. At the basis of its jurisdiction was the customary law, and actions were limited to events occurring within the borough. Barristers from the Inns of Court were often appointed as recorders of these courts. An appeal on writ of error lay from the borough court to the royal courts.

THE ECCLESIASTICAL COURTS

23. Canon law and the Church. Canon law is the body of ecclesiastical law formulated by the Roman Catholic Church, consisting largely of decrees of the Church Councils, writings of the Fathers of the Church, and epistles and bulls of the see of Rome. The great *Corpus Juris Canonici*, a twelfth century codification, was made up of the *Decretum* of Gratianus, the *Decretals* and the *Sext* of Gregory IX, and some other compilations of decrees. It was part of an attempt to establish the basis of a universal jurisdiction. Canon law was the essence of the great system of jurisdiction at the head of which was the papal court in Rome. Supreme judicial power was vested in the pope. The claim of the church to jurisdiction *in all matters* affecting its clergy and affecting the spiritual welfare of the laity was based on canon law.

24. Disputes between church and state. Between a church claiming absolute jurisdiction and a king demanding an exclusive loyalty from his subjects conflict was inevitable. (*See* II, 3, 13.)

(*a*) *Concordats* seeking to limit the areas of conflict between church and state were common features of medieval times. An important example was the legislation known as *the Constitutions of Clarendon* (*see* II, 13(*a*)) which attempted to settle some disputes between the crown and church.

(*b*) *The Reformation* (*see* III, 7) represented the culmination of the most serious dispute in this country between church and state. No concordat could end a dispute of this nature, and one of the results was a complete transfer to the crown of certain powers of jurisdiction exercised by the pope.

25. Ecclesiastical jurisdiction in the Middle Ages. The *courts Christian*, as the ecclesiastical courts were known, exercised the following extensive jurisdiction:

(*a*) *Jurisdiction concerning the affairs of the clergy and church property.* The church claimed the right to try and punish in its own courts clergy accused of felonies. Charges involving misdemeanours and non-criminal matters were heard in the lay courts. The quarrel between Beckett and Henry II arose out of the claim made by the church to exclusive jurisdiction over "criminous clerks." The church courts also heard matters concerning church buildings and other consecrated places. Disputes concerning the payment of (but not title to) tithes were heard by church courts.

(*b*) *Jurisdiction arising out of offences against religion and morality.* Blasphemy, heresy, drunkenness, contempt of the clergy, defamation, were some of the offences punishable in the church courts.

(*c*) *Jurisdiction in matters concerning marriage, legitimacy, intestacy and probate.*

(*i*) The determination of issues concerning marriage (*see* 26 below) passed entirely into the jurisdiction of the church courts during the twelfth century.

(*ii*) From the time of Henry II, the church courts had exercised an exclusive jurisdiction in the case of disputes concerning wills of personal property and the granting of probate. (It should be noted that oral wills were often made in the presence of a priest performing the final act of absolution.) In the thirteenth century jurisdiction was extended to disputes concerning intestacy. In 1357 the church courts were obliged to grant administration of an intestate's estates to one of his relations.

NOTE: The church courts were able to inflict a variety of punishments, all capable of being redeemed by penance: lesser excommunication, greater excommunication (a very severe penalty partaking in some ways of the nature of outlawry), exclusion from attendance at church, and fines.

26. Ecclesiastical jurisdiction in matrimonial matters. The church courts had a wide jurisdiction.

(a) *The following decrees could be granted:*

(i) *Restitution of conjugal rights*, on the grounds of desertion. Disobedience to the decree could result in excommunication.

(ii) *Nullity*, because of affinity, consanguinity, mental incapacity, force or error, lack or age, prior subsisting marriage. Annulment on the grounds of impotence was also granted.

(iii) *Divorce a mensa et thoro* (a type of judicial separation), on the grounds of adultery or cruelty.

(b) *Divorce a vinculo matrimonii* (*i.e.* the dissolution of a marriage initially valid) was not possible. After the Reformation the ecclesiastical courts declared, however, that they had the power to dissolve a marriage (which was no longer considered as a sacrament).

(i) In *The Marquis of Northampton's Case* (1542), this power was upheld by the Court of Bishops.

(ii) In *Foljambe's Case* (1602), Star Chamber declared that divorce by a church court did not dissolve the marriage absolutely.

(c) *A divorce a vinculo matrimonii could be obtained by private bill in Parliament.* In the eighteenth century a petitioner by private bill had to obtain first a decree *a mensa et thoro* on the grounds of adultery and, if a male, had to recover damages at common law in an action for criminal conversation.

27. The ecclesiastical courts enumerated. The most important of these courts were:

(a) *The Ordinary courts,* which originated in an ordinance of William I.

(b) *The post-Reformation High Court of Delegates.*
(c) *The post-Reformation Court of High Commission.*

28. The Ordinary courts. William I issued an ordinance which separated the ecclesiastical and civil jurisdiction of the courts. Sheriffs and other lay persons could no longer participate in the hearing of disputes based on church affairs, and bishops and archdeacons were forbidden to participate in the hearing of pleas in the courts of the hundred or the shire. These pleas were to be heard and determined by the bishop according to church law. From this ordinance issued the structure of the so-called *ordinary courts.*

(a) *The archdeacon's court.* The jurisdiction of the archdeacon arose from his position as bishop's deputy. He could enquire into the moral conduct of clergy and laymen, and could impose penalties of fines and penances. Appeal lay to the consistory court.

NOTE: Where a church court was exempted from the bishop's jurisdiction it was known as a *peculiar.*

(b) *The consistory court.* The consistory court for each diocese had appellate and first instance jurisdiction. It was presided over by the bishop's deputy, often his chancellor (in the Court of Canterbury he was known as the *commissary*), but the bishop had a right to hear a case personally after withdrawing it from his consistory court. In this court were heard matters concerning wills and probate.

(c) *The provincial Courts of the archbishop.* There were three metropolitan courts in the provinces of York and Canterbury.

(i) *The court of Canterbury* (also known as the *Court of Arches*, since its judge had the title of *Dean of the Arches*) heard appeals from dioceses in the province of Canterbury, and had first instance jurisdiction in some other cases. A similar court in the province of York was known as the *Archbishop's Court of Chancery*, the judge being called *principal*, or *auditor*.

(ii) *Courts of audience* in each province acted as courts of appeal.

(iii) *Prerogative courts of Canterbury and York* dealt with wills of testators who had left property in several dioceses.

NOTE (*i*) The *Papal Curia* in Rome stood at the summit of this system and exercised original and appellate jurisdiction. Litigants could ask the *Curia* to decide an action at any stage, whereupon the parties might be summoned to Rome, or a papal legate would be sent to hear the case at its place of trial.

(*ii*) Procedure in many ecclesiastical courts was very slow, was often conducted in Latin, and had certain features typical of chancery procedure. Thus, the action commenced with the issuing of a bill, known as a *libel*, there was no jury, and the parties could be examined by the judge.

(*iii*) In the courts of the dioceses and the provinces the judges were usually clergy learned in Canon Law appointed by the bishop, and known as *chancellors*.

29. The High Court of Delegates. Following the break with Rome, it became necessary to re-constitute the system of appeals from the archbishops' courts. Appeals had been made to the *Curia* at Rome, and these were now forbidden. In 1534 it was enacted that an appeal from the archbishops' courts was to be made to the king in chancery, and that the king (in line with the Pope's practice of appointing delegates to hear a case) would commission delegates to hear the appeal.

(*a*) The delegates, or judges, were known as *delegates of appeal*, and their court was known as the *High Court of Delegates*.

(*b*) A commission had to be appointed for each appeal and, hence, there were no permanent judges of the court, but merely *ad hoc* nominees in each case.

(*c*) The judges in the court were ecclesiastical lawyers and, occasionally, bishops. By the eighteenth century the court consisted of three common law judges and three lawyers learned in the civil law.

(*d*) Dissatisfaction with the court grew steadily, since the nominal fees of one guinea a day, paid to the civil lawyers by the successful party, attracted only junior practitioners, and there was little knowledge of canon law displayed by the common law judges. Precedent was rarely followed in the court, and reasons for judgments were rarely given. Decisions of the court could be challenged by a Royal Commission of Review.

(*e*) The Privy Council took over the court's jurisdiction under the *Judicial Committee Act*, 1833.

30. The Court of High Commission. The origin of this court may be found in the commissions granted for the enforcing of the religious policy of the state. Commissioners were nominated and were given extensive jurisdiction in spiritual matters. Thus, the ecclesiastical commissions of Elizabeth in 1559 nominated commissioners who had wide powers, including "from time to time . . . to reform, redress, order, correct and amend, in all places within this our realm of England, all such errors, heresies, crimes, abuses, offences, contempts and enormities, spiritual and ecclesiastical. . . ." The *Acts of Supremacy and Uniformity* were to be enforced against all in the realm. The court's jurisdiction extended throughout the country, and the commissioners became known as the court of high commission.

(*a*) In its early stages the court's work was of an informal nature, but after 1580 it sat in regular session with appropriate formality.

(*b*) Its judges were ecclesiastical lawyers and doctors of civil law. Three members, including one bishop, formed a quorum.

(*c*) It had no jurisdiction in matters of property.

(*d*) It could fine, imprison, and excommunicate.

(*e*) Its procedure, based on common law, commenced with the submission of *articles* on behalf of plaintiff or the commission. The accused was summoned by *letters missive* and was ordered to take an *oath ex officio*, before being informed of the charge against him. His oath declared that he would truly answer all interrogatories. The oath became one of the principal targets of the commission's many enemies; it was compared to some of the hated procedures of the Spanish Inquisition. The protection of the common law maxim that no person is bound to incriminate himself was denied to the accused person.

(*f*) In *Cawdrey's Case* (1591), the common law judges affirmed the court as proper and lawful.

(*g*) Attacks against the court and its procedure mounted. In 1610, the Commons' *Petition of Grievances* complained of the unlimited jurisdiction of the commissioners. "For that limit touching causes subject to this Commission, being only with these words, viz., 'Such as pertain to spiritual or ecclesiastical jurisdiction,' it is very hard to know what matters or offences are included in that number, and the other because it is unknown what ancient canons or laws spiritual are in force and what not."

(*h*) Letters patent were granted in 1611 so as to define with more precision the use of the *oath ex officio* and the types of crime which came under the court's jurisdiction.

(*i*) In 1641 the court was abolished by an Act which referred to "the great and unsufferable wrong and oppression of the King's subjects" caused by the commissioners. The abolition of the court was confirmed at the Restoration.

31. Later jurisdiction of the ecclesiastical courts. As religious toleration grew, the jurisdiction of the church courts in matters of morals and religious faith declined. The jurisdiction came to be centred around three matters: issues affecting the clergy, wills and probate, matrimonial matters. Legislation of 1857 was of particular importance.

(*a*) *The Court of Probate Act*, 1857, removed from the ecclesiastical courts jurisdiction concerning probate and wills of personal property, which then passed to the new probate court.

(*b*) *The Matrimonial Causes Act*, 1857, created the divorce court, which took over the jurisdiction of the ecclesiastical courts in matters concerning divorce.

NOTE: Ecclesiastical courts exist today. Consistory courts, presided over by a barrister-Chancellor, sit in each diocese. The *Court of Arches* and the *Court of Chancery* in York hear appeals from *consistory courts*. The final court of appeal is the *Judicial Committee of the Privy Council*. All questions concerning church property are dealt with according to the common law.

PROGRESS TEST 12

1. Outline the jurisdiction of the county court. **(4)**
2. What was the function of the *suitors* in the county courts? **(5)**
3. Outline the jurisdiction and constitution of the hundred courts. **(8, 9)**
4. Explain (*a*) *Sheriff's Tourn*, (*b*) *Articles of the Tourn*. **(10)**
5. Enumerate the seignorial courts. **(12)**
6. What was the jurisdiction of the baronial courts? **(14)**
7. Outline the origin of the franchise courts. **(15)**

8. Explain (a) *court baron*, (b) *court customary*.   **(20)**

9. Why did the seignorial courts decline?   **(21, 22)**

10. Outline ecclesiastical jurisdiction in the Middle Ages.   **(25)**

11. What were (a) the Ordinary courts, (b) the High Court of Delegates?   **(28, 29)**

12. What was the Court of High Commission?   **(30)**

CHAPTER XIII

THE CURIA REGIS AND THE COURTS OF COMMON LAW

CURIA REGIS—THE KING'S COURT

1. Background. In early times the king's judicial and administrative functions were not formally separated, and were carried out by him and his advisers in that part of his palace known as the *king's court*. The English *Curia Regis*, which may have developed under Norman influence from the Norman *Curia Ducis*, combined the functions of the *witan* (*see* I, **13**) and a royal council of advisers. It later developed into a powerful court of justice.

(*a*) In its early stages the *Curia* was concerned with administrative, as well as legal matters.

(*b*) Whereas the witan consisted of the king's "wise men," the qualification for membership under the Normans became tenure of land.

(*c*) Its members were the lay and ecclesiastical tenants-in-chief of the king, *i.e.* those who held their lands from him by tenure in barony, plus smaller landowners summoned at the king's pleasure.

2. Its importance. The *Curia Regis* was an institution of vital importance in the development of our law:

(*a*) Its work resulted in the centralised administration of justice in the realm.

(*b*) From it ultimately sprang the most important of our contemporary political and legal institutions:

(*i*) The large *curia* gave rise to Parliament.

(*ii*) The smaller *curia* developed into the great courts of common law.

3. Meetings of the Curia. Two kinds of meeting seem to have been held:

(*a*) *Meeting of the entire Curia.* On the three great festivals

159

of the year the king held his court (Easter at Winchester; Whitsun at Westminster; Xmas at Gloucester). These occasions, on which the king appeared in his full regalia, were known as the *crown wearings*, and were attended by his earls, abbots, bishops, knights and thegns. New legislation was enacted and disputes involving the great men of the realm were heard. The *Curia* thus acted in its administrative capacity and as a supreme court in the land.

(b) *Meetings of the smaller curia.* Regular government business, involving day-to-day administration, was transacted by a permanent group of the king's chief ministers, including his justiciar and chancellor. As their work developed, its specialised features, *e.g.* financial administration and control, came to be dealt with by groups of advisers who later formed the nucleus of the common law court system.

(*i*) The *Curia Regis* had powers to decide appeals, to hear cases removed from the hundred and shire courts, to administer the collection of the royal revenues, and to hear pleas concerning the king—the basis of subsequent common law court jurisdiction.

(*ii*) The later development of the king's council and the conciliar courts (*see* XIV) had its roots in the workings of the *Curia.*

4. Its jurisdiction. In essence the jurisdiction of *Curia Regis* was based on the king's supreme position in the hierarchy of the feudal system (*see* II, **7**) and on his duty to provide justice for all of his subjects who sought it.

(a) *The Curia Regis as a feudal court.* In his capacity as feudal lord the king was able to hear disputes which arose among his tenants-in-chief.

(b) *The Curia Regis as a manifestation of the king's residuary power of jurisdiction.* The ancient concept of kingship involved the king in a duty to ensure the internal peace of his realm and to act as a "fount of justice" for those who had failed to find justice elsewhere. Hence, in its judicial capacity, the *Curia Regis* adjudicated on breaches of the king's peace (*see* XVII, **14**) and heard pleas alleging that justice had been denied to plaintiff in the courts.

5. Curia Regis and the centralisation of justice. In time the royal courts took over much of the administration of justice from the local courts. Centralised royal justice was popular: the king's courts could enforce attendance and judgments; they could offer a rudimentary form of trial by jury which was preferred by many to the old forms of proof. The concentration of jurisdiction in the king's courts arose as a result of the following factors:

(a) The king's residuary powers of jurisdiction brought to his court many cases which had been determined unsatisfactorily elsewhere. Inherent in feudalism was the concept that a tenant who had been denied justice by his lord in his court could ask for a remedy in the court of his lord's lord.

(b) The power of the manorial courts declined as a result of the issue by chancery of writs of right in cases of disputes concerning freehold land. Later, under Edward I, issue of the writ became a preliminary stage of an action in the king's court.

(c) The king's courts, in the time of Henry III, were able to hear, in some circumstances, actions which had not been commenced by writ. This increased the popularity of these courts.

(d) An ordinance issued at Windsor by Henry II in 1179 offered, only in the royal courts, an alternative to the unpopular trial by battle. Defendant's case was to be considered by a group of impartial neighbours.

(e) Henry II's introduction of the Petty Assize (*see* VI, **17**) gave the king's court jurisdiction concerning the recovery of possession of land. This procedure was summary and, because of its relative speed, was popular.

(f) *The Statute of Gloucester*, 1278, was construed so that actions involving sums greater than 40s. were removed in most cases from the local courts. (*See* also XII, **6, 22**.)

THE DIVISION OF THE CURIA REGIS

6. Division of administration. As the work of the king's court increased the need arose for a division of functions. To the time of Henry II the *Curia Regis* remained one supreme court. But by the end of the reign of Henry III the judicial functions of the *Curia* were divided among several permanent courts.

7. The Courts of common law. The great common law courts which sprang from the *Curia Regis* were:

    (*a*) The Court of Exchequer (see **8–10** below)

    (*b*) The Court of Common Pleas (*see* **11–12** below)

    (*c*) The Court of King's Bench (*see* **13–17** below)

    (*d*) The Courts of Exchequer Chamber (*see* **18–20** below)

    (*e*) The General Eyre (*see* **21–23** below)

    (*f*) The Courts of Assize (*see* **24–28** below).

THE COURT OF EXCHEQUER

8. Origins. A type of treasury accounting can be traced back to Anglo-Saxon times, in, for example, the ascertaining by the king's officials of the bullion content of coin received as revenue (*blanching*). By the twelfth century the financial and revenue functions of the *Curia Regis* were carried out in the *scaccarium* (chessboard—so-called from the counters which, placed on chequered cloth, were used in accounting procedures). *The Curia Regis ad scaccarium* in the twelfth century summoned sheriffs to Westminster twice a year. The preliminary accounts were taken at Easter, the "final accounting" took place at Michaelmas.

    (*a*) In the process of collecting taxes and revenue disputes arose, and the settling of those disputes gave rise to the fiscal jurisdiction of the Exchequer.

    (*b*) The procedure of the Court of Exchequer was the subject of the *Dialogus de Scaccario*, written *c.* 1177 (*see* V, **20**).

9. Development of the court. The Exchequer had been the first offshoot from the *Curia Regis* in the reign of Henry I, and during the reign of Henry II it achieved distinctive status.

    (*a*) By the end of the thirteenth century the *Exchequer of Account and Receipt* (the forerunner of our Treasury) had become distinct from the Court of Exchequer (known also as the *Exchequer of Pleas*).

    (*b*) Special clerks (*barones scaccarii*) were appointed by Henry III to the exchequer, one of them being designated later by Edward I as *chief baron*. The chief baron, from the reign of Edward II, was a lawyer who acted as president of a group of exchequer barons who were specialists in the exchequer's legal work.

(c) In the sixteenth century the exchequer barons accompanied common law judges on circuit.

(d) The common law work of the court developed rapidly, largely by the use of *fictions* (*see* **10** below), and by the sixteenth century it had encroached on the work of the other common law courts.

(e) The equitable jurisdiction of the court had increased by the sixteenth century, and was exercised by the Treasurer, Chancellor of the Exchequer, and Barons. Exchequer of Pleas was held before the Treasurer and the Barons.

10. The jurisdiction of the court. The Court of Exchequer exercised three main types of jurisdiction: common law, equitable, fiscal.

(a) *Common law jurisdiction.* By the use of the exchequer writ of *Quominus* (*quo minus* = by which the less . . .) plaintiff could plead the fiction that he was a debtor of the king and could not repay that debt because of defendant's failure to repay him. The writ, used first c. 1320, allegedly concerned with the king's revenues, and hence within the scope of exchequer, was used by the court to extend its jurisdiction. The writ was later used so as to hear other matters which properly belonged to the jurisdiction of the Court of Common Pleas.

(b) *Equitable jurisdiction.* The writ of *subpoena*, used in chancery for the exercise of its equitable jurisdiction, was used in the sixteenth century by the exchequer. Exchequer judges gave decisions which were often based, as in chancery, on so-called natural justice.

(c) *Fiscal jurisdiction.* Suits by the king against his debtors were heard by the Court of Exchequer.

NOTE (*i*) Other reasons for the growth in the non-fiscal jurisdiction of the Court of Exchequer were: it was possible to recover there contract debts from executors (not possible elsewhere); the king could order that the affairs of certain merchants and clergy be heard there; the jurisdiction extended (unlike that of Common Pleas) to Wales; recognisances of debts could be enrolled in, and hence could be heard by, the court; the court's officials had the privilege of bringing actions against them into exchequer.

(*ii*) The equitable jurisdiction of the court passed to the Court of Chancery in 1842.

THE COURT OF COMMON PLEAS

11. Origins and development. Under Henry II there had been a large increase in the *communia placita* (pleas between subject and subject) heard by *Curia Regis* and the number of judges had been increased to eighteen. In 1178 the number was reduced to five (two clerks and three laymen). They were to sit as a permanent court, *in banco residentes*, to hear common pleas, and where they were unable to determine such cases, or where they failed to do justice, the cases were to be heard by the king (*coram rege*) and his council.

(*a*) Common pleas were pleas other than those which concerned royal rights.

(*b*) The court followed the king in his travels throughout the realm.

(*c*) Much inconvenience and great expense resulted to litigants by the court's not being in one fixed place. *Magna Carta*, 1215, c. 17, stated that common pleas should not follow the king's court, but should be held *in loco certo* (in some certain place).

(*d*) In the reign of Henry III the Court of Common Pleas separated from the *Curia*. Thus, in 1224 there came into existence two separate series of Rolls of the *Curia Regis*—the *Coram Rege Rolls*, and the *De Banco Rolls* which recorded common pleas.

(*e*) Under Henry III the Court of Common Pleas sat permanently in Westminster Hall, occupying the right hand side of the hall near the entry. Chancery sat at the southwest corner. King's Bench sat at the upper end of the southeast corner.

(*f*) The first Chief Justice of Common Pleas, Gilbert de Preston, was appointed in 1272. (Coke occupied this position in 1606.)

(*g*) The sole right of audience by the Court of Common Pleas passed to the serjeants-at-law (*see* XVI, 6). Their fees were very high and this accounted in part for the decline in the court's popularity.

(*h*) Senior clerks (*prothonotaries*) were appointed with the tasks of entering pleadings on the rolls of the court, assisting in the assessment of costs, and giving advice on technical matters.

(*i*) One section of the court concerned itself with deciding matters arising out of preliminary pleadings, another section (with a jury) decided the subsequent hearings.

12. The jurisdiction of the court. In the Middle Ages, the Court of Common Pleas had a very extensive jurisdiction and in that era it became the busiest of the common law courts. Its jurisdiction concerned the following matters:

(*a*) Pleas between the king's subjects in matters other than those touching royal rights. Actions for debts, covenant and detinue were heard by the court.

(*b*) Real actions, *i.e.* those concerning land.

(*c*) Actions involving the court's officials.

(*d*) The issuing of writs of *habeas corpus, certiorari, prohibition,* and *recordari facias*.

(*e*) Disputes removed from the manorial and communal courts by writs of *pone*.

(*f*) By use of the writ *quare Clausum fregit* ("whereas he has broken the close . . ."), the court was able to extend its jurisdiction in the time of Charles II. This fiction was based on a writ of trespass (a crown plea) which charged defendant with a fictitious trespass (which was not proceeded with at the hearing) to which was added an *ac etiam clause* (*ac etiam* = and also) stating the real allegation. The court concerned itself only with that which was alleged in the *ac etiam* clause.

NOTE (*i*) The Court of Common Pleas declined in importance for the following reasons: the old actions which it heard became unpopular; King's Bench and exchequer usurped the court's jurisdiction by the use of fictions such as *Quominus* (*see* **10**(*a*) above) and *Bill of Middlesex* (*see* VII **13**(a)); King's Bench and exchequer had powers of enforcing their judgments which derived from their concern with royal rights and which were denied to Common Pleas.

(*ii*) Under the *Judicature Act*, 1873, the court became a division of the High Court of Justice (*see* XI, **34**).

THE COURT OF THE KING'S BENCH

13. Origins and development. The last court to separate from *Curia Regis* was King's Bench. In its earlier stages it was, in effect, the smaller, or inner, *curia* (*see* **3** above) exercising a judicial function. In principle and in fact it was a court held before the king himself (*coram ipso domino rege*). In medieval times its title was "The Justices assigned for the holding of Pleas before the King himself."

(*a*) Separation from *Curia Regis* came *c*. 1230. One of the first to be appointed as Chief Justice (known in later times as Lord Chief Justice of England) was the celebrated Robert de Bruce.

(*b*) Until *c*. 1400 the court remained very closely connected with the affairs of the king and his Council—from this stemmed many of its powers of jurisdiction.

(*c*) The court followed Henry II and John on their travels, but in the absence of the king its functions often lapsed.

(*d*) In the late fourteenth century the court travelled through the realm in an attempt to carry out some of the functions of the Eyre (*see* **21** below). After 1400 it remained at Westminster.

(*e*) Until 1465 the king sat with his judges. James I asserted his claim to sit, but was dissuaded after argument by Coke.

(*f*) The growth of Star Chamber in the sixteenth century (*see* XIV, **6–13**) resulted in a loss of work by the court.

(*g*) Barristers gained a monopoly of audience in the court by the fifteenth century.

(*h*) Under the *Judicature Acts*, 1873–75 (*see* XI) the court became one of the divisions of the High Court of Justice.

14. Jurisdiction of the court. The jurisdiction of King's Bench was based on its function as a central court for the hearing of Pleas of the Crown, *i.e.* those offences said to have been committed *contra pacem Domini Regis, coronam et dignitatem suam* (against the peace of our lord the king, his crown and his dignity). This jurisdiction developed so that it was ultimately both criminal and civil, and included control of royal officials through the use of prerogative writs.

15. Criminal jurisdiction. The court's criminal jurisdiction was exercised at first instance and in an appellate and supervisory capacity.

(*a*) *As a court of first instance.* Jurisdiction extended to any county in which King's Bench was sitting. At such times the authority of the court superseded that of other judges in the county.

(b) *As a court of appellate and supervisory jurisdiction.* The court superintended, in a general way, the administration of criminal justice throughout the realm.

(i) *A writ of certiorari* could be used to transfer to King's Bench civil and criminal actions pending in other courts. The writ was available in matters which involved a particularly complicated and disputed point of law, or where a just hearing could not be obtained in the lower court. The case was then heard in King's Bench or was sent for trial at *nisi prius* (see 27 below), or was sent back to the county in which it had commenced.

(ii) *A writ of error* was available in the case of an error apparent upon the face of the record.

(iii) *Right of rehearing.* In the seventeenth century it was possible to claim a fresh hearing in King's Bench where there was an allegation of irregular proceedings in the lower court.

16. Civil jurisdiction. King's Bench civil jurisdiction was exercised at first instance and in an appellate capacity.

(a) *As a court of first instance.* Pleas affecting the crown were heard in King's Bench, as were cases originating in a writ of trespass (which alleged a breach committed *contra pacem regis*—against the king's peace).

(i) The growth of trespass on the case extended the court's civil jurisdiction.

(ii) Added growth in civil jurisdiction came from the use of fictions, particularly the use of the Bill of Middlesex (see VII, 13(a)).

(b) *As a court of appellate jurisdiction.* The court exercised this jurisdiction by means of motion for a new trial and writ of error.

(i) Motion for a new trial was available in the later stages of the court's development.

(ii) Writ of error was available in the case of an error apparent upon the face of the record. In 1285 the *Statute of Westminster II* gave parties the right to submit a bill of exceptions, in which could be stated objections to the decision of a judge on a matter of law, even where that decision had not been recorded. The right of King's Bench to hear a writ of error from the Court of Crown Pleas was abolished in 1830.

17. Jurisdiction over royal officials. King's Bench had the power of superintending matters concerning its own officials and other officers of the Crown. By the use of prerogative writs, such as those mentioned below, this control was exercised widely.

(a) *Certiorari*. This writ was used to remove a case from an inferior into a superior court. (*Certiorari* commands a court to "certify" a particular matter.)

(b) *Prohibition*. Used to restrain an inferior court from exceeding its jurisdiction.

(c) *Mandamus* ("we command"). Used to compel a court, or a public officer, to exercise proper functions.

(d) *Quo warranto* ("by what authority . . .?"). Used to enquire into the authority by which a public office was held, or a franchise claimed.

(e) *Habeas Corpus*. This writ was used to command a person who detained another in custody to produce that other person before the court.

THE COURTS OF EXCHEQUER CHAMBER

18. Background. Appeals in the Middle Ages were limited, in general, to cases in which the appellant established that he had been denied justice, *e.g.* as in the case of a formal error on the record. In order to establish a system of appeals, courts were created (*see* **19** below) known, at the time of their creation, as courts of Exchequer Chamber. The name may have originated in the fact that the common law judges occasionally met to discuss problems in a room adjoining the Exchequer. (The 1357 Act—*see* **19**(a) below—obliged the new court to sit "in any council room nigh the Exchequer.")

19. Enumeration of the courts. Coke, in his *Fourth Institute*, enumerates four courts known by the title of *Court of Exchequer Chamber*:

(a) *The Court of Error, created in 1357.*

(i) *Object*: to consider and determine errors from the common law side of the Exchequer (*i.e.* Exchequer of Pleas).

(ii) *Composition*: Lord Chancellor, Treasurer, together with Justices of King's Bench and Common Pleas "and other sage persons." Progress in the court was extremely slow because of the obligatory presence of the Chancellor and Treasurer. In 1588 it was enacted that they had to attend so as to deliver judgment, but the presence of either would suffice in the hearing of the case.

(b) *The Court created in 1585.*

(i) *Object*: to consider and determine errors from King's Bench in cases involving detinue, covenant, debt, account, trespass, action on the case. Appeal could be made from it to Parliament.

(ii) *Composition*: Barons of the Exchequer and Justices of Common Pleas.

(c) *The Court of Equity.*

(i) *Object:* to consider cases arising from the equitable jurisdiction of Exchequer.

(ii) *Composition:* Chancellor of the Exchequer, Barons of the Exchequer, Lord Treasurer.

(d) *The Court of assembly of the judges, which arose informally in the reign of Edward II.*

(i) *Object*: to discuss cases of particular importance or complexity.

(ii) *Composition:* The justices of the superior courts, serjeants-at-law (who participated in discussion, but did not give judgment), and counsel for the parties involved.

(iii) *The Court's decisions:* Resolutions of the Court were not judgments in the strict sense of that term, and no records were kept before the reign of Henry IV. But a resolution was considered as binding on the court from which the case had come. These decisions were regarded as binding precedents in the seventeenth century. "[It is] a known rule that after any point of law has been solemnly settled in Exchequer Chamber by all the judges, we never suffer that it shall be disputed or drawn in question again": per Herbert, C. J., in *Godden* v. *Hales* (1686) 11 S.T.1254.

20. Court of Exchequer Chamber, 1830. This court was set up by statute. Its object was to hear appeals from *all* the common law courts. Appeal lay from the court to the House of Lords. It was composed of the judges of the two common law courts, other than the court from which the appeal was being made. In 1873 its jurisdiction passed to the new Court of Appeal (*see* XI **34**(*d*)).

THE GENERAL EYRE

21. Background. Henry I had established the practice of sending some of the justices of the *Curia Regis* to the various counties to hear and determine criminal and civil pleas and to collect crown revenues. In 1176, at the Council of Northampton, the country was divided into six circuits for revenue and judicial purposes, and three itinerant justices were allocated to each of the circuits. These *Justices of the Eyre* (*eyre* = a hearing) met in the county court and exercised extensive functions of a supervisory, administrative and judicial nature. *The General Eyre* was a very thorough investigation of a county's affairs, which took place in the county towns regularly in the thirteenth and fourteenth centuries. It was looked upon as a local session of the king's court.

22. Organisation. A king's justice, acting under the commission *ad omnia placita*, presided over each Eyre, the members of which were occasionally divided into civil and criminal commissions. Approximately every seven years each county was subjected to a detailed inquiry into its affairs. A writ was sent to the sheriff which ordered a special session of the county court to be summoned to meet the king's justices.

(*a*) Each community in the county was to be represented.

(*b*) An account was to be presented by the sheriff of all the "doings, misdoings and non-doings" since the last Eyre had taken place.

(*c*) Articles of the Eyre (*capitula itineris*)—a series of interrogatories covering all the judicial and administrative affairs of the county—were administered, and answers were checked by the justices from the records.

(*d*) False answers, or answers not accurate in their details, resulted in fines. One of the important objects of the Eyre was to collect money for the crown, and no occasion was lost to impose a fine.

(*e*) Franchises had to be proved and claimed; a fine and forfeiture of the franchise followed failure to satisfy the justices in these matters.

(*f*) Failure of the community to apprehend its criminals resulted in an *amercement, i.e.* an arbitrary fine. (*Amercement* is derived from *estre à merci.*)

(*g*) The Eyre also exercised a type of equitable juris-diction, usually extended to poorer plaintiffs (*see* IX, **5**).

(*h*) County Court proceedings were postponed until the end of the Eyre, and the justices would hear any case which arose in the county during its sittings.

23. The end of the General Eyre. The Eyres were very unpopular, and Henry III was obliged to give a promise that they would be held only once in seven years. As Parliament grew in importance, the local information which had been provided at the Eyres became available in other ways. Addi-tionally, the practice of "compounding the eyre" (*i.e.* a county's representatives paying to the crown an estimate of the Eyre's fines) was increasingly tolerated. By the end of the thirteenth century, the sessions of the Eyre were growing longer, and the visits of the justices, who were overburdened with work, became less predictable. The last Eyre was held in the reign of Richard II.

THE COURTS OF ASSIZE

24. Background. The Norman kings sent representatives of the royal court—the royal justices—to travel the realm in order to hold sittings of the royal courts in various parts of the kingdom. These sittings were known as *assizes*. Note the other meanings attached to this term (*see* II **13**(*d*), *Note*). Under Henry I the main function of these itinerant justices was the hearing of criminal pleas. Under Henry II the realm was divided into circuits for the purpose of visits from the justices. The assizes grew in reputation and in popularity and Henry III was obliged to undertake to send justices of assize on circuit into the counties on two occasions each year.

25. The assize justices. The task of hearing the assizes fell primarily to the judges of the common law courts. Serjeants-at-law (*see* XVI, **6**) and non-lawyers were also given a royal commission which enabled them to exercise jurisdiction at assizes.

26. Magna Carta, 1215.

(*a*) *Magna Carta*, cc. 18, 19, stated that recognitions of *novel disseisin*, *mort d'ancestor*, and *darrein presentment* (*see*

VI, **18–20**), were to be held in the county where the lands in question were situated.

(*b*) The king, or chief justice in his absence, was to send two justices into each county on four occasions in the year, and these justices, together with four knights selected by the county court, were to hold the assizes.

(*c*) Prior to *Magna Carta* writs of assize had to be tried at Westminster, or had to wait for trial in their locality during the infrequent visits of the Justices in Eyre.

27. The Statute of Nisi Prius, 1285. This statute ordered that in a personal action which had originated in Common Pleas or King's Bench, the writ which commanded a sheriff to summon a jury to Westminster was to be designed so that the jury would assemble at Westminster *unless before* (*nisi prius*) *the date mentioned the issue had been dealt with by the justices of assize in the county concerned.*

(*a*) One of the most important reasons for this enactment was the difficulty encountered by juries travelling from distant counties to Westminster.

(*b*) The trial at *nisi prius* was not a trial of the entire action. The pleadings would be heard at Westminster, and the verdict of the jury at the assize was sent by the commissioner to Westminster so that judgment might be entered. At this time a commissioner of assize was not empowered to enter judgment. At a later date the entire trial could be conducted at the assize.

(*c*) By 1328 *nisi prius* had been extended to real actions.

28. The commissions conferring criminal jurisdiction. Following the *Assizes of Clarendon and Northampton*, criminal offences could be tried by judges and others acting by virtue of the royal commissions of *oyer and terminer*, and *general gaol delivery*.

(*a*) *Oyer and terminer* ("to hear and determine"). The commissioners were ordered to hear and determine such charges (usually involving serious crimes, such as treason and felonies) as were presented before them by the grand juries of the county.

(*b*) *General gaol delivery.* The commissioners were ordered to deliver from the county gaols, and to try persons imprisoned therein and awaiting their trial.

PROGRESS TEST 13

1. What was the importance of the *Curia Regis* in the development of our law? (2)
2. Outline the jurisdiction of the *Curia Regis*. (4)
3. Enumerate the courts of common law which sprang from the *Curia Regis*. (7)
4. What was the origin of the Court of Exchequer? (8)
5. Outline the jurisdiction of the Court of Exchequer. (10)
6. What was the origin of the Court of Common Pleas? (11)
7. Explain (a) *quare clausum fregit*, (b) *ac etiam clause*. (12)
8. Outline the jurisdiction of the early King's Bench. (14)
9. Enumerate the courts known by the title of Court of Exchequer Chamber. (19, 20)
10. What was the General Eyre? (21, 22)
11. Explain the importance of *Nisi Prius*, 1285. (27)
12. What was *oyer and terminer*? (28)

CHAPTER XIV

THE KING'S COUNCIL AND THE CONCILIAR COURTS

THE KING'S COUNCIL

1. Background. Following the separation from the *Curia Regis* of the three great Common Law Courts of Exchequer, Common Pleas, and King's Bench (*see* XIII), the king continued to exercise his residual jurisdiction through the *council*. This council, whose functions were to provide advice, to adjudicate, and to administer, consisted of the king's chief officers of state and household, his judges, barons, bishops, and others who acted as counsellors. Given shape by Henry III, and developed by Edward I, the king's standing (or "continual") council exercised very extensive powers.

2. Development of the council in the Middle Ages and under the Tudor dynasty. The council had wide jurisdiction in the Middle Ages, and later became a tool in the hands of the Tudors who were seeking to consolidate absolutist powers.

(*a*) *In the Middle Ages*, the council concerned itself with matters outside the common law, *e.g.* cases involving foreign merchants (where affairs likely to impinge on relations with foreign countries would be within the council's particular knowledge), with actions in which the common law failed to provide adequate remedies (in which cases it granted a kind of equitable relief), and with those matters which touched on the king's own interests. The council also gave advice to the courts on matters of importance.

(*i*) *Exercise of the jurisdiction.* A *subpoena*, derived from the writ of *quibusdam de certis causis*, commenced civil proceedings by ordering the attendance of defendant, who was not informed of the nature of the charge. The trial was not in accordance with common law procedures, hence evidence could be obtained from the parties by detailed interrogation. (Note that *witnesses* only, and *not the litigants*, could give

174

evidence at common law.) In a criminal trial the council used the procedure of the *crimina information*, which dispensed with the need for a jury. After 1352 the council lost the power to impose capital punishment, nor could it adjudicate on matters concerning freehold land. But it could imprison, fine, and order severe mutilation, of a kind which caused great popular hatred. Its jurisdiction extended to Wales and Ireland.

(*ii*) *Opposition to the jurisdiction.* Complaints against the council's activities were prolonged and vigorous. Thus, in 1331, it was declared that "no man should be attached by any accusation . . . against the form of the Great Charter." In 1352, it was enacted that "none shall be taken by petition or suggestion made to our lord the King or to his Council, unless . . . by indictment or presentment of good and lawful people. . . ." Further enactments followed petitions by the Commons, who looked upon the council as a willing ally of the crown in its exercise of the prerogative, which, all too often, involved the exercise of unrestrained power.

(*b*) *Under the Tudors* the main political task was the creation of a strong central government. The council was well constituted to aid in this task. In this period there developed the offshoots of the council—the great *conciliar courts*, and the *Privy Council* created by Henry VIII.

(*i*) *The Privy Council* was a small body of the king's trusted advisers, concerned mainly with state matters. The Ordinances of the Council of 1526 distinguished its executive from its judicial aspects. Henceforth the executive branch was to attend the king constantly, the judicial branch was to remain at Westminster. In 1540 the Privy Council was given its own clerk and minute book, and the separation of Privy Council and Star Chamber (*i.e.* that part of the Council which sat at Westminster) may be said to have been effective from that date.

(*ii*) *The Star Chamber*, an important conciliar court, is considered at **6–13** below.

3. Further development of the council. With the intensification of conflict between the crown and Commons, the council became the centre of controversy.

(*a*) *Under the Stuarts.* The council, a creature of the royal prerogative power, was disliked by Parliament and by the common lawyers. Common lawyers saw in some of the activities of the council, and in the workings of the conciliar courts, a subversion of some of the great common law doctrines which they considered fundamental to the administration of justice.

(b) *The Act of 1641.* In 1641, the Long Parliament passed an Act "for the regulating of the Privy Council and for taking away the court commonly called the Star Chamber." It also abolished some of the local courts of the council (*see* **17–18** below), stating that "the Council Table hath of late times assumed to itself a power to intermeddle in civil courts and matters only of private interest between party and party, and have adventured to determine of the estates and liberties of the subject, contrary to the law of the land and the rights and privileges of the subject." It was enacted that "neither his Majesty nor his Privy Council have or ought to have any jurisdiction, power or authority by English bill, petition, libel or any other arbitrary way whatsoever to examine or draw into question, determine or dispose of the lands, tenements, hereditaments, goods or chattels of any of the subjects of this kingdom, but that the same ought to be tried and determined in the ordinary courts of justice and by the ordinary course of the law."

(c) *After 1641.* The jurisdiction of the council was manifested after 1641 only in the appellate work of the Privy Council, which remained the appellate court for the Colonies. After 1660 the Privy Council's jurisdiction was vested in a small committee.

(i) *As the British Empire grew*, so appeals to the Privy Council increased, and its work became important once more.

(ii) *The Privy Council Act*, 1832, transferred to the Privy Council the appellate jurisdiction of the Court of Admiralty (*see* XV, **8–12**) and the Court of Delegates (*see* XII, **29**).

(iii) *The Privy Council Act*, 1833, amended by the *Judicial Committee Act*, 1844, established the Judicial Committee of the Privy Council, which today hears, *e.g.* appeals from ecclesiastical courts, admiralty, medical tribunals, some courts outside the United Kingdom. (The Privy Council today is concerned merely with executive acts of a formal nature. Its members include the Lord President, cabinet and ex-cabinet ministers, holders and former holders of high judicial and church office.)

THE CONCILIAR COURTS

4. Origins. During the Tudor period much of the jurisdiction exercised by the council passed, as a deliberate policy, to specialised judicial bodies such as the Star Chamber. The conciliar courts thus created exercised a jurisdiction which stemmed essentially from their connections with the king and his council.

5. The principal conciliar courts. These were:

(*a*) The Court of Star Chamber (*see* **6–13** below).
(*b*) The Court of Chancery (*see* IX).
(*c*) The Court of Requests (*see* **14–16** below).
(*d*) The Local Councils (*see* **17–19** below).

THE COURT OF STAR CHAMBER

6. Its name. The origin of the court's name is not clear. Two suggestions as to this origin are:

(*a*) The court sat in a room, the ceiling of which was decorated with gilded stars (*camera stellata*: *chambre d'estoiles*).
(*b*) The contracts of Jewish merchants, which were known as *starra*, were kept in a chamber in which the king's council conducted its work.

NOTE: There is a reference to a meeting of the king's council in 1453 "*in the sterred chambre.*"

7. The Act of 1487. At its creation, the court exercised the criminal jurisdiction of the king in his council.

(*a*) *In 1487 an Act "to punish divers misdemeanours" was passed.* It stated: "The King . . . remembereth how by unlawful maintenances, giving of liveries signs and tokens, and retainders by indenture promises oaths writing or otherwise, embraceries of his subjects . . . by great riots and unlawful assemblies, the policy and good rule of his realm is almost subdued. . . ." The Act empowered the Chancellor, Treasurer, Keeper of the Seal (or two of them), together with a bishop and temporal lord of the council and the two chief justices of King's Bench and Common Pleas, to call before them "the said misdoers" for examination and punishment.

(Henry VIII added to the members the Lord President of the Council.)

(b) *The Act did* not *create Star Chamber, which, in fact, met before 1487.* The words *"pro camera stellata"* appended to the Act as a marginal title were added after 1487. (It was believed for a long period that the Act of 1487 was the statutory origin of Star Chamber, so that when the Chamber was abolished that Act was repealed.)

(c) The Act may have merely recognised the existence of the Chamber.

8. Developments. The origin of the court is not in any Act, and its jurisdiction derived and developed from the authority of the king's council to receive petitions for the redress of complaints. Its separation from the council may be dated from 1540 (*see* 2(b)(i) above).

(a) The court had been formed in order to deal with riots and disturbances and "to bridle such stout noblemen or gentlemen which would offer wrong by force to any manner of men and cannot be content to demand or defend the right by order of law": Sir Thomas Smith, in *De Republica Anglorum* (1565).

(b) To this criminal jurisdiction, which proved very effective in maintaining order in a political situation which promised chaos, civil jurisdiction was added.

(c) The court's civil jurisdiction declined, however, as action on the case grew in popularity.

(d) As Star Chamber took upon itself the responsibility for the punishment of offences such as conspiracy and criminal libel, so it added to the development of the common law.

9. Jurisdiction.

(a) *Criminal.* This jurisdiction was nowhere defined either by statute or ordinance. In general, the Chamber sought: to keep order in the realm; to punish those who sought to create riot and disturbance; "to repress the insolence of the noblemen and gentlemen of the north part of England, who being far from the King and the seat of justice made almost as it were an ordinary war among themselves and made free their law" (Sir Thomas Smith).

Matters such as attempts to commit crimes, with which

the Chamber dealt, were not considered as criminal offences at common law. Breaches of proclamations, perjury and forgery, were also punished by the Chamber. Perjury had hitherto been merely an ecclesiastical offence, and only certain types of forgery, such as forgery of the coin of the realm, had been punished. Star Chamber did not usually try felonies which involved capital punishment.

(b) *Civil.* Many types of dispute were brought before Star Chamber, often to save time and expense. In such cases the procedure of the Chamber resembled that of the Court of Chancery.

(c) *Other types of case.* Star Chamber also heard some cases concerning ecclesiastical matters and the law merchant (*e.g.* detention of ships, disputes between corporations).

10. Procedure. The Chamber's procedure in criminal cases was of an entirely different nature from that of the common law. In essence the procedure was of an *inquisitorial* kind.

(a) The Attorney-General filed an information against defendant, or plaintiff addressed a bill to the king praying for a remedy.

(b) The court would issue process (*i.e.* summon defendant by *subpoena*), or would non-suit the plaintiff.

(c) Defendant's answer had to be signed by counsel.

(d) Defendant was subjected to interrogatories on oath.

(e) Witnesses gave evidence on affidavit. Defendant was not allowed to examine them.

(f) Judgment was given by the members of the court in ascending order of importance. (Sir Thomas Smith writes of the defendant, who, "being called to answer . . . shall be so charged with such gravity, with such reason and remonstrance, and of those chief personages of England, one after another handling him on that sort, that, what courage soever he hath, his heart will fall to the ground.")

(g) The Chamber's decision was recorded in its books and in a document given to the successful party.

NOTE: It is not clear whether the Star Chamber resorted to torture during the trial. Compare, for example, the views of Holdsworth, Vol. V, and Elton, Chapter 6 (*see* Bibliography).

11. Penalties. The usual penalty was a heavy fine. The court could not impose the death penalty, nor could it confiscate property. A frequent punishment, which was responsible for much public hostility, was whipping and mutilation.

The following examples of judgments in some of the celebrated cases heard by the Chamber will suffice as illustrations:

(a) 1630. Alexander Leighton (father of a future Scottish Archbishop) was fined £10,000, degraded, whipped, put in the pillory, had one ear cut off, his nose slit, his cheek branded, and was imprisoned for life. His offence: the writing of *An Appeal to Parliament*.

(b) 1637. William Prynne, barrister, fined £5,000, degraded, ears cut off, pilloried and imprisoned. His offence: the writing of a book alleged to have insulted the queen.

(c) 1638. John Lilburne, the future heroic figure of the Parliamentary army, whipped, pilloried, imprisoned for three years. His offence: refusal to swear to an interrogatory during the hearing of a charge alleging distribution of anticlerical pamphlets.

(d) 1638. Sir Thomas Wiseman, fined £17,000, degraded, pilloried, ears cut off, imprisoned during the king's pleasure. His offence: slandering the court.

12. Star Chamber as a "court of criminal equity." The general jurisdiction of the Chamber was analogous to that of Chancery, in that it arose in part from a failure of existing courts to do justice. Other resemblances were:

(a) Proceedings commenced with a bill, not with a writ.

(b) There was no jury.

(c) Execution was made not *in rem*, but *in personam*.

(d) Evidence was given on oath.

(e) Written pleadings were used.

(f) The court exercised a discretion in giving judgment.

13. Decline and disappearance of Star Chamber. The Chamber had been, in some respects, popular and had provided a relatively swift form of hearing. Coke, in his *Fourth Institute*, said of it: "It is the most honourable court (our Parliament excepted) that is in the Christian world, both in respect of the judges of the court and of their honourable proceedings according to their just jurisdiction and the ancient and just orders of the court. . . . This court . . . doth keep all England in quiet."

(a) Growing unpopularity resulted from its harsh and

arbitrary sentences and from its association with the king's unpopular policies in the 1630's. Its intolerance inflamed Puritan sentiment, and its very existence was seen by the common lawyers as a threat.

(b) In 1641 the Court of Star Chamber was abolished (see 3(b) above).

THE COURT OF REQUESTS

14. Origin and development. The Court of Requests was a court of equity which grew out of the jurisdiction of the king's council. It was concerned, in particular, with petitions from the poor, affairs of persons of the king's household, and with matters not sufficiently important for the Court of Chancery.

(a) In 1390, an Order in Council transferred the hearing of petitions which came from poor people to a committee of the council, over which the Lord Privy Seal presided.

(b) The court may have been modelled on the French *Chambre des Requêtes*.

(c) In 1485 a bill for its abolition was dropped by Parliament.

(d) It was confirmed by statute in 1487.

(e) Wolsey set it up in the White Hall as a separate court.

(f) In 1590 the Court of Common Pleas granted a prohibition against it.

(g) In *Stepney* v. *Flood* (1598)—*see* IX, 15(e)—it was declared that the Court of Requests "had no power of judicature."

(h) The court continued in existence until the summer of 1642, when its sittings were suspended. After the Restoration it was not formally abolished, but Charles II did not revive it, possibly because of its close association with the council.

15. Jurisdiction. The court exercised the civil jurisdiction of the king in council, but in time, perhaps because of its swift and cheap procedure and the reputation of its judges, it began to poach upon the preserves of the common law, thus arousing the antagonism of the common lawyers. A body which had been in its origins "the court of poor men's causes" began to concern itself with mercantile, matrimonial and admiralty causes, with tenants' rights, and with quasi-criminal matters.

16. Composition of the court. In 1483 a second clerk of the council was appointed to be responsible for the petitions and supplications of poor men. The Committee of the Council, headed by the Lord Privy Seal, was controlled, after 1550, by two Ordinary Masters of Requests, and, in 1562, by additional Masters Extraordinary. (The ordinary Masters were paid £100; the extraordinary Masters received nothing, but were recompensed with fees, etc.)

(*a*) One part of the court often accompanied the king on his travels, the other part remained at the White Hall.

(*b*) The Masters of Requests appointed after the Restoration had no judicial duties.

NOTE: The Court of Requests must not be confused with the eighteenth-century *Courts of Requests or of Conscience*, set up by statute in various towns to hear small causes (*i.e.* not exceeding 40*s.*). These courts employed a form of trial without jury, and were abolished by the *County Courts Act*, 1846.

THE LOCAL COUNCILS

17. Council of the North. This Council may have had its origins in a small committee set up by the Duke of Gloucester to administer the north of England on behalf of Edward IV. It was established, without an Act of Parliament, in an attempt to deal with an area in a remote part of the country subjected to great lawlessness. It had fifteen members, including peers, lawyers and churchmen.

(*a*) Its methods resembled those of the Star Chamber.

(*b*) It had criminal and civil jurisdiction, exercised concurrently with the King's Council and Star Chamber, derived from commissions of the peace and oyer and terminer (*see* XIII, 28). Its common law jurisdiction enabled it to hear matters of felony and treason.

(*c*) The regulations for the Council of the North, 1484, state: "the said Council [shall] have authority and power to order and direct all riots, forcible entries, variances, debates and other misbehaviours against our laws and peace committed and done in the same parts."

(*d*) The Council developed an equitable jurisdiction; the Court of Chancery sent cases arising in the north to York for the Council's decision. This equitable jurisdiction was pronounced illegal by the common law judges in the reign of Elizabeth I.

(e) It covered the counties of York, Westmorland, Durham, Cumberland, and Northumberland.

(f) It was abolished in 1641 (*see* **3**(b) above).

18. The Council of the Marches. (The Marches were those parts of south and east Wales conquered by the Lords Marcher—originally vassals of the Conqueror—in 1067–1280, and then taken from Welsh rule, but not made part of the realm until the mid-sixteenth century.) Wales was a troubled and violent area for a long period. The Council arose, like the Council of the North, from Edward IV's administrative council. It was reconstructed by Wolsey in 1525.

(a) It acted as the chief court of Wales. The court at Ludlow (held there from the time of Henry VIII to 1689) controlled the administration of justice in Wales, Monmouth, Shropshire, Gloucester, Hereford, and, until 1569, Cheshire.

(b) Its jurisdiction was civil and criminal. It had received commissions of the peace, *oyer and terminer*, and could hear cases of felony and treason.

(c) It often employed torture as a regular part of its procedure.

(d) It resumed its work after the Restoration, but was finally abolished in the reign of William and Mary.

(e) Its jurisdiction often conflicted with that of the four Courts of Great Sessions, set up in Wales by Henry VIII in 1543. These courts administered law and equity in civil cases, and had jurisdiction in criminal cases. They were abolished in 1830.

19. Council of the West. This short-lived Council (April 1539–June 1540) had jurisdiction over Cornwall, Devon, Somerset and Dorset, and was to hold four sessions every year at Tavistock, Wells, Dorchester and Exeter. Its jurisdiction extended to riots, sedition and "non-conformity," and it afforded remedies to very poor litigants. It disappeared with the fall of its originator, Thomas Cromwell.

NOTE: *The Courts of the Counties Palatine.* The Counties Palatine (*palatinus* = belonging to the palace) were counties on whose owners were bestowed sovereign rights, including the right to pardon wrongdoers and to appoint judges. "The owner [of a County Palatine] hath in that county *jura regalia* as fully as the King had in his palace, from whence all justice ... flowed": Coke, in his *Fourth Institute*. Each of these counties (Chester, Durham, Lancaster) had its own court. The King's writ did not extend there, and writs were in the name of the county. Henry VIII asserted the royal right to pardon in the palatinates. Ordinary royal writs issued from Westminster to the Chancellor of the County Palatinate who issued a mandate to the sheriff.

(*i*) *Durham.* A charter was granted by William the Conqueror to the Bishop of Durham. The jurisdiction was transferred to the crown in 1836. In 1873 the Court of Pleas at Durham was abolished under the *Judicature Acts* and its jurisdiction transferred to the High Court. The Durham Chancery is in existence today.

(*ii*) *Lancaster.* A charter was granted by Edward III to John of Gaunt in 1377. The county was annexed permanently to the crown in 1461. The Court of Common Pleas, Lancaster, was abolished in 1873. The Chancery Court of Lancaster exists today.

(*iii*) *Chester.* Granted by William to his nephew, Hugh Lupus, the county reverted to the crown in the reign of Henry III. It became a principality conferred on the king's eldest son in the time of Richard II. In 1830 the offices of Chief and Second Justices of Chester were abolished.

PROGRESS TEST 14

1. What was the importance of the council to the Tudors?   **(2)**
2. What was the effect of the Act of 1641?   **(3)**
3. Enumerate the principal conciliar courts.   **(5)**
4. Outline the criminal jurisdiction of the Court of Star Chamber.   **(9)**
5. Outline the procedure used in Star Chamber.   **(10)**
6. Why was Star Chamber described as a "court of criminal equity"?   **(12)**
7. Outline the jurisdiction of the Court of Requests.   **(15)**
8. Give an account of the work of (*a*) the Council of the North, (*b*) the Council of the Marches.   **(17, 18)**

CHAPTER XV

COURTS MERCHANT AND MARITIME, THE HIGH COURT OF PARLIAMENT AND MISCELLANEOUS COURTS

THE LAW MERCHANT

1. Its nature. Law merchant "is neither more nor less than the usages of merchants and traders . . . ratified by the decisions of courts of law which, upon such usages being proved before them, have adopted them as settled law": per Cockburn, C. J., in *Goodwin* v. *Robarts* (1876) L.R.10 Ex.337. The development of trade, internally and externally, involved contact with legal principles not always embodied in the practices of the common law. Trading customs, rules concerning merchants' transactions, which had the force of unwritten customary law, became recognised in time by our common law. The law merchant comprised:

(*a*) *Regulations*, often local in nature and origin, concerning matters such as the holding of markets and fairs.

(*b*) *Trading customs* recognised universally by merchants, *e.g.* the practice whereby a document executed by X could create an obligation which could be enforced against X by any person in possession of it. (The common law did not recognise at this time the negotiable instrument which was payable to bearer.)

(*c*) *The law maritime*, which purported to regulate relations between shippers, masters and their mariners.

(*i*) The sea laws had a common origin in the *Lex Rhodia* (derived from the maritime laws of Rhodes).

(*ii*) The compilation of the customs centred on Barcelona was known as the *Consulato del Mare* (*c.* 1340) and was looked upon as maritime law pertaining to the Mediterranean.

(*iii*) *The Visby sea laws* (*c.* 1240) were those observed in the North Sea and the Baltic.

(*iv*) *The Laws of Oléron* (*c.* 1190)—*Rôles, Jugements et Lois d'Oléron*—were a collection of ancient customs and rules recognised by the maritime court of Oléron, an island off La Rochelle. Oléron was, for a time, a possession of the English kings, and these laws, which were adopted by Richard I, were promulgated there by Eleanor, Queen of England and Duchess of Aquitaine.

NOTE: There are very few remaining original treatises on law merchant. Those which exist include the fourteenth-century *Red Book of Bristol*, the *Black Book of the Admiralty*, and the *Oak Book of Southampton*.

2. Law merchant and equity. There were similarities between the two systems:

(*a*) Equity, in its early development, drew some of its principles from so-called natural justice. Law merchant drew upon the practices of international merchants, *i.e.* a type of *jus gentium* (law of nations).

(*b*) Procedure in courts merchant and in chancery was of a summary nature.

(*c*) Both systems were complementary to that of the common law.

(*d*) Both systems took into account the doctrine of notice, and protected a *bona fide* purchaser.

(*e*) Both systems paid relatively little attention to the sanctity of the sealed agreement, or to consideration (*see* XXII). Intention, rather than form, was of decisive importance.

(*f*) Both systems recognised the assignability of *choses in action*, *e.g.* debts.

(*g*) Parties to the action, who were denied the opportunity of giving evidence at common law, could be heard as competent witnesses in chancery and in the courts merchant.

3. The courts merchant. The two important courts merchant were the "*Piepowder" Courts of the Fairs and Boroughs*, and the *Courts of the Staple*. They were local courts and endured until the nineteenth century, when the economic conditions in which they had thrived had changed radically.

4. The Piepowder courts. The name originated in *pieds poudrés*, referring probably to the dusty feet of the merchant litigants.

(*a*) *Markets of the fairs and boroughs*. The market was a

prominent feature of medieval commerce, much of which was limited to the places and days of the markets. Fairs provided occasions for the holding of markets. The right to hold a fair or a market, and the right to the incidental tolls and taxes, was often based on a franchise, or royal grant, made to a borough corporation or a lord of the manor. The franchise carried the right to hold a court and to take any profits made therein.

(b) *Jurisdiction*. The jurisdiction extended to actions concerning breach of contract, petty offences, and to almost all matters arising in (and often around) the area in which the fair was held. It did not extend to actions concerning land and pleas of the crown.

(c) *Composition of the court*. The mayor of the borough, with his bailiffs, presided over the court. In the case of a franchise, the president would be the owner's steward. Merchants acted as assessors.

(d) *Procedure*. The piepowder courts, in that they administered the law merchant, and not the common law, were not hampered by the slow and technical rules of the common law courts. Procedure was swift, the laws of evidence were relaxed so that interested parties were accepted as competent witnesses. The courts were in session for the duration of the fair, and judgments were given without delay.

(e) *Decline of the jurisdiction*. The general decline of these courts set in as communications improved, so that local trading and local markets began to lose their significance. Particular causes of the decline were:

(i) A decision of the Court of Common Pleas in 1467, to the effect that a writ of error could be brought from the piepowder courts to the common law courts. This diminished the control exerted by merchants over their courts.

(ii) A statute of Edward IV in 1477, confining the jurisdiction of the court to matters arising only within the place and duration of the fair or market. This immediately limited the scope and significance of the courts' work.

NOTE: The Bristol Tolzey Court (*see* 25 below) is a remaining survival of the piepowder court.

5. The courts of the staple. Staples were towns appointed by Edward I and Edward II to be exclusive markets for certain staple products of the realm, *e.g.* wool, tin, lead, leather.

(*a*) *The Statute of the Staple*, 1353, created, within the staple towns, courts of the staple, which were intended to settle disputes among merchants (particularly those from abroad) engaged in commercial transactions.

(*b*) The judges in these courts were the mayor (who was obliged to know the law merchant) and two constables, or justices. Debts, breaches of contract, and trespass could be settled in these courts.

(*c*) Where a jury was used, and both parties were foreign merchants, it would consist entirely of foreigners. In such a case two foreign merchants were allowed to act as assessors. Where only one of the parties was a foreigner, half of the jury consisted of foreigners.

(*d*) There was a right of appeal to the chancellor.

(*e*) The jurisdiction of the court declined as the staple system became of decreasing importance in the commercial affairs of the realm.

THE LAW MERCHANT, CHANCERY AND THE COMMON LAW

6. Law merchant and chancery. *See* 2 above. The jurisdiction of the local courts was limited territorially, but this limitation did not apply to chancery. Hence merchants sent some petitions to chancery, but the delay inherent in procedure produced inconvenience for merchants, for whom a swift settlement of disputes was necessary.

7. Law merchant and the common law. In the sixteenth century the extended use of the action on the case allowed the common law courts to hear such actions based on merchants' customs. In time many of these customs were absorbed into the common law.

(*a*) In the case of contracts made abroad, the common law courts employed a fiction that the contract had been made at some place within its jurisdiction. This was done by stating that the contract had been made, say, in Hamburg, "to wit in the parish of St. Mary-le-Bow."

(*b*) By the end of the seventeenth century some customs became judicially noticed, and in future cases they were not required to be proved.

(c) The work of Chief Justices Holt and Mansfield in the eighteenth century was of great importance in the assimilation of the law merchant and the common law. They used juries of merchants and established the rule that immemorial usage need not be proved in the case of a mercantile custom, provided that the custom is not in opposition to any statute or accepted custom or rule.

NOTE: The contribution of the law merchant to English law may be seen in the existing law of agency, negotiable instruments, insurance and partnership.

THE HIGH COURT OF ADMIRALTY

8. The office of admiral. The office of Lord High Admiral appeared in the reign of Edward I. William de Leyburne, in 1297, was known as *Admiral de la Mer du Roy d'Angleterre*. In 1306 Edward appointed three admirals with jurisdiction over the southern, eastern, and western coasts. In the fourteenth century the office of admiral was made permanent. The jurisdiction of the admiral extended at first only to his fleet, but by the mid-fourteenth century it had extended considerably.

9. Origins of the High Court of Admiralty. Following the naval victory at Sluys in June, 1340, control of the Channel, with responsibility for the maintenance of order in that area, passed to Edward III. The admirals and their deputies held courts which sat at the main ports. Gradually these courts made encroachments upon the jurisdiction of the courts merchant. In 1360 an Admiral of all the Fleets took office, with the duties of acting as Commander of the Navy, Minister of Marine, and President of the Court of Admiralty. Early in the fifteenth century the courts were absorbed by one High Court.

10. Admiralty jurisdiction. Originally the jurisdiction of Admiralty Courts extended to certain crimes (particularly piracy) and to matters of prize. But the court soon began to exercise a civil jurisdiction. In its early stages of development the court used a procedure resembling that of the common law, but at a later stage continental practices, derived in part from Roman law, were introduced.

(a) *Criminal jurisdiction.* This had its origins in the *Jurisdiction of the Admiral Act*, 1391, which gave the court power to try piracy and other offences committed at sea or on board ship below the bridges of the great rivers.

(*i*) In 1536 an Act "for the punishment of pirates and robbers of the sea" declared that "treasons, felonies, robberies, murders and confederacies" committed within the admiral's jurisdiction were henceforth to be tried by commissioners who were to be appointed by the crown, and who were to proceed "as if such offences had been committed upon the land." These commissioners acted as common law judges.

(*ii*) The jurisdiction of the commissioners passed to the Central Criminal Court in 1834.

(*b*) *Civil jurisdiction.* This may have originated in those petitions to the council which were then referred to the admiral. By the reign of Richard II, the general opposition to the judicial functions of the council had resulted in complaints and petitions against the Court of Admiralty, alleging, in particular, encroachment on the courts of the boroughs. As a result, two restraining Acts were passed.

(*i*) In 1389 it was enacted that "the admirals and their deputies shall not meddle from henceforth of anything done within the realm, but only of a thing done upon the sea, as it hath been used in the time of the noble prince King Edward."

(*ii*) In 1391 it was enacted that "of all manner of contracts, pleas and quarrels, and other things rising within the bodies of the counties as well as by land as by water, and also of wreck of the sea, the admiral's court shall have no manner of cognizance, power, nor jurisdiction," and that these matters "shall be tried, determined, discussed and remedied by the laws of the land, and not before nor by the admiral, nor his lieutenant in any wise."

NOTE: These statutes were repealed in 1879.

11. Developments in the fifteenth and sixteenth centuries. At the beginning of the fifteenth century it was enacted that where an action had been commenced wrongfully in the Court of Admiralty, double damages might be awarded—an indication of Admiralty's continued practice of hearing merchants' cases. The court was far from inactive.

(*a*) From *c.* 1520 the court sat at Orton Key, near London Bridge, later moving to Doctors' Commons (*see* XVI, **14**(*b*)(*iii*)).

(*b*) Doctors of civil law practised not only in the church

courts, but in the Court of Admiralty. At one time, the offices of Dean of the Arches (*see* XII, **28**(*c*)(*i*)) and judge of the Court of Admiralty were held by one and the same person.

(*c*) The Court of Delegates (*see* XII, **29**) acted as a court of appeal in Admiralty cases. This jurisdiction was transferred to the Privy Council in 1832.

(*d*) By the use of the fiction *super altum mare* (on the high sea) the court continued to exercise a relatively wide jurisdiction. This fiction, first used in the time of Henry VI, involved an allegation that a transaction, or an offence, had taken place "at sea," whereas it had, in fact, taken place in England.

(*e*) Henry VIII and Elizabeth extended the jurisdiction of the court, but it was during Elizabeth's reign that the common lawyers commenced their attack upon its work.

(*f*) In 1540 it was enacted that the court should deal with matters affecting damage to cargo.

(*g*) In 1575 the court was given jurisdiction in the case of contracts arising abroad.

12. Developments in the seventeenth and eighteenth centuries. This era opened with mounting attacks by the common lawyers upon the court. Coke's opposition was unyielding.

(*a*) Following a debate in the Council in 1632, the court was allowed a limited jurisdiction in cases involving contracts and charterparties, but this was granted in the face of hostility from the common law judges.

(*b*) During the Commonwealth a committee under Cromwell was responsible for naval affairs.

(*c*) After the Restoration the king held the office of Lord High Admiral.

(*d*) By 1660 the jurisdiction of the court was more restricted than ever before and was virtually limited to a concurrent jurisdiction with the courts of common law in cases of contract and civil wrongs arising on the high seas.

(*e*) In the eighteenth century the court lost its jurisdiction in matters concerning insurance, charterparties, and contracts made abroad.

(*f*) The prize jurisdiction of the court grew in importance in the eighteenth century, and under Lord Stowell the court enjoyed a period of revival. Acts of 1840 and 1861 gave wide jurisdiction to the court in cases concerning shipping.

NOTE (i) In the reign of George IV, the powers of the Lord High Admiral vested in the Lords Commissioners of the Admiralty.

(ii) *The County Courts Admiralty Jurisdiction Acts*, 1868–69, transferred minor cases from the Admiralty to the county courts.

(iii) Under the *Judicature Act*, 1873, the court was merged into the High Court of Justice.

THE HIGH COURT OF PARLIAMENT

13. Origins of the jurisdiction. (The jurisdiction of Parliament today is exercised by the House of Lords.) After the establishment of a Parliament by Edward I, the barons kept some of the powers which they had exercised when the national assembly consisted of them alone. Until the fifteenth century they had continued to meet as the *Magnum Concilium* and the powers exercised there, which included judicial powers, were transmitted eventually to the House of Lords.

(a) In 1399, the Commons accepted that they possessed no right to interfere in any judicial matters, except those affecting legislation and taxation.

(b) In 1485 it was decided that jurisdiction in error (*i.e.* appeal from the King's Bench) belonged not to Parliament, but to the House of Lords. Such jurisdiction was considered as being derived from the powers of *the King and his Council in Parliament*, and the Commons could not claim to have been a part of the Council.

14. The jurisdiction of the House of Lords. The Lords exercised civil and criminal jurisdiction at first instance. Appellate jurisdiction was exercised in the Middle Ages by the Lords sitting as a Court of Review.

15. Civil jurisdiction. In the fourteenth and fifteenth centuries, jurisdiction at first instance in civil cases was exercised by the council, rather than by Parliament. In the time of the Stuarts, the Lords were exercising this jurisdiction in increasing measure.

(a) *Skinner* v. *E. India Co.* (1666) 6 S.T.710. The crown referred to the Lords a petition by Skinner against the E. India Co., as a result of which the company was ordered to pay him £5000. The company complained to the Commons who resolved that the Lords had acted illegally. The Lords then resolved that the Commons' proceedings in this case were "a breach of the privilege of the House of Peers." Conferences between the Commons and Lords failed to resolve the dispute, and the Commons proceeded to vote Skinner into custody and to resolve that anyone who executed the order of the Lords would be "deemed a betrayer of the rights and liberties of the Commons." The Lords then ordered the imprisonment of the deputy chairman of the E. India Co. Eventually the king ordered the erasing from the journals of Parliament of the proceedings.

(*b*) From that date the Lords have not exercised any original jurisdiction in civil cases.

16. Criminal jurisdiction. *Magna Carta*, 1215, *c*.39 (*see* II, **15**) had declared that a man was entitled to the judgment of his peers—"*judicium parium suorum.*" The word "peer" (which meant "one of the same rank") came to be interpreted as referring to the barons, since they alone were able to maintain and enforce the right to be tried by their peers. A later rule, in 1441, limited such a trial to charges of felony and treason.

(*a*) Where Parliament was in session the trial took place before the House of Lords.

(*b*) When Parliament was not in session the trial was held in the Court of the Lord High Steward. Decision was by a majority of at least twelve. The Lord High Steward sat as a judge and did not vote. The trial of Lord Delamere for treason in 1686 was the last case heard by this court, which became obsolete in 1948.

(*c*) Two trials for felony have taken place in the House of Lords during this century: Earl Russell, tried and convicted of bigamy in 1901; Lord de Clifford tried and acquitted of manslaughter in 1935. Trial by peers in cases of treason and felony was abolished by the *Criminal Justice Act*, 1948, *s*. 30.

(*d*) The Commons, from 1376, had the power to impeach at the Bar of the House of Lords. The Commons prosecuted, the Lords passed sentence. Celebrated cases of impeachment involved Lord Bacon, the Duke of Buckingham, Archbishop Laud, Warren Hastings. The last case to be tried involved Lord Melville, impeached in 1806 on a charge of malversation in the Admiralty. The power to impeach remains, but the growth of the doctrine of cabinet responsibility has rendered it obsolete.

(e) The Lords retain jurisdiction in matters involving their privileges through the Committee of Privileges.

17. Appellate jurisdiction. The Lords now exercise an appellate jurisdiction in civil and criminal cases.

(a) *Civil.* Jurisdiction to review dates from the Middle Ages.

(i) Jurisdiction in error lay from King's Bench and the exchequer.

(ii) Jurisdiction in error in chancery was settled in the seventeenth century. In 1621 the Lords had declined to review a decision of the chancellor. In *Shirley* v. *Fagg* (1675) 6 S.T.1122, the Commons had voted that there could be no appeal to the Lords from courts of equity. The subsequent dispute between the Houses (exacerbated by the fact that Sir John Fagg was a member of the Commons) was allowed to lapse, and the Lords' appellate jurisdiction in matters of equity continued.

(iii) Appeals from the common law side of chancery were established by the seventeenth century.

(iv) In 1707 the Lords became a court of appeal from the Court of Session at Edinburgh.

(v) In 1800 the Lords regained a right to hear appeals from courts in Ireland, a right which they had given up in 1782.

(b) *Criminal.* This appellate jurisdiction was conferred only in 1907 by the *Criminal Appeal Act.*

18. Exercise of the jurisdiction. In the nineteenth century it was settled as a constitutional convention that lay peers do not participate in the hearing of appeals.

(a) The conviction and appeal of the Irish Nationalist leader O'Connell in 1844 settled this issue. Tory peers indicated their intention to vote on appeal, so as to support O'Connell's conviction. The President of the Council, Lord Wharncliffe, urged them not to do so, warning that, if they cast a vote, "the authority of this House as a court of justice would be greatly impaired." His advice was followed.

(b) The abolition of the Lords' appellate jurisdiction was

enacted in the *Judicature Act*, 1873 (*see* XI, **34**(*d*)). The Act was to become effective in 1875, but in the interim period Disraeli, who had succeeded Gladstone, decided that the appellate functions of the Lords should be retained.

(*c*) The present position is that for an appeal to be heard, there must be present at least three of the following: the Lords of Appeal in Ordinary, the Lord Chancellor, and those peers who have held high judicial office (as defined by the *Appellate Jurisdiction Act*, 1876).

MISCELLANEOUS COURTS

19. General. The courts mentioned at **20–26** below are minor courts of some historical interest. Some of these courts continue to exercise a jurisdiction at the present time.

20. Courts of the Stannaries. Stannaries were the districts in Cornwall and Devon in which tin was mined.

(*a*) By ancient charter, dating from Edmund, Earl of Cornwall, the tin miners were exempted from any jurisdiction other than that of the stannary courts, except in cases affecting life, limb, or land.

(*b*) Stannary courts were set up in the two counties, and met every three weeks.

(*c*) The Vice-Warden of the Stannaries presided over the stewards who formed the courts.

(*d*) Appeal lay to the Lord Warden of the Stannaries and to the Privy Council.

(*e*) In 1836 the jurisdiction of the stewards was ended.

(*f*) In 1855 the Stannaries Courts of Devon and Cornwall were consolidated.

(*g*) In 1873, under the *Judicature Act*, the jurisdiction of the Lord Warden was transferred to the Court of Appeal.

(*h*) In 1896 the *Stannaries Courts Abolition Act* transferred the jurisdiction to the county courts of Cornwall.

21. Court of Augmentations. The court was created by statute in 1536, and was known as the *Court of the Augmentations of the Revenues of the King's Crown*.

(*a*) It was to administer the rents, farms, tenements, revenues and profits of the dissolved monasteries.

(*b*) The court consisted of a chancellor, treasurer and other officials who were empowered to make grants under the court seal.

(*c*) Henry VIII dissolved the court, but later re-constituted it.

(*d*) Mary, in 1554, united the court with the Exchequer.

22. The Court of Wards and Liveries. The court was established by Henry VIII, and received statutory powers and its seal in 1540.

(*a*) It was concerned with wards who held *in capite* of the crown.

(*b*) Its jurisdiction extended only to land held by military tenure.

(*c*) It was empowered to manage the property of wards, to act as their guardians, and to levy fines in the case of a ward's marriage without the consent of the king.

(*d*) It was abolished under the *Abolition of Tenures Act*, 1660.

23. The Court of Chivalry. This court, also known as the *Curia Militaris*, Court of Honour, and Court of the Constable and Earl Marshal, was probably founded at the Norman Conquest.

(*a*) Its jurisdiction was controlled by a statute of the reign of Richard II.

(*b*) It enforced some aspects of military discipline and settled disputes between military men (*e.g.* concerning ransoms) by a form of summary jurisdiction.

(*c*) It also heard appeals of treason, *e.g.* the appeal brought in 1398 by the Duke of Hereford against the Duke of Norfolk.

(*d*) The earl marshal and constable proceeded "according to the customs and usages of the court . . . *secundum legem armorum*" (Coke: *Fourth Institute*).

(*e*) The court sat at Arundel Castle, or in the Painted Chamber at Westminster.

(*f*) The office of constable was abolished in 1521, after the execution of Buckingham.

(*g*) The earl marshal's right to hold the court and to adjudicate in cases involving precedence and heraldic arms was confirmed by Charles II. The right to bear arms could originate only in a grant from the king, made by his heralds. Such a right could be confirmed by the Court of Chivalry if use since time immemorial were proved.

(*h*) There was an appeal to the crown in disputes involving armorial bearings.

(*i*) Penalties were usually monetary fines, or imprisonment for contempt. The court could also order a party to ask his opponent's forgiveness.

(*j*) The court's issuing of proclamations of martial law was pronounced illegal by the *Bill of Rights*, 1689.

(*k*) In 1737, the court tried what was afterwards considered to be its last case, but the jurisdiction was revived, surprisingly, in *Manchester Corporation* v. *Manchester Palace of Varieties* (1955) 2 W.L.R. 440, where the dispute concerned the display by a theatre of the city's coat-of-arms.

24. The Salford Hundred Court. This court, which is in existence today, was formed by an amalgamation in 1868 of the Manchester Court of Record and the Salford Hundred Court (one of the most ancient of the hundred courts—*see* XII, **7**).

25. The Tolzey Court of Bristol. This was originally a court of the bailiffs of the Bristol Hundred, being amalgamated later with the court of the Lord Steward. Its separate existence was revived by Richard II, and its sessions today are held under a charter granted in 1710 by Queen Anne. (Note that in Bristol may also be found the only existing court of *piepowder*— *see* **4** above.)

26. The Liverpool Court of Passage. This ancient court, created by charters from Charles I and William I to deal with imports and exports passing through the port of Liverpool was held originally by the mayor and bailiffs.

(*a*) In 1834 the *Court of Passage Act* enacted that the court should not sit without an assessor.

(*b*) In 1893 the judge of the court was given the powers of a High Court judge sitting in chambers, under the *Liverpool Court of Passage Act*.

PROGRESS TEST 15

1. What was the general nature of the law merchant? **(1)**

2. What were (*a*) *Consulato del Mare*, (*b*) *Laws of Oléron*? **(1)**

3. Explain the composition and jurisdiction of the piepowder courts. **(4)**

4. What were the courts of the staple? **(5)**

5. What were the origins of the jurisdiction of the Courts of Admiralty? **(9, 10)**

6. Explain the fiction *super altum mare*. **(11)**

7. How did the jurisdiction of the Lords originate? **(13, 14)**

8. What was the significance of (*a*) *Skinner* v. *E. India Co.* (1666), (*b*) *Shirley* v. *Fagg* (1675)? **(15, 17)**

9. Outline the development of the Courts of the Stannaries. **(20)**

10. What were (*a*) the Court of Wards and Liveries, (*b*) the Court of Chivalry? **(22, 23)**

CHAPTER XVI

LAWYERS, JUDGES AND JURIES

THE LAWYERS

1. General. The legal profession, in the strict sense of that term, did not exist until the medieval period. The growth of a profession whose members were allowed—very slowly at first—to represent litigants in the courts, was the result, in large measure of:

(*a*) The growth in the number of courts, the increasing number of litigants, and the general expansion of the legal system;

(*b*) The increasing technicalities of the law, and of court procedure;

(*c*) The increasingly specialised nature of the system of pleadings.

2. General development of the legal profession. The origins of the modern profession, with its division of barristers and solicitors, may be discerned in the fifteenth and sixteenth centuries. For our purpose we shall consider the development in two stages:

(*a*) The period up to and including the fifteenth century, in which *counters*, *narrators*, and *serjeants-at-law* appear;

(*b*) The period following the fifteenth century, during which the modern profession took shape.

THE PERIOD TO THE END OF THE FIFTEENTH CENTURY

3. Background. Proceedings in the early courts were generally informal, and the litigants presented their own cases.

(*a*) With the increased use of the writ and the growth of the writ system (*see* **VI**), procedure became more formal.

(*b*) By the time of Henry II litigants were allowed to

appear personally or by a substitute who might be a relative or friend, known as a *responsalis* (answerer).

4. The attorney. In Bracton's day the *attorney* had appeared.

(*a*) He was appointed in court by the litigant and his pleadings were considered as binding on that litigant.

(*b*) Attorneys were eventually considered as officers of the court in which they practised, and several were attached to the Court of Common Pleas and the King's Bench.

(*c*) In 1292 Edward I ordered education in the law to be given to attorneys' "apprentices." After that date enrolment as an attorney was confined to those who had received the appropriate education.

(*d*) In 1402 it was enacted by statute that all who wished to be enrolled as attorneys were to be examined by a body of judges.

5. The narrators and conteurs. As actions became more complicated, the conduct of a case tended to fall into two parts: the preparatory stages, and the oral presentation of the case to the court.

(*a*) The preparatory work was performed by the attorney; the oral presentation became a specialist matter and was left to the *narrator* or *counter* (or *conteur*).

(*b*) The professional narrator existed during the reign of Edward I.

(*c*) From the profession of narrator was to emerge the barrister.

6. The serjeants-at-law. From the narrators and *conteurs* there sprang the great Order of Serjeants-at-Law in the fourteenth century, *The Statute of Westminster*, 1275, refers to *serjeant-counters* (i.e. *conteurs*); the term *serjeants-at-law* (*servientes ad legem*) appears about 1310.

(*a*) By the end of the fourteenth century the serjeants had a monopoly of audience in the Court of Common Pleas, and judges were being chosen exclusively from the Order. Thus, 58 of 86 serjeants between 1400–1500 became judges.

(*b*) The serjeant was appointed by patent from the king. His appointment was a great ceremonial event, marked by a lavish entertainment and feast which was sometimes attended by the king. (So expensive was this event that some refused the royal patent, and in 1412 a £1000 fine was imposed for such a refusal.)

(c) The serjeants ranked as knights and wore a distinctive dress, characterised by the white lawn coif. (It was symbolic of their status that they were not obliged to doff the coif even in the royal presence.)

(d) The serjeants, including those who had become judges, lived at Serjeants' Inn. Stands against the pillars in St. Paul's were used as meeting places for them and their clients.

7. The apprentices and barristers. The term *apprentice* had a very specialised meaning when applied to the early legal profession. It denoted either those narrators who were not serjeants-at-law, or, more rarely, the student members of the Inns of Court (*see* **8** below). The first sense of the term was implied in a statute of 1379 which stated that "every serjeant and great apprentice of the law" was to be taxed on the level applicable to a baron; other apprentices who followed the law were to pay one-half of that rate; apprentices "of less estate" were to pay one-sixth.

(a) In the Inns of Court lived the *barristers*, known as *utter* (or *outer*) *barristers*. Their name was derived from the bar or form in the outermost part of the hall in which sat the senior students who argued in the *moots* (*i.e.* the mock courts).

(b) The barristers had audience in the King's Bench (in which they achieved a monopoly after 1400), the exchequer, and, occasionally, in Common Pleas where they sometimes assisted the serjeants.

(c) The students were known as *inner barristers*.

(d) Some attorneys were members of the Inns (but *see* **10** below).

(e) The barristers were governed through their Inns by committees of senior members, known as *benchers*.

8. The Inns of Court. The four great Inns carried on the traditions of the law schools which existed in London in the twelfth and thirteenth centuries.

(a) *Gray's Inn.* The site of the inn was let by the Dean

of St. Paul's to Reginald de Grey, chief justice of Chester, in the thirteenth century. The Inn began to function as a legal institution *c.* 1320–30.

(*b*) *Lincoln's Inn.* The records of Lincoln's Inn commence in 1422, the inn having been sited originally in Shoe Lane. There is a legend that the inn's name is derived from the Earl of Lincoln, who, in Edward II's reign, brought professors of the law to settle and teach there.

(*c*) *The Inner and Middle Temples.* Roger Blom, *nuncius* of the Knights Templars (suppressed in 1312) let some of his houses, standing at the north of the Temple to professors of the common law in 1326. The two inns were granted the premises in perpetuity by a grant of James I in 1609.

9. The Inns of Chancery. With a growth in the number of students at the Inns of Court, a number of smaller Inns, known as *Inns of Chancery*, were founded. They were attached to the Inns of Court—Staple Inn and Barnard's Inn were affiliated to Gray's Inn, Clifford's Inn and Clement's Inn to the Inner Temple, and New Inn to the Middle Temple.

THE LATER ERA

10. The attorneys. Following the sixteenth century, the attorneys began to separate in function from the barristers. Up to this period attorneys and barristers had conducted cases together. Henceforth the attorney acted as a middleman between client and barrister, and a rule was formulated whereby a barrister could not work directly for a client. The attorneys concentrated on conveyancing and the drafting of pleadings. In the mid-sixteenth century they were excluded from membership of the inns and, in time, amalgamated with the solicitors (*see* **11** below). Here was the beginning of the split in the legal profession which exists today.

11. The solicitors. The lawyers mentioned so far practised in the courts of common law. In the sixteenth century there had grown up the Courts of Chancery, Star Chamber and Admiralty, and in those courts there were no attorneys, since their functions were undertaken by the staff of the courts. In the fifteenth and later centuries the solicitor acted as the litigant's agent, charged with the task of commencing proceedings.

(a) In 1729 it was enacted that admission to the profession of attorney or solicitor required an apprenticeship under articles of five years.

(b) In 1739 attorneys, solicitors and proctors (see **14** below) combined to form the *Society of Gentlemen Practitioners in the Courts of Law and Equity.*

(c) By the mid-seventeenth century solicitors who had been entered on the Roll of the Court of Chancery were considered to be performing functions equivalent to those of the attorneys.

(d) In 1831 the *Society of Gentlemen Practitioners* and other associations formed the *Law Society* which today controls the education and admission of solicitors.

12. The Serjeants. The prominent position occupied by the serjeants did not endure. In 1758 members of Serjeants' Inn in Fleet Street joined the Serjeants' Inn in Chancery Lane. In 1877 the Order was dissolved, and Serjeants' Inn was sold.

13. The barristers. The role of the barristers grew in importance as the King's Bench and exchequer came to enjoy an enlarged jurisdiction. In 1852 the *Council of Legal Education* was created to control examinations for the Bar. In 1894 the *General Council for the Bar* was formed.

14. Proctors and advocates. In the Church courts (see XII, 23-31) practitioners were known as *proctors* and *advocates.* They also practised in the Court of Admiralty (see XV, 8-12).

(a) *Proctors.* They performed duties similar to those performed by solicitors.

(i) They were empowered to institute and withdraw proceedings by a *proxy,* which was signed by the party to the action, attested and deposited in the registry of the court.

(ii) Following the abolition of the jurisdiction of the Church courts in matrimonial and testamentary matters, the proctors were awarded compensation (under the *Court of Probate Act,* 1857, and the *Matrimonial Causes Act,* 1857, s. 69) and were allowed to practise not only in the probate and divorce courts, but in courts of common law and equity.

(*iii*) Under the *Judicature Act*, 1873, *s*. 87, proctors were given the title of *solicitors of the Supreme Court*.

NOTE: The Treasury Solicitor who today represents the Crown in the Probate, Admiralty and Divorce Division is known as the *Queen's Proctor*.

(*b*) *Advocates*. They performed the functions of serjeants-at-law and barristers, their title being derived from canon and civil law.

(*i*) Henry VIII had forbidden the study of canon law in 1538, and had founded professorships of civil law at Oxford and Cambridge. A degree of Doctor of Civil Law from one of these universities became essential for admission (by the Archbishop of Canterbury) to practise in the church and admiralty courts.

(*ii*) The doctors of civil law who practised in these courts had formed themselves, in 1511, into an association of Doctors of Law.

(*iii*) After 1567 their headquarters (known as *Doctors' Commons*) was on the south side of St. Paul's churchyard.

(*iv*) Some of the doctors acted as judges.

(*v*) In 1768 they obtained a charter which incorporated them as *The College of Doctors of Law exercent in the Ecclesiastical and Admiralty Courts*. The college consisted of a president and those doctors who had been elected as fellows. 34 Proctors (*see* (*a*) above) were attached to the college.

(*vi*) The upsurge of civil law, which, in the sixteenth century, had seemed to promise much was not maintained, and the work of the advocates declined. The *Matrimonial Causes Act* and the *Court of Probate Act* marked the end of the jurisdiction of the ecclesiastical courts in which the doctors had practised in matrimonial and testamentary cases.

(*vii*) Under the *Court of Probate Act*, 1857, the college surrendered its charter and was dissolved.

LAW OFFICERS OF THE CROWN

15. The king's attorneys and solicitors. In the thirteenth century the *king's legal representatives* began to make their appearance in the courts. It was their task to represent the royal interest, for example by taking over from private appellors the prosecution in a criminal case. At a later date a serjeant would be engaged in a civil case to plead the king's cause, where that was involved.

(a) In 1247 Lawrence del Brok was retained as the king's permanent attorney in King's Bench.

(b) The king's attorney wrote and kept memoranda of the cases involving the interests of the crown (enrolled by him on the *Controlment Rolls*) and was known as the *Clerk of the Crown and Attorney of King's Bench,* or *The Coroner of England.*

(c) In 1315 Edward II retained four serjeants to act for him. Their functions extended to the Courts of Common Pleas, Exchequer, Chancery and Parliament (to which they were summoned together with other judges). By custom these officials were obliged to give their services free of charge to litigants in extreme poverty.

16. Attorney-general and solicitor-general. By the end of the fifteenth century, the royal attorneys and solicitors had been replaced by a single solicitor-general, and by a single attorney-general (William Husee, in 1472). From 1530 the solicitor-general succeeded the attorney-general.

(a) They were appointed at first not from the ranks of the barristers, but from the solicitors and attorneys.

(b) The king's serjeant, who pleaded the king's cause in the courts, was appointed from the senior serjeants.

(c) The Tudors appointed as attorney-general and solicitor-general barristers who were not serjeants (probably because of the serjeants' common law, and, hence, anti-royal prerogative, background).

(d) Their functions included advising the council and prosecuting on behalf of the state.

(e) In the sixteenth century and first half of the seventeenth century, the attorney-general attended the House of Lords, where he gave assistance in the House's work. The solicitor-general sat as a member of the House of Commons.

(f) The chief law officers were often promoted to the chancellorship or to the position of chief justice. (Although the custom was that judges had to be members of the Order of Serjeants, non-serjeants were promoted to the position of judge and, simultaneously, were created members of that Order.)

17. King's counsel. Towards the end of the sixteenth century the Crown's law officers were assisted in their work by senior barristers (usually of a political persuasion acceptable to the crown). They were created *king's counsel learned in the law*, and were obliged to give their services to the crown when asked to do so. In Elizabeth's reign they ranked in precedence next to the serjeants. By the eighteenth century they had ceased to be consulted by the crown. Their duties to the crown had become merely nominal. The title of *king's counsel* was reserved, from that time, as a title of distinction conferred on prominent barristers.

THE JUDGES

18. Early stages of development. In the communal and feudal courts of the Middle Ages there were no professional judges. The body of suitors (*see* XII, **5**) gave its judgments based on the local customary law. In the king's courts there were, at first, no judges.

(*a*) As procedure became complicated, and as the royal courts increased their area of jurisdiction, professional judges became essential for the proper working of the courts.

(*b*) Henry II appointed *Commissioners in Eyre* to act as judges, and by the end of his reign a group of justices in the king's court was in existence.

(*c*) In the twelfth century the royal justices were headed by a *justiciar*, a high official who acted in the absence of the king as his viceroy.

(*d*) In the communal and feudal courts the suitors became mere jurors who found on the facts, the court's judgment being given by the lord's steward or the sheriff's bailiff.

19. Further developments. In the twelfth century the royal judges had been found from among clerks in the royal household and the chancery. Most were churchmen who lacked practice and learning in the law.

(*a*) The salaries of the early judges and their successors were very small, and fees from litigants made up their income. As a result the courts competed with one another and judges were exposed to bribery and its consequences.

(*b*) *Magna Carta*, 1215, *c.* 45, stated that the king would appoint as justices, constables, sheriffs and bailiffs, only such "as know the law and mean duly to observe it." This clause was omitted from the Charter of 1216.

(c) During the reign of Edward I almost half of the body of judges had been drawn from the serjeants-at-law who, for many years to come, were to provide the sole recruits to the bench.

(d) In 1289 there was a great scandal involving charges of corruption against the bench, as a result of which the Chief Justice of the King's Bench was heavily fined, and the Chief Justice of Common Pleas left the country.

(e) From the time of Edward II the proportion of ecclesiastics among the judges began to decline.

20. The fourteenth century. In 1328 the *Statute of Northampton* enacted that no royal command issued under the Seal should disturb the course of the common law, and that the judges should ignore any such command. For the next decade the judges sought to enforce the terms of this enactment.

(a) Between 1340–50 the judges declared on several occasions that statutes were to be interpreted rigidly, that the discretion of the bench was very restricted, and that any change in the law must come not from their endeavours, but from Parliament.

(b) In 1340 it was enacted that where the judges had failed to arrive at a decision because of the difficulty of a case, a commission of non-lawyers was to decide that case.

(c) From about the middle of the fourteenth century the pattern became clear: Parliament was to legislate, and the judges were to interpret that legislation.

21. "Durante beneplacito nostro"—the judges under the Stuarts. Judges held office only during the king's pleasure (*durante beneplacito nostro* = during our good pleasure) and, during the reigns of James I and Charles I, the judges, perhaps in the knowledge that their tenure of office depended on the whims of a royal despot, tended to favour the royal prerogative. In principle, a judge who held office under such a patent could demand that the king "show cause" by writ of *scire facias*, but, in practice, only one judge, Walter, C. B., did so, in 1629. (The king refused the writ and Walter was suspended from office.) Coke soon came into conflict with James I on these matters.

(a) *The Case of Commendams* (1616). An action was brought by two persons against Bishop Neile of Lincoln, contesting the legality of a royal grant to him of two benefices to be held *in commendam* (*i.e.* together with his bishopric). During the proceedings the king learned that plaintiffs' counsel had challenged the royal right to bestow a *commendam*. James was angered and he ordered Coke and the other judges hearing the case not to hear any action in which the question of his prerogative was raised. The judges answered that they felt bound by their oaths to disregard an order of this nature. They were summoned before the king, and all, except Coke, complied with the king's wishes. Coke was censured and later suspended from office.

(b) As a result the common law judges became even more dependent than before upon the "good pleasure" of the king.

22. "Quamdiu se bene gesserint." Following the defeat of the royal cause in the civil war, the judges held office under a patent which made their tenure *dependent on their good behaviour*.

(a) In 1668 Charles II, and, later, James II, reverted to the practice of James I in appointing judges *durante beneplacito nostro*.

(b) In 1679 it was enacted under the *Habeas Corpus Act, s.* 10, that a judge was not to be liable for any judicial act or omission, except for a refusal to issue a writ of *habeas corpus* during vacation.

(c) William (1689–1702) appointed his judges *quamdiu se bene gesserint* but declined to make this provision the basis of a statute.

(d) The *Act of Settlement*, 1701, declared that: "Judges' commissions shall be made *quamdiu se bene gesserint* and their salaries ascertained and established, but upon the address of both Houses of Parliament it may be lawful to remove them." (In fact no English judge has been removed under the procedure of the Act.)

(e) From that time the independence of the judges was assured. (Their salaries are now a permanent charge on the Consolidated Fund.)

JUSTICES OF THE PEACE

23. Origins of the office. The decline of the old communal courts, the decline of the Eyre, the growth in criminal law and jurisdiction, and the increased burden of civil cases thrust upon the justices of Assizes, meant that some other type of judicial officer was needed to deal with the vast increase in crime. The office of justice of the peace was created with this need in mind. Sir Thomas Smith wrote, in *De Republica Anglorum*, of the justices: "There was never in any commonwealth devised a more dulce and gentle nor a more certain way to rule the people whereby they are always kept as it were in a bridle of good order and sooner looked into that they should not offend than punished when they have offended."

(*a*) In 1195 a royal decree had been issued by Archbishop Hubert Walter, Chief Justiciar of Richard I, commanding certain knights to receive oaths for the preservation of the peace from all men above the age of fifteen.

(*b*) In 1252, 1253, and 1264, *custodes pacis* were appointed, and in 1285 they were ordered to enforce the *Statute* of *Winchester* and to receive presentments of breaches of the peace.

(*c*) In 1327 conservators of the peace—soon to be known as *justices of the peace*—were appointed in each county. Their task was to keep records of allegations of crime, to arrest suspects and to imprison them until the royal justices arrived to try them.

(*d*) In 1328 they were empowered to punish offenders.

24. Developments. The powers of the justices were increased considerably in an era in which lawlessness was rife and catastrophes such as the Black Death made the enforcement of law a very urgent matter.

(*a*) In 1345 the justices were empowered to hear and determine allegations of trespasses against the peace and felonies.

(*b*) In 1349 the Black Death had the effect of drastically reducing the number of labourers. As a result labourers were in a position to demand increased wages. *The Ordinance of Labourers*, 1349, and other statutes, were passed so as to fix rates of wages (". . . servants and labourers will not and for long time have not been willing to serve and labour without outrageous and excessive hire . . . so that husbandmen and tenants cannot pay their rents or hardly live on their lands": *Statute of Richard II*, 1388, *c*. 4.) The justices of the peace were given the important task of ensuring that the statutes were observed.

(*c*) In 1362 a statute was enacted which required the justices of a county to meet four times a year—the origin of Quarter Sessions.

(*d*) The power of the justices to convict summarily was increased considerably in the fifteenth century.

(*e*) In 1439 it was enacted that the requirement for appointment as a justice of the peace was possession of lands or tenements to a value of £20 p.a. (This was raised in 1732 to £100 p.a., the statute declaring that "the constituting of persons of mean estate to be justices of the peace may be highly prejudicial to the public welfare." The property qualification was ended by the *Justices of the Peace Act*, 1906.)

25. The Tudor "maids of all work." Under the Tudors the power and number of the justices of the peace expanded considerably. They were made responsible for the enforcement of many regulations concerning local government. From an average of ten justices to a county, the number rose to between forty and fifty.

(*a*) In 1494 the justices were empowered to hear complaints against the sheriff and his officers concerning alleged extortions practised in the county courts. This element of control over the sheriffs indicates the growing power of the justices.

(*b*) In 1554 and 1555 the justices were empowered to conduct the preliminary examination of indictable crimes and to send a written record to the court in which the accused man was to be tried.

(*c*) *The Statute of Artificers*, 1563, "touching divers orders for artificers, labourers, servants of husbandry, and apprentices," was administered by the justices, who were to hold two inquiries each year into the operation and effect of the statute.

(*d*) The commission of the peace, which was issued every

year and which, together with statutes, formed the basis of the justices' powers, was revised in 1590. The new commission:

(*i*) Gave the justices authority to hold regular sessions;

(*ii*) Ordered the sheriff to provide men for the empanelling of juries;

(*iii*) Designated one of the justices as keeper of the records (*custos rotulorum*);

(*iv*) Authorised the justices to enforce statutes concerning the keeping of the peace, and to demand sureties for good behaviour;

(*v*) Authorised the justices to enquire into felonies and offences, subject to the presence of one of a quorum (*i.e.* a group of justices of experience "in whom was especial trust reposed");

(*vi*) Allowed justices to try cases on indictment.

(*vii*) Forbade the justices to give judgment in very difficult cases unless there was present a justice of the bench or assize.

NOTE: The control of the *Poor Law* in 1597 was a very heavy burden placed upon the justices of the peace. The justices were required to appoint overseers, but an amending Act of 1601 stated: "If any persons shall find themselves grieved by any act done by the overseers, then it shall be lawful for the justices of the peace, at their general quarter sessions, to take such order therein as shall be thought convenient."

26. The heyday of the justices.

From the mid-seventeenth century to about 1825 the justices had a great influence in the judicial affairs of the community. Their administrative functions were also very extensive. But by the end of the eighteenth century the pattern of local government was beginning to change. In 1834 the Poor Law powers of the justices were transferred to the Poor Law Commissioners, and statutes took away from the justices almost all of their administrative powers.

NOTE: (*i*) *In* 1848 *four bills concerning the work of justices of the peace were introduced* by the Attorney-General. The bills were: to facilitate the performance of the justices with respect to persons charged with indictable offences, to facilitate the performance of the duties of justices with respect to summary convictions and orders, to protect the justices for acts done in the execution of their office, and to regulate the holding of special

H

and petty sessions. The first three bills became law in 1848, the fourth in 1849.

(*ii*) *Payment of the justices.* During the Middle Ages the justices were paid 4*s.* per day at Quarter Sessions. In time, because of the fall in the value of money, the practice grew up of not accepting payment, and the position of justice became, in effect, honorary. In the seventeenth and eighteenth centuries the unauthorised practice of accepting fees emerged, and an author of that period wrote of the "trading justices" who profited by this. In 1855 payment was abolished.

(*iii*) *Control of justices of the peace* was by means of the prerogative writs issued from King's Bench.

THE CORONERS

27. Origins. In 1194 Richard I appointed three knights and one clerk as *custodes placitorum coronae* (keepers of the pleas of the crown). (Note that pleas of the crown were prosecutions in criminal matters, brought in the name of the crown which, according to Blackstone's expression, was supposed to be "the person injured by every infraction of the public rights of the community." *See* XVII, **13**.)

(*a*) Their appointment may have been intended as a check on the growing powers of the sheriffs.

(*b*) They were (until 1888) usually elected by a body of freeholders in the county court.

(*c*) Originally four were elected in each county, and one in each *commote* (*i.e.* judicial district) in Wales.

28. Development. The work of the coroners increased swiftly, but received a check in *Magna Carta*, 1215, *c.* 24, which stated that no sheriff, constable, coroner or bailiff was to hold pleas of the crown.

(*a*) *The Statute of Westminster*, 1275, declared that none but "lawful and discreet knights" should fill the office of coroner. The qualification was later fixed at lands to the value of £20 p.a., *i.e.* the land holding which qualified a tenant for knighthood.

(*b*) *Their duties were numerous* and included the following:

(*i*) The keeping of rolls of persons suspected of crimes,

which were presented to the king's justices during the Eyre (*see* XIII, **21**) so as to check the accuracy of the presentments.

(*ii*) The holding of inquests into wrecks, treasure trove and royal fish (*i.e.* whales and sturgeon caught on or near the coast).

(*iii*) The conducting of outlawry proceedings (*see* XVII, **24**) in the county courts.

(*iv*) The hearing of appeals of felony and of approvers (*see Note* below)—such matters being enrolled and presented at the Eyre. (After 1554 coroners were obliged to make written records of their hearings and inquiries.)

(*v*) The hearing of abjurations of the realm (*see* XVII, **26**).

(*vi*) The hearing of matters involving deodands (*see Note* below).

(*c*) In 1887 the *Coroners Act*, *s*. 44 (which re-enacted *Magna Carta*, *c*. 24) took away a number of the above powers (which had become obsolete) from the coroners. Coroners are now appointed by county and borough councils.

NOTE: (*i*) An interesting power of the medieval coroner was his right to receive a writ which would ordinarily have been addressed to the sheriff, when that sheriff had an interest in the matter which was the subject of the writ.

(*ii*) *Approvers* were informers and self-confessed criminals who, in the hope of being pardoned, were allowed an appeal of felony and trial by battle. In the thirteenth century they had to win five battles and were hanged if a battle was lost.

(*iii*) *Deodands* (*deo* = to God, *dandum* = given). In the early Middle Ages the practice grew of surrendering to the king or lord of the manor any animate or inanimate thing which had brought about a death (on the principle *omnia quae movent ad mortem sunt deodanda*). So, an axe used to slay a person, or a vessel filled with milk in which a child was drowned, would be surrendered. The deodand was sold by the lord or king and the money received was used as a "gift to God," being employed, for example, in the saying of prayers for the soul of the deceased. After the Reformation the money was usually given to the relations of the dead person or to a charity. In 1841 a railway carriage was surrendered to a lord of the manor after a fatal railway accident at Sonning. In 1846 deodands were abolished.

JURIES

29. Origins. The jury has its origin in the calling together of a number of persons by a royal official and the charging of those persons with the duty of answering specific questions. The English jury system may have its origins in one or more of the following prototypes:

(a) *The Anglo-Saxon gathering of the doomsmen.* It was the task of the doomsmen to give judgment and to declare the customary law.

(b) *The Law of Wantage.* In c. 997 Ethelred ordered, in a law issued at Wantage, that twelve senior thegns were to bring before the local courts information concerning those suspected of crimes.

(c) *The Frankish jury.* In 829 the Emperor Louis, son of Charlemagne, ordered that the rights of the crown were to be ascertained by hearing unbiased statements made on oath by local witnesses in the local courts.

(d) *The Norman Inquisition.* The Normans inherited many features of the Frankish system of government, and their dukes and kings developed the method of ascertaining rights by inquisition, *i.e.* by obtaining sworn information from those with particular knowledge of the matter in question.

30. The inquisitorial system in England. The Norman type of inquisition was introduced into England following the Conquest. An outstanding example of its use was in the compilation of Domesday Book (*see* II, **9**) based on sworn information gathered locally.

(a) Henry II extended trial by inquisition so that it became available not only to the government for administrative purposes, but to private individuals.

(i) In 1164 the *Constitutions of Clarendon, c.* 9, enabled the procedure of the inquest to be used to settle the nature of tenure in certain cases.

(ii) In 1180 trial by inquest was allowed as an alternative to battle in the case of a writ of right.

(b) It is to Henry II and his introduction of the various assizes (*see* VI) that we owe the development of the early jury system.

THE DEVELOPMENT OF THE CRIMINAL JURY

31. Background. From early times the crown had concerned itself with the punishment of criminal acts, not only from motives of ensuring strong government, but because the trial of criminal acts, which often resulted in monetary fines, was a profitable matter. Hence the kings were concerned that local offenders should be brought to justice.

(a) *The Law of Wantage* (see **29** (b) above) gave to the twelve thegns the functions of a public prosecutor, *i.e.* they had to accuse on oath those suspected of crime. The establishment of guilt was left to procedure by ordeal or compurgation. Hence the thegns acted as a type of grand jury.

(b) Under the *Assizes of Clarendon*, 1166, and *Northampton*, 1176, it was declared that an inquiry was to be held in every county and in every hundred by twelve lawful men (*i.e. legales homines*—men who had not been convicted of any offence) as to the crimes in their neighbourhood. They were to present these crimes in the county courts. They did not decide the guilt or innocence of the accused. The persons presented were usually submitted to the water ordeal (see XVII, **18**). These juries of presentment were the prototype of the Grand Jury.

(c) At a later date, in the fourteenth century, the sheriff was ordered to bring together twenty-four men from the county to answer for its affairs.

(d) The later procedure of the grand jury was based on its duties as an accusing jury. After hearing the case against the accused the jury retired and found either a "true bill" of indictment, or "ignored" the bill. In the former case the accused (after 1215) was sent for trial by a petty jury (see **32**(a) below). In the latter case the jury threw out the bill by writing on it *"ignoramus"*. (A famous instance of a jury's *"ignoramus"* was in 1861 at the trial of Shaftesbury for treason.)

NOTE: The presenting of a bill of indictment passed to the justices of the peace in 1554. The grand jury was abolished except for a few cases, by the *Administration of Justice Act*, 1933, and finally abolished by the *Criminal Justice Act*, 1948.

32. The effect of abolition of the ordeal. The Church had for long opposed the trial by ordeal, and in 1215 Pope Innocent

III, in the Fourth Lateran Council, prohibited the clergy's participation in the rites associated with the ordeal. In effect, therefore, the ordeal was abolished. The problem then arose as to the provision of a substitute system; it was solved by the use of the *petty jury*.

(*a*) There had been introduced before 1215 a process of occasionally allowing a second jury (known as a *petty jury*) to consider the findings of the accusing jury and to pronounce on the guilt or innocence of the accused. In the time of Henry III this became an accepted procedure.

(*b*) An accused person could refuse trial by petty jury, but in such a case he could be imprisoned under the provisions of the *Statute of Westminster*, I, 1275, *c.* 12, which ordered that such persons were to be "remanded to a hard and strong prison (*prison forte et dure*)."

(*i*) The phrase *prison forte et dure* was misconstrued so as to read *peine forte et dure*, and by the 16th century it was used to permit the practice of forcing an accused to accept jury trial by torturing him. The torture took the form of piling heavy weights on his body until he accepted trial, or died.

(*ii*) This practice was abolished in 1772 and was replaced by a plea of guilty. The last fatal torture of this nature took place in 1658. In 1827 it was enacted that a plea of not guilty was to be entered when an accused person remained mute.

(*c*) In 1352 it was enacted that a member of the grand jury could not be a member of the petty jury in the trial of a misdemeanour or a felony.

THE DEVELOPMENT OF THE CIVIL JURY

33. Background and development. The procedure of the sworn inquest was used by William and Henry I mainly for administrative matters. Cases of its use in civil actions occur during the reign of Henry I when *probi et legales homines* were summoned to testify to matters occurring within their neighbourhood, of which they were presumed to have particular knowledge.

(*a*) Under Henry II the introduction of the Petty and Grand Assizes (*see* VI, **16–20**) involved the procedure of the inquest for the deciding of civil disputes.

(*i*) *The Petty Assizes* (*see* **VI, 17–20**) required the trying of a dispute by twelve knights of the neighbourhood.

(*ii*) *The Grand Assize* (*see* **VI, 16**) allowed the choice between trial by battle and decision by twelve knights.

(*b*) Under Henry III the assizes were held at least twice in the year, and the model of the assize procedure was used for the basis of future juries in civil actions.

THE DEVELOPMENT OF THE JURY FROM RECOGNITORS TO JUDGES OF FACT

34. The jury as recognitors. In the time of Henry II, and for a considerable time after that, the jury were considered as *recognitors, i.e.* men who were to decide matters of fact and law *on the basis of their own personal knowledge.*

(*a*) The task of the *recognitor* was to arrive at a decision on the main matter in dispute. Members of the jury relied on their own knowledge and were not concerned with matters outside that knowledge.

(*b*) Where they did not, or could not, know whether the alleged facts were true or not they were dismissed and ordered to return within a few weeks in possession of the facts. In some cases they were joined, or replaced, by *recognitors* who knew the facts, *i.e.* who were *witnesses.*

(*c*) Henry III allowed special witnesses to join the jury on certain occasions.

35. The jury acting on evidence.

(*a*) Under Edward III witnesses gave testimony, but did not participate in the process of arriving at a verdict. The jury was beginning here to act on evidence in addition to its own knowledge.

(*b*) Under Henry IV all evidence had to be given at the bar of the court.

(*c*) From 1562 a witness could be compelled to appear and to testify in court.

36. Later developments.

(*a*) In 1702 it was decided by Queen's Bench that a jury had to inform the court where it gave a verdict on its own knowledge, so that the jurymen could testify as witnesses if necessary.

(b) In 1816 it was held that a fresh trial could be ordered where a judge directed a jury to find on the basis of its personal knowledge.

NOTE: The requirement that a civil jury should come from the county involved was abolished in 1705.

THE "OBSTINATE JURY"

37. Control of the jury by attaint. A jury which gave a verdict considered to be wrong was, in early times, held to be guilty of perjury. In such a case the jury members were liable to a writ of attaint.

(a) The writ applied only to civil juries.

(b) A jury of 24 persons was summoned, with the task of trying the first jury for perjury, the punishment for which could be imprisonment and confiscation of goods.

(c) By 1361 the writ was made available in any action (except a criminal matter) tried by jury.

(d) The writ ceased to apply to the Grand Assize and fell into general disuse. In 1583 Sir Thomas Smith spoke of attaints, saying that "they be very seldom put in use."

(e) The writ was abolished in 1825.

38. Star Chamber. *See* XIV, 6–13. Star Chamber imprisoned and fined juries which returned verdicts considered as "perverse," particularly in political cases. Thus, in 1544, eight members of the London jury which acquitted Sir Nicholas Throckmorton of high treason were fined heavily and imprisoned.

39. The seventeenth century. Interference with "obstinate" verdicts of juries was particularly marked in the seventeenth century.

(a) In December, 1667, Lord Chief Justice Keeling was brought to the bar of the Commons (". . . a chair was set for him, but he stood . . .") to answer complaints that he had fined and imprisoned juries and had spoken of *Magna Carta* in indecent terms. The House resolved that such fines and imprisonments were illegal.

(b) In King's Bench, judgment was given in 1670 in the

historic case of *Edward Bushel*. Bushel was the foreman of a jury which had acquitted the Quakers, Penn and Mead, who had been charged with preaching to an assembly, contrary to the *Conventicle Act*, 1664. The jury members were each fined 40 marks by the Recorder of London, but Bushel refused to pay, was imprisoned and sued by writ of *habeas corpus*. Chief Justice Vaughan ordered that the imprisonment was to end. His judgment brought to an end the punishment of jurors for a verdict against the judge's direction. (This would not apply, of course, to a corrupt verdict.)

(c) Per Vaughan, C. J., "To what end is the jury to be returned out of the vicinage whence the cause of the action ariseth? . . . To what end must they have such a certain freehold, and be *probi et legales homines*, and not of affinity with the parties concerned? . . . To what end must they undergo the heavy punishment of a villainous judgment, if, after all this they implicitly must give a verdict by the dictates and authority of another man, when sworn to do it according to the best of their own knowledge?"

40. Further development in the case of libel.
In 1764 Lord Mansfield ruled that the court alone (and not the jury) should decide upon the criminal nature of a libel. But in 1792, against the wishes of all the judges, *Fox's Libel Act*, a declaratory Act (*i.e.* one which declares the existing law on a particular subject) gave to the jury in a trial for criminal libel the duty of deciding whether or not the words in issue were defamatory. Thus, the powers of the jury were increased.

NOTE: The Court of Appeal has power today to order a new trial in the case of a perverse jury verdict.

41. Importance of the jury system.
The jury system, which originated in the exercise of royal powers for administrative purposes, became in the course of its development, an integral part of English constitutional and political liberties. It remains a basic constituent of our legal system. "Whenever a a man is on trial for serious crime, or when in a civil case a man's honour or integrity is at stake, or when one or other party must be deliberately lying, then trial by jury has no equal": per Lord Denning, in *Ward* v. *James* (1966) 1 Q.B.273.

PROGRESS TEST 16

1. Who were the *conteurs*?   **(5)**
2. Explain the terms (*a*) serjeants-at-law, (*b*) utter barristers, (*c*) inner barristers.   **(6, 7)**
3. What led to the separation of attorneys and barristers?   **(10)**
4. Who were the proctors?   **(14)**
5. How did the office of attorney-general originate?   **(15, 16)**
6. Account for the origin of King's counsel.   **(17)**
7. Explain the significance of the term *durante beneplacito nostro*.   **(21)**
8. What was the importance of the *Case of Commendams* (1616)?   **(21)**
9. What was the origin of the office of justice of the peace?   **(23)**
10. What were the duties of the early coroners?   **(28)**
11. How may the jury have originated?   **(29)**
12. What was the effect of the abolition of the ordeal?   **(32)**
13. Explain the terms (*a*) *prison forte et dure*, (*b*) *recognitors*. **(32, 34)**
14. What was the significance of *Bushel's Case* (1670)?   **(39)**

PART FIVE

THE DEVELOPMENT OF CRIMINAL
LAW AND TORT

CHAPTER XVII

THE EARLY GROWTH OF CRIMINAL LAW

THE MEANING OF CRIME

1. The criminal law. Criminal law is concerned with the defining, trial and punishment of crimes and has its historical sources in common law and legislation. Crimes are, in essence, those wrongful acts or omissions considered by the community, acting through Parliament and the judges, as being so injurious as to warrant a particular and special procedure, known as criminal procedure.

(*a*) The community does not seek to punish *all* wrongful acts. Some acts (such as adultery, for example) may be generally regarded as wrongful, but are not classed as crimes.

(*b*) The community's concept of what constitutes crime varies from time to time. Thus: suicide ceased to be a crime with the passing of the *Suicide Act*, 1961; incest (never a crime at common law, although an offence under ecclesiastical law) became a statutory offence only in 1908.

(*c*) In contemporary society the state, *i.e.* the elected government, is able to declare that certain modes of behaviour shall be considered as criminal conduct. "The domain of criminal jurisprudence can only be ascertained by examining what acts at any particular period are declared by the State to be crimes, and the only common nature that they will be found to possess is that they are prohibited by the State and that those who commit them are punished": per Lord Atkin in *Proprietary Articles Trade Assoc.* v. *A.-G. of Canada* [1931] A.C. 310.

2. The constituents of criminal conduct. We may describe a crime as:

(*a*) An act or omission brought about by human conduct,

(*b*) which is harmful and which the State wishes to prevent, and

(*c*) which renders the person responsible liable to a punishment as the result of proceedings which are usually initiated by the State, and

(*d*) which are designed to ascertain the nature, extent, and legal consequence of that responsibility.

THE DISTINCTION BETWEEN CRIME AND TORT

3. Torts. Torts are essentially civil wrongs (*see* XIX, **1**), *i.e.* wrongs which are redressed by proceedings in the civil courts, such as, for example, private nuisance. Some types of conduct may be, at one and the same time, criminal and tortious. Thus, assault and false imprisonment are crimes and may give rise to actions in tort.

4. Crime and tort. Some of the principal differences between crime and tort are:

(*a*) Different types of proceedings are involved; a civil proceeding begins with a complaint, a criminal proceeding with an information.

(*b*) The crown may pardon a crime, but it may not pardon a tort.

(*c*) The consequences of a crime differ from those of a tort. The law of torts is concerned essentially with compensation where a right has been infringed, but the criminal law is concerned with sanctions involving punishment.

(Note the anomalous case of the award of exemplary damages in tort. "There are certain categories of case in which an award of exemplary damages can serve a useful purpose in vindicating the strength of the law, and thus affording a practical justification for admitting into the civil law a principle which ought logically to belong to the criminal": per Lord Devlin in *Rookes* v. *Barnard* [1964] A.C. 1129.)

5. Origin of the distinction. In early law the state was concerned primarily with the protection of its subjects. Wrongs which struck at the safety of the state (*e.g.* treason) were considered as meriting, without exception, very drastic punishment. In other cases some kind of compensation was considered as a suitable remedy for wrongs suffered.

(a) Some wrongs were considered to be crimes involving punishment by the officers of the king. Other wrongs were considered as emendable, usually by compensation to those affected by the injurious act.

(b) The Assize of *Novel Disseisin* (*see* VI, **18**) introduced the concept of estimating the damage suffered by plaintiff in monetary terms.

(c) By the time of Edward II the process of arrest did not apply in the case of a civil wrong in which violence had not been used.

(d) Hence, at an early date, some of the distinctive features of crime and tort had been established: crime—generally the more serious offences which involved arrest and punishment; torts—generally wrongs considered to affect the private individual, as opposed to the community in general, and capable of being remedied by an award of monetary damages.

THE CONCEPT OF MENS REA

6. Actus non facit reum, nisi mens sit rea. (An act itself does not constitute guilt unless it has been done with a guilty intent.) In the modern criminal law the commission of a crime involves, in general, an *actus reus* (*i.e.* the forbidden act) and *mens rea* (a guilty mind, *i.e.* intention, or recklessness as to the circumstances and the consequences of the act).

(a) Until the twelfth century this concept played a relatively minor role in the formation of the criminal law, although it was recognised by the common law.

(b) Acceptance of the implications of the maxim meant that, at common law, a man was not considered guilty of a criminal offence unless his state of mind was "blameworthy."

7. The early law. Criminal intention rarely featured in that part of Anglo-Saxon law concerned with the punishment of crime.

(a) Where X injured or killed Y it is very probable that strict liability and strict accountability attached to X, no matter what the circumstances may have been. But *see* XIX, 6.

(*b*) The law concerning *deodands* (*see* XVI, **28,** *Note* (*iii*)) stems from the notion of responsibility attaching to the cause of an injury.

(*c*) The obligation to make compensation for the so-called emendable crimes attached strictly to the offender.

8. Norman innovations. By the end of the twelfth century the concept of strict liability had undergone some modification, *e.g.*

(*a*) The influence of the church, which emphasised the importance of the mind in acts which were sinful, was growing, and was playing a part in the jurisdiction exercised by the Courts Christian.

(*b*) *Leges Henrici Primi* (*see* V, **12**(*b*)) allowed for the exemption from strict criminal liability of the insane and (in some cases) infants.

9. Later developments.

(*a*) Succeeding centuries witnessed a progressive movement to the idea of criminal intention as playing an important part in establishing liability. Thus, pardons were granted in cases involving death as the result of misadventure and in cases of a crime having been committed in self-defence (*Statute of Northampton*, 1328). Bracton, in his writings, seems aware of the importance of establishing an intention to commit an offence when considering the guilt of a thief.

(*b*) In the fourteenth and fifteenth centuries it was declared that a crime committed under duress during a period of war might be excused, and that the commission of a felony involved "malice aforethought"—a significant step forward in the development of criminal liability.

(*c*) *R.* v. *Levett* (1638) Cro. Cas. 538, established the importance of mistake of fact in determining criminal liability. William Levett was indicted for the homicide of Frances Freeman, having fatally stabbed her under the impression (mistaken, as it turned out) that she had entered his buttery so as to steal. "It was resolved that it was not manslaughter; for he did it ignorantly, without intention of hurt to the said Frances."

THE EARLY CRIMINAL LAW

10. Before the Conquest. Anglo-Saxon laws concerning wrongs are mentioned briefly at I, **19,** and are considered in detail below.

11. The blood feud. The early Anglo-Saxons allowed a process of vengeance, or blood feud, with the object of avenging the wrong not only upon the wrongdoer, but also upon his kin.

(*a*) The process was an attempt by the community to limit the area of vengeance, so that it ceased to be merely indiscriminate.

(*b*) The type of vengeance permitted was determined largely by the nature of the injury.

(*c*) The vengeance was "controlled" by custom. Thus, the killing of a *thegn* might be avenged finally by the slaying of six *ceorls*.

(*d*) By the time of Alfred it was possible to demand a money price, rather than to pursue blood vengeance (*see* **12** below). Alfred also attempted to delay the execution of vengeance. (In his Laws he also decreed: "A man who knows his enemy to be at home shall not fight him before he has demanded satisfaction. . . . If he cannot besiege him, let him go to an alderman for help; if the alderman will not help, let him go to the king before attacking his adversary.")

(*e*) A century later, the Laws of Edmund enacted that the wrongdoer should be allowed a year in which to make compensation.

12. The tariff of compensation. Anglo-Saxon laws formulated a detailed tariff of money payments to the person injured, or his relatives. For example, Alfred's Laws enact: ". . . if a great toe be struck off, let twenty shillings be paid to him as *bot* [*i.e.* a graduated compensation for injury] . . . if the little toe be struck off, let five shillings be paid to him."

(*a*) *Wergild* (*wer* = a man; *gild*, or *geld* = payment) was an estimate in money terms of appropriate compensation based on a person's rank in the community. For a king's *thegn* it was 1200 shillings, for a *ceorl* it was 200 shillings.

(*b*) *Wite* was a fine payable to the king for breaches of the law.

(*c*) The highest *bot* was payable in the case of bodily disfigurement.

(*d*) The law provided no means of enforcing payment, but non-payment might result in outlawry (*see* **24** below).

(*e*) Some offences were considered *botless*, *i.e.* so grave in their nature and consequences that they could not be atoned for by a monetary penalty. These were offences considered by the king to be so serious that they were punished with mutilation or death. Alfred stated, for example, that treason against a lord could not be pardoned (*see* XVIII, **17**).

13. Pleas of the crown. Pleas of the crown were wrongs which were considered to be personal to the king and to the dignity of his royal office.

(*a*) The commission of such offences usually involved a fine payable to the king (a useful method of obtaining revenue for the crown).

(*b*) Cnut enumerates some of these pleas as: "*mundbryce* and *hamsocn*, *forsteal* . . . and *fyrdwite*," (*i.e.* breach of legal protection, attacking an enemy in his house—or housebreaking—assault and neglect of one's military duties).

14. The king's peace. The king's peace, the breach of which was an offence, was an important development in the extending of the responsibility of the crown for the punishment of crime. (In general, every freeman "had his peace," *i.e.* a right to freedom from violence, etc., which attached to his dwelling place.) The king's peace attached at first to his palace and 3000 paces beyond, and to the four great roads.

(*a*) The king's peace extended throughout the realm on the occasion of a church festival.

(*b*) An act of violence at these times was punished by a special fine (*wite*).

(*c*) In the eleventh and early twelfth centuries, the king's peace was considered to have ended temporarily on the death of the king. But on the death of Henry I the suspension of the peace led to "tribulation in the realm, for every man that could forthwith robbed another." To avoid a repetition of this lawlessness, on the death of Henry III, the great nobles proclaimed the king's peace, although the new king was in Palestine. From that time the king's peace was not considered as being in suspension at the time of a king's death.

NOTE: At a later date, in the fourteenth century, certain criminals were considered at being outside the king's peace. Thus, one who was attainted of *praemunire* (see II, 21(c)), was not under that peace, and the slaying of such a person was not considered to be murder (until Elizabeth's reign).

THE ORDEAL

15. Background. *See* I, **22,** and XVI, **32.** The ordeal is found in a number of primitive societies. In England its origins are pre-Christian, but by medieval times it had become closely associated with the church.

(a) The ordeal was essentially an appeal to a supernatural power to intervene in the natural order by a sign which would make manifest the guilt or innocence of an accused person.

(b) In medieval times it was considered as a veritable *dei judicium* (divine judgment).

(c) It was submitted to by the accused, and (very rarely) by the prosecutor.

16. Ordeal by the hot iron. The accused was obliged to carry a heated iron weighing one pound (later increased under the Laws of Athelstan to three pounds) for nine steps.

(a) This took place in church during the mass.

(b) After three days the priest removed bandages which had been placed around the hand and pronounced the innocence of the accused if the wound were healed, and pronounced his guilt if the wound were not healed.

(c) A variant was to make the accused walk over nine red-hot ploughshares—a procedure carried out in the trial of the mother of Edward the Confessor, Queen Emma, and the Bishop of Winchester, accused of familiarity—or to dip the hand into boiling water.

17. Ordeal of the cursed morsel. This was often used in the case of clergy who were on trial.

(a) The priest, in church, prepared a *corsnaed*, or "trial

slice" of consecrated bread and cheese, sometimes containing a feather.

(b) Standing at the altar, he administered the morsel to the accused, declaring that if the accused were guilty his throat would be choked by the angel Gabriel.

(c) Guilt was pronounced if accused appeared unable to swallow the morsel.

18. Ordeal by water. This ordeal (echoes of which were apparent in the ducking of witches in later eras) began with an appeal by the priest to the accused to confess his guilt.

(a) If accused insisted that he was innocent, he was taken out of the church, bound with a rope, and let down into the water.

(b) If he sank down to a knot tied in the rope he was considered to be innocent, otherwise he was judged guilty.

NOTE: The ordeal was virtually abolished in 1215. *See* XVI, 32.

FELONIES AND MISDEMEANOURS

19. Meaning of the terms. The classification of criminal offences ranged in gravity from treason, through felonies, to misdemeanours.

(a) In general, a felony at common law was an offence which involved a forfeiture of the felon's land and goods and the death penalty. Today the term has general application to a category of crimes considered as less heinous than treason, and more serious than misdemeanours. (But *see* the *Criminal Law Act*, 1967, at **23,** *Note*, below).

(b) A misdemeanour is a crime which is not as serious as a felony, and which was generally punished at common law by fine and imprisonment.

NOTE: *Derivation of the term "felony."* One derivation suggests the Latin *fel*, having the sense of "one filled with venom." Another suggestion is that the word is derived from *fee, i.e.* a property held under a feudal tenure, and *lon*, a price; hence, the word suggests a crime, the "price" or penalty being loss of property.

20. Development of the distinction. In the Anglo-Saxon era there were no felonies or misdemeanours. Most crimes were either *emendable* (by the payment of compensation) or *non-emendable* (*botless*)—see **12**(*e*) above.

(*a*) The concept of felony may have been introduced at the Conquest to categorise the more serious offences.

(*b*) *The Assize of Northampton*, 1176 (*see* II, **13**(*d*)(*ii*)) refers to "murder and other felony."

(*c*) By the thirteenth century a unique procedure characterised trials for felony; thus:

    (*i*) The punishment was very severe—mutilation or death.

    (*ii*) The convicted felon forfeited his property to his lord, or in some cases to the crown.

    (*iii*) His right to inherit or transmit land by descent was lost (*see* **21**(*e*) below).

(*d*) Non-felonious offences, which were breaches of the king's peace, were known later as misdemeanours. The procedure which attached to the trial of a misdemeanour differed from that attached to a felony; thus:

    (*i*) The punishment was an *amercement* or a *fine*; an *amercement* was in the discretion (*à merci*) of the court, a *fine* was fixed.

    (*ii*) There was no benefit of clergy (*see* **27** below).

    (*iii*) There was no forfeiture of property.

21. Forfeiture. At common law, the lands and property belonging to a person convicted of treason were forfeited to the king absolutely. The lands of a person convicted of petty treason (*see* XVIII, **19,** *Note*) or felony escheated (*i.e.* reverted) to his lord.

(*a*) Escheat was subject to the right of the crown to hold the land for *ann, jour et wast, i.e.* one year, one day, including the right to commit waste.

(*b*) *Magna Carta*, 1215, *c.* 32, stated that the king should not hold the lands of a convicted felon except for a year and a day (waste is not mentioned), and that at the end of the period the lands were to be given up to the lords of the fees.

(*c*) In 1814 forfeiture of land was limited (save in the cases of treason and murder) to the life interest of the felon.

(*d*) Until 1870 the personal property of the felon was liable to be forfeited to the crown.

(e) *Attainder*, which involved a loss of civil rights and "corruption of the blood," meant that the felon lost his right to inherit or transmit land by descent. *The Forfeiture Act*, 1870, declared: "No confession, verdict, inquest, conviction, or judgment of or for treason, or felony, or felo de se, shall cause any attainder, or corruption of the blood, or any forfeiture or escheat."

22. Capital punishment. The penalty for a felony was, until the nineteenth century, death. In practice, felons were not always executed.

(a) By the end of the eighteenth century, according to one estimate, only one felon in eight was executed.

(b) The Crown's prerogative of mercy was often exercised on condition that the felon was transported for life to the Australian colonies.

NOTE: In 1768, judges of Assize were given a discretionary power to order the transportation of certain felons for any suitable term. Transportation was abolished in 1853.

(c) Fictions were used so as to avoid the death penalty.

(i) Distinctions were made based on the value of a stolen article. If the article had a value of more than 12d., the felon, in and following the reign of Henry I, could be punished with death. If the article had a value under 12d., the offence became a *petty larceny*, which did not carry the death penalty.

(ii) Juries often gave fictitious assessments of the value of stolen property so as to make the stealing a non-capital petty larceny. In *R*. v. *MacAllister* (1808), a jury declared on oath that a Bank of England £10 note was worth 39s.; accused was a woman charged with the capital offence of stealing property to the value of 40s. in a dwelling house.

(iii) See also benefit of clergy at **27** below.

(d) In the decade following 1827, the death sentence was abolished for many felonies.

23. The practical effects of the distinction between felony and misdemeanour. The differentiation of these offences was apparent in the following matters:

(a) Until 1703 a person accused of felony was not allowed

to call any witnesses in his defence, nor was he allowed, until 1836, the services of counsel. One accused of misdemeanour was not penalised in these ways.

(b) No misdemeanour was punished with death. Almost all felonies carried the death penalty.

(c) Felony resulted in forfeiture. No misdemeanour carried this penalty.

(d) Differences in trial procedure (e.g. in the oaths taken by the jurymen) continued until the nineteenth, and into the twentieth century.

NOTE: The wheel has now come full circle. *The Criminal Law Act*, 1967, states: "All distinctions between felony and misdemeanour are hereby abolished. . . . On all matters on which a distinction has previously been made between felony and misdemeanour, including mode of trial, the law and practice in relation to all offences cognisable under the law of England and Wales (including piracy) shall be the law and practice applicable at the commencement of this Act in relation to misdemeanour." (s. 1)

OUTLAWRY, SANCTUARY AND ABJURATION

24. Outlawry. Outlawry was a procedure whereby an offender was placed outside the protection of the law. In England the procedure was in use from the time of Alfred in the case of some serious crimes.

(a) Outlawry resulted in the outlaw's being considered attainted (*see* 21 (e)above). His property was forfeited and he lost all civil rights, becoming, in effect, *civiliter mortuus*.

(b) The penalty was used where, for example, an accused man refused to appear in court, or attempted to evade justice by disappearing, or failed to pay *wergild* (*see* 12(a) above).

(c) It was extended in the late Middle Ages to cases arising from private actions. In these circumstances it did not involve escheat of land, or even summary capital punishment. Thus, a writ of trespass had as its ultimate sanction the threat of outlawry.

(d) The procedure of outlawry involved summoning accused to four consecutive sittings of the county court. On his final failure to appear he was pronounced an outlaw, the sentence stigmatising him as an animal to be hunted and to be struck down if encountered—*"gerit caput lupinem"* (he bears the head of a wolf).

(*e*) He could be captured by any person and killed if he resisted.

(*f*) On capture he could be hanged on proof of his sentence of outlawry.

(*g*) Edward III enacted that an outlaw could be put to death only by a sheriff. The killing of an outlaw by anyone other than the sheriff was murder, except where the killing took place while the outlaw was attempting to evade capture.

(*h*) The person outlawed in civil proceedings lost his right to sue in the courts, nor could he enforce any legal rights. He was personally liable, however, upon any cause of action.

(*i*) Outlawry in civil proceedings was abolished in 1879; criminal outlawry had been obsolete long before it was formally abolished by the *Administration of Justice Act,* 1838, *s.* 12.

25. Sanctuary.

The right of sanctuary was the right available under certain circumstances to an accused or convicted person whereby he could seek refuge within a consecrated place in which neither criminal nor civil processes could be executed.

(*a*) The right is mentioned in the Laws of Ethelbert (*c.* 600).

(*b*) There was a detailed procedure of sanctuary. The fugitive had to confess his crime to a priest, surrender any arms, pay a fee to the church, and state the details of his crime.

(*c*) Within 40 days he had to appear, dressed in sack-cloth, before the coroner (*see* XVI, 28), confess, and swear to leave the realm (*see* 26 below). Attainder of blood and forfeiture followed.

(*d*) The Normans allowed two types of sanctuary: *general,* which belonged to all churches, and *peculiar,* which resulted from the grant of a royal charter. 22 such chartered sanctuaries existed, *e.g.* at Derby, Durham, St. Martin's le Grand and St. Mary le-Bow in London, Ramsey, Winchester, York. The general sanctuary afforded protection only to those guilty of a felony; the peculiar sanctuary protected those accused of felony and treason.

(*e*) In 1540 Henry VIII curtailed this privilege and established eight cities of refuge in Wells, Northampton, Norwich,

Derby, York, Lancaster, Westminster and Manchester (later transferred to Chester).

(*f*) James I abolished the right of sanctuary for criminal offenders in 1623.

(*g*) In London unofficial sanctuary continued in the area of Whitefriars, where arrests required a writ from the Lord Chief Justice.

(*h*) An Act of 1697, and an amending Act in 1723, finally abolished these rights.

NOTE: Sanctuary was not available in the case of condemned criminals and clerks, or in the case of the offence of sacrilege.

26. Abjuration. Abjuration of the realm was an alternative to outlawry and was introduced by the Normans. It involved an oath to leave the country for ever.

(*a*) The fugitive who had sought sanctuary, on confessing his felony to the coroner, took an oath to leave the realm.

(*b*) He was told by the coroner of the nearest port from which he was to leave the country, and was promised safe conduct there.

(*c*) In 1529 Henry VIII ordered the branding of those who had abjured the realm, so that they could be recognised (and hanged) if they returned.

(*d*) The abjurer was given only a short time in which to reach the port. In the time of Edward III, for example, nine days only were allowed for one abjurer to reach Dover from Yorkshire, on foot.

(*e*) The abjurer, dressed in a conspicuous white robe, and carrying a wooden cross, had to keep to the king's highway, and was forbidden to halt for more than two nights in any place.

(*f*) An abjurer might return to the realm if pardoned by the crown.

BENEFIT OF CLERGY

27. Background. Benefit of clergy was a privilege by which clergymen were exempt from the criminal process. The twelfth century witnessed many disputes between the ecclesiastical and the lay courts. *The Constitutions of Clarendon*, 1164, (*see* II, **13**(*a*)), allowed "criminous clerks" to be brought before the king's court, then to be tried by a church court and degraded upon proof of guilt, and then to be handed once more to the king's court for punishment.

(a) In the thirteenth century the clerk was obliged to "plead his clergy" when brought for trial. He was handed over to the church court (usually to be tried by a process involving compurgation—*see* VI, 9) when his plea had been accepted.

(b) In 1352 the privilege was allowed to secular clerks, the test being literacy. The claim of benefit of clergy involved the test of ability to read the so-called "neck verse," which was the first verse of Psalm LI (*"Miserere mei, Deus"*— "Have mercy upon me, O God").

(c) In the fourteenth century the procedure was varied, so that an accused person could be tried and could plead his clergy after conviction.

(d) In Edward III's reign, benefit of clergy was not available in cases of highway robbery.

(e) In 1490, laymen who were allowed benefit of clergy were branded on the hand, and could not claim the benefit on a future occasion.

(f) In 1531 benefit of clergy became no longer available in cases of robbery and murder (*see* XVIII, 4(f)).

(g) Under William III, the benefit was extended to women in 1692.

(h) In the reign of Anne, claim of benefit of clergy no longer depended on a literacy test (1707).

(i) Blackstone states that in his day there were 160 felonies in which benefit of clergy could not be claimed.

(j) *The Criminal Law Act*, 1827, abolished benefit of clergy.

PROGRESS TEST 17

1. What was the origin of the distinction between crime and tort? **(5)**
2. What role was played by the concept of criminal intention in early law? **(7)**
3. Explain the significance of the blood feud. **(11)**
4. What was the *tariff of compensation* in Anglo-Saxon law? **(12)**
5. Explain the procedure in the *ordeal of the cursed morsel*. **(17)**

6. How did the distinction between felonies and misdemeanours originate?   (20)

7. Explain the terms (a) *ann, jour et wast*, (b) *attainder*.   (21)

8. What was the procedure in outlawry?   (24)

9. Under what circumstances could the right of sanctuary be claimed?   (25)

10. What was meant by *abjuration*?   (26)

11. Explain the term *benefit of clergy*.   (27)

CHAPTER XVIII

THE DEVELOPMENT OF THE COMMON LAW CRIMES OF HOMICIDE, LARCENY, AND TREASON

HOMICIDE

1. Meaning of the term. Homicide is the unlawful killing of a human being. Coke, in his *Third Institute*, gives the following definition of murder: "Murder is when a man of sound memory, and of the age of discretion, unlawfully killeth within any county of the realm any reasonable creature *in rerum natura* under the king's peace, with malice aforethought, either expressed by the party or implied by law, so as the party wounded, or hurt, etc. die of the wound or hurt, etc. within a year and a day after the same."

2. Homicide in the Anglo-Saxon era. The Anglo-Saxons regarded the unlawful slaying of a member of the community as a most heinous offence. Even the unlawful killing of a slave by his master was punishable under the Laws of Alfred.

(*a*) An unlawful killing gave rise to a blood feud or *wergild* (*see* XVII, **11, 12**).

(*b*) Some types of killing excited great horror, *e.g.* that which had been planned with deliberation and in which the victim was trapped in ambush. A crime of this particular type was considered unemendable.

3. Homicide following the Conquest. Under the early Norman kings, homicide became a plea of the crown, and, as a felony, it resulted in a forfeiture of the felon's property.

(*a*) *Murdrum.* The conquered did not take easily to the Conquest, and there were many killings of local rulers and their servants, who had been installed by William. The Norman answer to this threat was the introduction of *presentment of Englishry* and *murdrum.*

(*i*) The hundred in which a Norman had been slain was liable to a very heavy fine if the murderer had not been caught. The fine was known as *murdrum* (derived from *morth*—a secret killing). The name *murdrum* came to signify the killing.

(*ii*) Where it could be proved that the murdered person was English, and not Norman, the fine was not levied. The presumption was that the person slain was a Norman, unless a *presentment of Englishry* was made, *i.e.* unless proof could be given that the person slain was English. The proof usually required an inquest and a declaration by the dead man's four nearest relatives.

(*b*) The Normans did not distinguish at first between murder and manslaughter.

> NOTE: By custom *murdrum* was not payable in Kent or Cornwall.

4. Later developments.
In the twelfth–sixteenth centuries came important developments.

(*a*) After the *Assize of Clarendon*, 1166, the distinctions between the unlawful killing of Englishmen and Normans began to fade, and the term *murder* took on its present meaning of a deliberate killing.

(*b*) In 1267 it was declared that no murder fine would be imposed in the case of a death *per infortunium*. But a homicide in self-defence or by misadventure resulted in a forfeiture of property and necessitated a royal pardon.

(*c*) In 1328 a statute was enacted which limited pardons in cases of homicide to misadventure or self-defence.

(*d*) In 1340 *presentment of Englishry* and *murdrum* were abolished.

(*e*) In 1390 it was enacted that charges of "slaying in ambush, in assault, or of malice aforethought" should not be the subject of a general pardon by the crown.

(*f*) The developing concept of malice aforethought was given expression in an enactment of Henry VIII in 1531, removing benefit of clergy (*see* XVII, 27) in the case of "wilful murder with malice prepensed." From that time the crime of murder was clearly established as involving wilful killing with malice aforethought.

5. Suicide.
Self-slaughter was a felony (*felonia de se*) and, hence, resulted in the forfeiture of the goods belonging to the

person who had killed himself (*felo de se*). (Under common law rules the corpse of the suicide was transfixed with a stake and was buried along a highway. In 1824 burial of a suicide, without any funeral service, was allowed between 9 p.m. and midnight. It was not until 1882 that the *Interments Act* ended these practices.) Forfeiture of the property of a *felo de se* ended with the *Forfeiture Act*, 1870.

NOTE: The common law considered also as *felonia de se* the killing of a person by his own hand during the course of attempting to kill another.

LARCENY AND ASSOCIATED CRIMES

6. The meaning of "stealing." A person steals who without the consent of the owner fraudulently, and without a claim of right made in good faith, takes and carries away anything capable of being stolen, with intent, at the time of such taking, permanently to deprive the owner thereof: *Larceny Act*, 1916, *s.* 1.

(*a*) It should be noted that this is a statutory definition of *stealing*; the Act nowhere defines *larceny* as such.

(*b*) Bracton defined theft as: "*contrectatio rei alienae fraudulenta, cum animo furandi, invito illo domino cuius res illa fuerit*" (the fraudulent handling of another person's thing, without his agreement, with the intention of stealing it).

(*c*) Taking and carrying away have always been essential in the crime of stealing property; hence it was necessary at common law that the thing stolen should be tangible. A debt, for example, could not be stolen at common law. Anything which could be considered as corporeal could be stolen: *R.* v. *White* (1853) Dearsley, 203—gas was held larcenable at common law.

7. The common law rules concerning stealing. The common law evolved a number of rules concerning the crime of stealing, the more important of which are mentioned below:

(*a*) The *actus reus* (*see* XVII, **6**) involved:

(*i*) The seizing of property;
(*ii*) The carrying away of the property;
(*iii*) Lack of consent of the owner.

(*b*) The seizing and carrying away need not necessarily be by the person accused: *R.* v. *Pitman* (1826) 2 C. & P. 423.

(*c*) Asportation is complete when the object is removed even slightly from its original position: *R.* v. *Lapier* (1784) 1 Leach 320.

(*d*) The thing stolen must have an owner—larceny was considered at an early stage as involving a removal *vi et armis* of property from its owner.

(*e*) Land, and things which "savour of the realty" were considered incapable of being stolen. Thus, a crop of growing corn was held not larcenable. For many centuries the cutting down of a tree was held not to be a larceny: *The Forester's Case* (1338).

(*f*) A taking was not larceny where the intention to steal was formed after the taking.

8. General development of the law. From the time of Henry I some forms of stealing were punishable with death.

(*a*) As a felony, larceny should have been invariably a capital offence. But in fact distinctions between various types of larceny soon began to appear. The distinctions were based on the monetary value of the property stolen.

(*b*) Where stolen property was worth only twelve pence or less, the stealing was considered as a *petty larceny*, not punishable with death. The stealing of property worth more than twelve pence was a *grand larceny*, punishable with death.

(*c*) In the following centuries the device of benefit of clergy (*see* XVII, 27) complicated the law of larceny.

(*d*) In the first half of the nineteenth century, larceny ceased to be a capital offence.

(*e*) In 1827 the distinction between petty and grand larceny was ended.

9. Mitigation of the severity of the law. Benefit of the clergy and petty larceny represented ways in which the severity of the law concerning larceny was lessened. Mitigation resulted also from other matters:

(*a*) The common law judges strained the law so as to discover reasons which would place the stealing of certain types of article outside the scope of larceny, *e.g.* some domestic animals, growing crops, were held not larcenable at common law.

(b) The judges applied ingenious arguments to the notional reduction of the value of stolen property. Thus, in 1553, Hales, J., is reported as casting doubt on the possibility of precious stones being larcenable property, "because they be not of price with all men; howsoever some do hold them dear and precious."

(c) Juries often valued stolen property at below a value which would have supported a conviction leading to the death penalty. (*See* XVII, 22(*c*)(*ii*).)

10. "Breaking bulk." At common law a bailee (*i.e.* a person to whom the possession of goods is entrusted by the owner) who acted dishonestly had some immunity, since he was considered to be in lawful possession of the goods. Hence, appropriation by the bailee was not stealing at common law.

(a) In the *Carrier's Case* (1473), the Star Chamber considered the following matter: X had bargained with Y, a foreign merchant, to carry Y's bales and other property to Southampton. X dishonestly took and carried the goods to another place where he opened the bales, converted some of the goods therein to his own use, and then disposed of them. The question to be decided was whether or not this was a felony.

(b) *Per* Brian, C. J.: "It seems to me that it cannot [be called a felony]. For when he has possession lawfully by the bailment and delivery of the other party, it cannot afterwards be called felony or trespass: for no felony can be except with violence and *vi et armis*; and what he himself had he could not take *vi et armis* or *contra pacem*."

(c) *Per* Hussey, the King's Attorney: "It is felony where one feloniously claims the property without cause, with intent to defraud him in whom the property is *animo furandi*. And here, despite the bailment, the property remained in him who made the bailment."

(d) The justices assembled reported to the Chancellor in Council that in the opinion of most of them it was felony.

(e) In 1857 dishonest conversion by a bailee was made a statutory offence.

11. Nemo dat quod non habet. (No one can give what he has not got). Under the common law a thief could not confer ownership of the stolen goods on any person. Two exceptions to this rule were formulated under common law. Where a person gives a thief valuable consideration for the stolen property, not knowing of the theft, that person may acquire a good title to it:

(a) If the stolen property is money or a negotiable instrument, or,

(b) If the property was transferred to him in *market overt* (*i.e.* in a lawfully established market on market day, or, later, in the City of London)—an interesting vestige of the rules thought necessary to protect merchants in the medieval fairs and markets.

12. Robbery. Robbery was, at common law, the felonious taking of money or goods from another by violence or by putting him in fear. In 1348, larceny with violence was declared a capital offence even though the robber might have taken property worth less than twelve pence.

13. Burglary. (*Burge-breche* = breach of a borough). In early times burglary was the breaking by night into a house, a church, the gates or walls of a town. (In ancient law the walls of a town were considered *res sanctae*, *i.e.* things under divine protection. The violation of city walls was a capital offence under Roman law, and legend has it that Romulus, founder of Rome, killed his brother, Remus, for leaping the city walls.)

(a) At common law, burglary became the breaking and entering of a dwelling house by night with the intent to commit a felony therein, whether the felony was committed or not.

(b) In 1547 it was enacted that housebreaking "to the dread of the inmates," and larceny from a church, and horse-stealing, were to be excluded from benefit of clergy.

(i) Towards the end of the eighteenth century judges were given discretion to substitute transportation for capital punishment.

(ii) *The Larceny Act*, 1827, made burglary punishable with death, and removed the possible alternative of transportation.

(iii) Burglary ceased to be a capital offence in 1837.

I

(c) In 1583 all the justices assembled at Serjeants' Inn resolved that entry to a household might be constituted by the mere insertion of an instrument. The report states: "An actual case was mentioned, which was this: in the night, one who meant to shoot another, in a house, broke a hole through the wall of a house and shot at him through the hole with a gun, and missed him; which was adjudged to be burglary."

(d) In 1594 it was resolved by all the justices and barons of the exchequer assembled at Serjeants' Inn that, for the purpose of the offence, a house remains a dwelling house if occupied habitually by members of a household, even while that household is absent temporarily, ". . . for the house of everyone is the proper place to preserve his goods, although no person be there."

14. Embezzlement. (Derivation: *besillier* = to ravage). Embezzlement is the conversion to his own use by a servant or clerk of property which he has received on behalf of his master.

(a) In 1529 the "imbezilment" of goods delivered into the possession of a servant by his master was declared to be a felony.

(b) The felony did not apply, however, to the case of goods received from a third party on the master's account.

(c) *R.* v. *Dingley* (1687). X was employed to sell goods for Y, his master. X received 160 guineas for these goods from a purchaser. He (X) deposited ten guineas in his room and took away the rest when he was discharged by Y. He later returned at night to Y's house, broke in, and took away the ten guineas. It was *held* that the taking away of the money was not a felony, since, although it was Y's money in right, it was X's money in possession.

(d) *R.* v. *Bazeley* (1799) 2 Leach 835. B, a bank cashier, was charged with feloniously stealing a bank note for £100. C had paid in £137 to the bank on his own account. B received this money from C, put £37 in the appropriate bank drawer, and put a £100 note in his pocket. Later that day B used the note to discharge an acceptance of his own. It was *held* that B had committed no felony, inasmuch as the £100 had never been in the possession of the bank.

(e) Largely as a consequence of this case an Act was passed in 1799 which declared to be a felony the embezzlement by a servant or clerk of property received by him for his employer, even though the property had not reached the actual possession of the employer.

15. Fraudulent conversion. When a servant acquired physical control of, and full ownership in property which it was his duty to hand to his master, or to dispose of in his master's interests, the common law had no remedy where the servant failed to carry out that duty. It was only in 1811 and 1861 that the law recognised conversion of a criminally fraudulent nature.

16. False pretences. At common law the cheating of a person by a lie or false representation did not amount to an offence unless the cheating had been carried out by "a device of a tangible nature" and was such that ordinary care would not have sufficed as a protection. "Shall we indict one man for making a fool of another?": per Holt, C. J., in *R.* v. *Jones* (1704) 2 Ld. Raym. 1013. In 1757 the obtaining of property by false pretences became a statutory offence.

TREASON

17. "The most heinous of all crimes." Breach of allegiance to one's overlord, which was the essence of treason (*tradere* = to betray) was punishable by death under the ancient laws of Alfred and Aethelred. "Almighty God adjudged [no mercy] to those who scorned him," declare Alfred's Laws; hence there was to be no mercy for those who were guilty of treachery to a lord. "If anyone plots against a king's life," declare the Laws, "directly or by harbouring his exiles, he may forfeit his life and everything he owns."

NOTE: Benefit of clergy never applied to treason.

18. The early common law. Prior to the time of Edward III, the law of treason was not clearly defined.

(*a*) All the king's subjects from the age of fourteen had to swear an oath of allegiance if they were requested to do so, but allegiance was expected even from those who had not taken the oath.

(*b*) Breach of allegiance was punished, but the judges

decided in an arbitrary manner whether particular actions constituted such a breach.

(*i*) Segrave, in Edward I's reign was convicted of treason because he had appealed to the French courts.

(*ii*) John Geberge of Royston, who assaulted a messenger of Edward III and detained him until he paid £90, was held to have committed a treason.

19. The Statute of Treasons, 1351. In the reign of Edward III, the barons petitioned against the arbitrary nature of the courts' decisions upon treason, and the *Statute of Treasons*, which limited high treason to seven modes, was passed. No other action was to be adjudged as treason by the courts unless with the agreement of the king and Parliament. The seven heads of treason were:

(*a*) Compassing or imagining the death of the king, queen or heir. "Compassing" was interpreted to mean "bringing about," "imagining" meant "planning and plotting." Some overt deed was necessary:

(*i*) The twenty-nine regicides tried in 1660 were charged with compassing the death of Charles I, his execution being considered as the overt act which proved the compassing.

(*ii*) Spoken words were not necessarily an overt act. Thus, in the case of *Hugh Pyne* (1628) Cro. Car. 117, Pyne was acquitted on a charge of treason, having declared aloud: "Before God, he [the king] is no more fit to be King than Hickwright [an old and simple shepherd]." But "words of persuasion to kill the king" were held to constitute an act of overt treason in *R.* v. *Charnock* (1694) 2 Salk. 631.

(*b*) Violation of the king's consort, eldest daughter, or wife of his heir.

(*c*) Levying war against the king in his realm. "War" was taken to include a forcible disturbance involving a large number of people, intended for some general purpose: *Damaree's Case* (1709) Foster, 213.

(*d*) Being adherent to the king's enemies in his realm, giving them aid and comfort in the realm or elsewhere: *R.* v. *Casement* [1917] 1 K.B.98.

(*e*) Counterfeiting the king's great seal or money.

(*f*) Bringing counterfeit money into the king's realm.

(Offences (*e*) and (*f*) were reduced to felonies under the *Coinage Offences Act*, 1861, and the *Forgery Act*, 1913.)

(*g*) Slaying the chancellor, treasurer, or the king's justices.

NOTE: The Act defined as *petty treason* the slaying of a master by his servant, of a husband by his wife, or of a prelate by a person who owed him allegiance. These became ordinary murders under the *Offences against the Person Act*, 1828.

20. Further developments. In the centuries which followed the *Statute of Treasons*, many new offences were made treasons.

(*a*) Henry VIII made statutory additions to the law of treason, *e.g.* "to slanderously and maliciously publish and pronounce, by express writing or words, that the King . . . should be heretic, schismatic, tyrant, infidel or usurper of the crown" (1534: "An Act whereby divers offences be made high treason"), and "forging and counterfeiting of the King's sign manual or privy signet" (an Act of 1536).

(*b*) Most of Henry VIII's statutory treasons were repealed in 1553 by the *First Treason Act* of Mary.

(*c*) In 1702 it was enacted that to endeavour to deprive or hinder the next successor to the throne from succeeding was a treason.

(*d*) In 1707 it was declared treason to maliciously, advisedly and directly by writing or printing, maintain and affirm that any person has a right to the crown otherwise than according to the *Acts of Settlement*, or that crown and Parliament cannot pass laws to limit the succession to the throne.

(*e*) *The Treason Act*, 1796, extended the definition of treason so as to include plots to harm or kill the king or his successors, if such plots were expressed by publishing any printing or writing, or by any overt act or deed. These "constructive treasons" became felonies under the *Treason Felony Act*, 1848.

21. Trials for treason. Those accused of treason and brought to trial laboured under considerable disadvantages. Even Judge Jeffreys was moved to complain, in *R*. v. *Rosewall* (1684): "I think it is a hard case that a man should have counsel to defend himself for a twopenny trespass, and his witnesses examined upon oath.; but if he steal, commit murder or felony, nay, high treason . . . he shall neither have counsel, nor his witnesses examined upon oath." *The Treason Act*, 1696, changed this situation:

(a) The prisoner was entitled to have a copy of the indictment five days before the trial.

(b) He was entitled to a list of the intended jury panel two days before the trial.

(c) He was allowed the assistance of counsel.

(d) He was allowed witnesses who could be examined on oath.

(e) There could be no conviction unless the prisoner confessed voluntarily in open court, or his guilt was established by two witnesses on oath.

(f) Prosecutions for treason (except in the case of an actual plot to slay the king) were limited to a term of three years from the alleged commission of the offence.

NOTE: All of these rules are now abolished, and procedure in the case of a trial for treason was revised by the *Treason Act*, 1945.

22. Misprision of treason.

This was a common law misdemeanour committed by one who knew, or had reasonable cause to know, that another had committed treason, and who failed to disclose this information to the proper authority. A conviction could bring imprisonment for life and forfeiture of the offender's goods and profits from his land during his life. From 1552–54 the offence was considered high treason. *The Forfeiture Act*, 1870, did not affect forfeiture for this particular offence.

23. Punishment.

The death penalty for treason was carried out with remarkable ferocity:

(a) The traitor was dragged to the scaffold on a hurdle, hanged, but cut down alive, disembowelled, then beheaded and quartered, the head and quarters being at the disposal of the Crown.

(b) The King could dispense with all parts of this punishment except the beheading.

(c) In 1814 it was declared that beheading and quartering were to follow death by hanging.

(d) In 1870 beheading and quartering were abolished.

PROGRESS TEST 18

1. Explain (*a*) *murdrum*, (*b*) *presentment of Englishry*.   **(3)**
2. What were the common law rules concerning stealing?   **(7)**
3. How was the severity of the law of larceny mitigated?   **(9)**
4. Explain the importance of the *Carrier's Case* (1473).   **(10)**
5. What was meant by burglary at common law?   **(13)**
6. What was the origin of the felony of embezzlement?   **(14)**
7. Why was treason considered as "the most heinous of all crimes"?   **(17)**
8. What were the seven heads of treason under *the Statute of Treasons*, 1351?   **(19)**
9. What was the effect of the *Treason Act*, 1696, upon a trial for treason?   **(21)**

CHAPTER XIX

THE DEVELOPMENT OF TORTS

THE ELEMENTS OF TORT

1. The meaning of a tort. A tort is a civil wrong which results from the infringement of a legal right (not arising exclusively out of trust or contract), the remedy for which is an action for unliquidated damages (*i.e.* damages which are not agreed in advance, but are left to be assessed by the court).

2. Tort, crime, breaches of contract and trust. The wrongs which form the subject matter of the law of torts must be distinguished from:

(*a*) *Crimes.* The criminal law is concerned basically with the punishment of the offender; compensation of the injured person is not of primary importance. But the essence of an action in tort is the compensation of the injured party; punishment as such is not within the contemplation of plaintiff. *See* XVII, 3–5 for the distinctions between crime and tort.

NOTE: It is possible for an action to be at one and the same time a crime and a tort. X steals Y's purse—the crime is larceny, the tort is conversion. An assault may result in criminal proceedings or a civil action in tort.

(*b*) *Breaches of a contractual agreement.* The liability which arises in contract emerges as the result of the agreement of the parties to the contract. But liability in tort flows from the infringing of a right fixed by law.

(*c*) *Breaches of trust.* Trust, and the breaches arising from it, are essentially matters arising in equity. But tort arises out of the common law.

3. Damage, motive, and malice in tort. Two concepts are of particular importance in tort: *damnum* (damage suffered); *injuria* (a legal wrong).

(a) *Damnum sine injuria* (damage sustained without a legal wrong). One who suffers damage of this kind is not necessarily entitled to maintain an action in tort.

(b) *Injuria sine damno* (a legal wrong resulting in no damage). In some very few cases an actionable tort may result without any proof of actual damage (*e.g.* slander, which is actionable *per se* in certain restricted circumstances, as where there has been an imputation of unchastity to a woman).

(c) *Motive*. The motive for the action complained of is generally immaterial in tort.

(d) *Malice*. In some torts (*e.g.* defamation) malice may be a material factor, but generally it is immaterial. Thus, a lawful act will not become unlawful because it has been carried out with malicious intentions.

4. General sources of the law of torts. The most important source is the common law. Legislation has contributed much. Equity has affected the growth of tort only secondarily, *e.g.* by its development of the injunction.

TORTS AND THE FORMS OF ACTION

5. The writ system. The historical significance of the forms of action and the writ system in the development of tort is of importance.

(a) For a long period a plaintiff had a right of action only if there was in existence some form of action (or writ) which was appropriate to his case.

(b) Before the fourteenth century, personal actions complaining of wrongs were usually based on a variant of the writ of trespass (*see* VII), *e.g.* trespass to the person, to land, or to goods.

(c) Following the fourteenth century, new forms of action emerged. As a result plaintiff could bring an action based on the infringement of newly-recognised rights, and there appeared specific wrongs such as libel and nuisance.

(d) The writ system disappeared under the *Common Law Procedure Act*, 1852. It was no longer necessary for plaintiff to select a particular and recognised form of action. Plaintiff could now set out in his pleadings the relevant facts on which he based his allegation of a tortious act, and it was left to the court to decide whether or not he had a remedy.

INTENTION AND LIABILITY IN TORT

6. The early law. *See* XVII, **7**. Assume that, in early times, D caused some injury to P. Was D liable in all circumstances? Was D's liability absolute, or was there, in early law, any understanding and acceptance of the concept that D's liability was to be determined by the circumstances surrounding the case? There are two schools of thought:

(*a*) *The "absolute liability" school* (as represented by Holdsworth). It is maintained that in the early law intent was of no relevance in deciding the liability of an alleged wrongdoer. The early courts lacked the sophistication necessary to "look behind" a deed; the deed was everything, the mental element behind the deed, nothing. It sufficed that a deed had been performed. The performer acted at his peril.

(*b*) *The "strict liability" school* (as represented by Winfield). It is suggested that, although the concepts and procedures of the early law were peremptory and harsh, yet liability was no more than strict. It was not absolute. It is suggested, further, that the early law was moving in a direction which would allow of the modification of liability by surrounding circumstances. Thus:

(*i*) The Laws of Aethelred (*c*. 1000) contain a comment which indicates that in forming a judgment, careful discrimination ought to be made between age and youth, wealth and poverty, in inflicting penalties. The case of an offender who acted as an involuntary agent is to be distinguished from that of the person who offends voluntarily and with intention.

(*ii*) The Dooms of Cnut contain a similar statement.

7. Intention, liability and trespass. For trespass generally, *See* VII. Trespass was based essentially on a wrong committed *vi et armis contra pacem domini regis*.

(*a*) *Trespass to the person*: an offender could argue that he committed the act in self-defence.

(*b*) *Trespass to property*: self-defence was unlikely to be raised as a motive, and strict liability, with no reference to intention, came to be the rule.

(c) *Trespass on the case*: a successful action in trespass on the case often demanded some proof that defendant had *caused* the wrong complained of. There is scope here for the concept of intention. Thus, in an action for deceit, the intentions of defendant, based on his knowledge at the time of the alleged deceit, were relevant.

8. The Case of Thorns. This celebrated case, *Hull* v. *Orynge* (1466), which involves fifteenth-century attitudes towards intention and liability in trespass, is of great interest.

(a) *The facts*: D was clipping a thorn hedge, which stood on his land. Some of the clippings fell on the adjoining land of P, D's neighbour. D then entered on P's land in order to collect and remove the clippings.

(b) *The problem*: Was D's entry an actionable trespass?

(c) *The argument*: The plea that the clippings fell on P's land against D's will was not accepted. "When a man does something he is bound to do it in such wise that by his acts no damage ensues to others": *per* Brian, C. J. Choke, J., commenting on D's plea that the clippings fell on P's land against D's will, said: ". . . that is no good plea, but he must say that he could not do it in any other manner or that he did all that was possible to keep them [on his own land], otherwise he will be answerable for damages." D suggested that his entry on P's land could be justified by analogy with an entry for the purpose of collecting any of his cattle which might have strayed there from the highway. This, too, was rejected.

(d) *The judgment*: We do not know with certainty whether judgment was given for the plaintiff, but it would seem that the weight of opinion was such as to support his case. The case was used in later times to support the contention that where a trespass had resulted in any harm, the trespasser was liable, no matter what his intention, if the trespass might have been avoided in any manner: *Weaver* v. *Ward* (1616) Hob. 134.

9. Later developments. In *Basely* v. *Clarkson* (1682) 3 Lev. 37, unintentional mistake was rejected as a defence to an action for trespass to land. But in *Tuberville* v. *Savage* (1669) 2 Keb.545, however, intention was considered as of some relevance in trespass to the person. X put his hand on his sword, saying to Y, "If it were not assize-time I would not take such language from you." X's action was held not to have constituted an assault, since his words implied that no assault was intended. "The declaration of [X] was that he would not assault him [Y], the judges being in town."

10. The nineteenth century. The concept of strict liability in trespass continued.

(*a*) In *Leame* v. *Bray* (1803) 3 East., Grose, J., declared: "Looking into all the cases. . . . I find the principle to be, that if the injury be done by the act of the party himself at the time, or he be the immediate cause of it though it happens accidentally or by misfortune, yet he is answerable in trespass."

NOTE: Inevitable accident as a defence in tort was further considered in *Stanley* v. *Powell* [1891] 1 Q.B.86. P, a member of a shooting party, fired at a bird. The pellet touched a tree and glanced off, hitting S. P was held not liable for trespass to the person, the harm being accidental, and due neither to negligence nor lack of caution. The authority of this decision was accepted in *National Coal Board* v. *Evans* [1951] 2 K.B.861.

(*b*) In *Rylands* v. *Fletcher* (1868) L.R.3 H.L.330, the question of strict liability was considered.

(*i*) *The facts*: Defendants employed independent contractors to construct a reservoir on their land. Negligence of the contractors resulted in a failure to block up shafts on the site which communicated with mines belonging to the plaintiff. When the reservoir was filled the water burst the shafts and flooded plaintiff's mines.

(*ii*) *The judgment*: Defendants, who were neither vicariously liable for the negligence of the independent contractors, nor themselves negligent, were held liable. "We think that the true rule of law is, that the person who for his own purposes brings on his lands and collects and keeps there anything liable to do mischief if it escapes, must keep it in at his peril, and, if he does not do so, is *prima facie* answerable for all the damage which is the natural consequence of its escape": *per* Blackburn, J., in the Court of Exchequer Chamber. A proviso of the House of Lords stated that the rule would have application only if there had been a non-natural use of the land.

(*iii*) *Defences to the rule*: The judgment continues: "He [defendant] can excuse himself by showing that the escape was owing to the plaintiff's default; or perhaps that the escape was the consequence of *vis major*, or the act of God."

NEGLIGENCE IN TORT

11. The meaning of negligence. Negligence has come to have two separate meanings in the law of torts:

(*a*) It may mean total or partial inadvertence to conduct, or to the consequences of that conduct. "Negligence is the omission to do something which a reasonable man guided upon those considerations which ordinarily regulate the conduct of human affairs would do, or doing something which a prudent and reasonable man would not do": *per* Alderson, B., in *Blyth* v. *Birmingham Waterworks Co.* (1856) 11 Exch.781.

(*b*) It may refer specifically to the modern tort of negligence, in which a successful plaintiff must show the existence of a duty of care owed to him by defendant, a breach of that duty, and resulting damage to him.

12. The early period. There seems to be little evidence of liability for negligence as such in the early courts. But from the middle of the fourteenth century bailees were held liable for fraud and negligence. In the fifteenth century the celebrated *Marshal's Case* (1455) decided that a bailee (in this particular case, the marshal of a prison) was liable to the person on whose order a prisoner had been committed. The bailee pleaded that the prisoner had been released by "the king's enemies," who had broken into the prison. From argument on the case emerged the point that a bailee would not be liable for a matter arising out of an act of God or an act of the king's foreign enemies. In *Southcote's Case* (1601) 4 Co. Rep. 83b it was declared that a bailee was an insurer of the goods with which he had been entrusted by the owner. (This was rejected in *Coggs* v. *Bernard* (1703).)

NOTE: The modern position is that a bailee is liable for gross negligence in the case of a culpable default where the bailment is entirely for the bailor's benefit; he is liable even for slight negligence, *e.g.* failure to take care, where the bailment is solely for the bailee's benefit: he is liable for ordinary negligence where the bailment is for the common benefit of bailor and bailee.

13. Common callings. In the medieval era a special liability was imposed on those who followed certain occupations, *e.g.* innkeepers, farriers, smiths, common carriers.

(*a*) He who followed a common calling was obliged to accept work and could be prosecuted in the event of a refusal.

(*b*) From the time of Edward III, an innkeeper was liable for negligence in the case of theft from his premises, or in the case of damage caused to goods belonging to his guests.

(*c*) Common carriers were liable for damage to goods or for loss resulting from theft.

(*d*) Liability for loss was not absolute, however. Defendant might establish that there was no *defectus custodiae* (default of keeping).

14. Later developments.

(*a*) *Mitchil* v. *Alestree* (1676) 1 Vent. 295. Defendant exercised a horse, which to his knowledge was unruly, in Lincoln's Inn Fields. A person passing by was injured, and defendant was held liable for the injury. The important point established was that defendant's liability did not arise merely because of his knowing that the horse was unruly, but because his action in exercising the horse was very likely to result in an injury to some person. The widening of the concept of negligence as a result of this judgment was of much importance in the development of torts.

(*b*) In the nineteenth century it came to be established that plaintiff in an action founded on negligence had to show a duty of care owed to him by defendant. In *Langridge* v. *Levy* (1837) 2 M. & W. 519, X sold Y a defective rifle. X knew of the defect, but warranted the rifle to be in good condition. Y informed X that the rifle would be used by Y's son, who was afterwards injured when the gun burst. X was held liable to the plaintiff, Y's son.

NOTE: The modern principle defining the existence of a duty

of care was stated in *Donoghue* v. *Stevenson* [1932] A.C. 562, by Lord Atkin. A duty of care is owing to one's neighbour. "Who, then, in law, is my neighbour? The answer seems to be—persons who are so closely and directly affected by my act that I ought reasonably to have them in contemplation as being so affected when I am directing my mind to the acts or omissions which are called in question."

PROGRESS TEST 19

1. What was the importance of the writ system in the development of tort?   **(5)**

2. How far was liability for a wrong absolute in the early law?   **(6)**

3. What was the importance of the *Case of Thorns* (1466)?   **(8)**

4. Consider the development of the concept of strict liability in (a) *Leame* v. *Bray* (1803), (b) *Rylands* v. *Fletcher* (1868).   **(10)**

5. What was the legal significance of "common callings" in the medieval era?   **(13)**

6. Explain the significance of *Mitchil* v. *Alestree* (1676).   **(14)**

CHAPTER XX

PARTICULAR TORTS: TRESPASS, CONVERSION, DECEIT AND DEFAMATION

TRESPASS

1. General. Trespass, from which originated many of the personal actions, is mentioned at VII, 1–2.

(*a*) The writ first made its appearance *c.* 1250.

(*b*) It was based on an allegation of *vi et armis*.

(*c*) It was enforced by the threat of outlawry (*see* XVII, 24).

(*d*) During the time of Edward III writs of trespass were issued in which the *vi et armis* clause was not used. Plaintiff was considered as bringing an *action upon his case*, or *upon the special case*.

(*e*) The action on the case separated from trespass, so that, for example, the fifteenth century writer Fitzherbert was able to treat these as distinct types of action.

(*f*) From case developed, *e.g.* case for words (libel, slander), case for deceit, trover and assumpsit.

2. The modes of trespass. The wrongs which trespass sought to remedy were of three general types:

(*a*) Trespass to the person.

(*b*) Trespass to land.

(*c*) Trespass to chattels.

TRESPASS TO THE PERSON

3. General. From trespass to the person sprang in time specialised torts such as assault, battery, and false imprisonment.

(*a*) *Assault and battery.* *Assault* was considered as an act

258

by defendant which caused plaintiff to fear the infliction of immediate and unauthorised bodily harm. *Battery* was considered as the unauthorised and intentional application of force to a person. Even a slight application of force sufficed, *e.g.* the throwing of water. "The least touching of another in anger is a battery": *per* Holt, C. J., in *Cole* v. *Turner* (1704) 6 Mod.149. The battery complained of had to be direct; thus, in *Dodwell* v. *Burford* (1670) 1 Mod.24, X struck Y's horse which then galloped away and threw Y. Y was then injured by Z's horse which trampled on him. It was held that Y could not recover damages in trespass from X.

(*b*) *False imprisonment.* "Every confinement of the person is an imprisonment whether it be in a common prison or in a private house, or in the stocks, or even by forcibly detaining one in the public streets": Blackstone. The *Termes de la Ley* (*see* V, **28**(*a*)) spoke of the party so restrained as "a prisoner, so long as he hath not his liberty freely to go at all times to all places whither he will, without bail or mainprize."

TRESPASS TO LAND

4. General. The essence of trespass to land was any interference with the land or with any right in the land.

(*a*) In its early stages the action for trespass to land did not bring recovery of possession of the land, but merely damages. Recovery of possession could be obtained through the Assize of *Novel Disseisin* (*see* VI, **18**).

(*b*) *Contra pacem* had no application in the case of a wrong committed unintentionally or in the case of an omission.

(*c*) Defendant could maintain a claim of right, *e.g.* based on his assertion that he had entered plaintiff's land to gather crops which belonged to him.

(*d*) A plea of lawful justification might have sufficed, as where defendant entered plaintiff's lands in order to put out a fire which threatened defendant's property.

(*e*) Trespass *vi et armis* had no application to a case arising out of non-feasance: *Shapcott* v. *Mugford* (1696) 1 Ld. Raym.187.

5. The growth of nuisance. The tort of nuisance arises from an interference, not justified at law, with the use or enjoyment of land or of some right over it. Blackstone defined it as "any thing done to the hurt or annoyance of the lands, tenements, or hereditaments of another."

(a) *The assize of nuisance.* This assize developed as a supplement to the assize of novel disseisin. It provided for damages and an order of abatement, and was available for a loss of profit resulting from an interference by defendant with plaintiff's incorporeal rights, and, by Bracton's time, for any interference with plaintiff's land which made it uninhabitable. It could be employed where the act complained of was performed on defendant's land. The assize was available only to a freeholder and could be brought only against a freeholder.

(b) *The writ of quod permittat prosternere.* This was available to a freeholder where the land on which the nuisance arose had since been alienated. The writ (and the assize of nuisance) were abolished under the *Real Property Limitation Act*, 1833, *s.* 36.

(c) *Public nuisance.* This was interference with a communal right (*i.e.* the so-called "common nuisance") and became a plea of the crown.

(d) *Action upon the case for nuisance.* This action probably originated in the reign of Henry VI. Prior to its use, remedies for nuisance were not available in the case of a person suffering from a public nuisance, or in the case of nonfreeholder occupiers. Nor was the assize available in a case arising from omission. Action on the case provided a relatively simple process and was available to lessees. By the sixteenth century it had begun to supplant the assize. A disadvantage of the action was that it gave rise only to damages, and not to abatement.

TRESPASS TO CHATTELS

6. General. The tort of trespass to chattels occurs when there is any wrongful interference with the possession of those chattels. Prior to the appearance of the writ of trespass the principal remedies had been:

(a) The appeal of felony (*see* **7** below).

(*b*) The action based on an allegation of unlawful detention (*see* **8** below).

7. The appeal of felony (*appellum de felonia*). The appellant
had to allege that his chattels had been seized "*. . . in felonia,
vi et armis et contra pacem Domini Regis.*"

(*a*) The appeal was usually followed by proof of trial by
battle (*see* VI, **10**).

(*b*) It could be brought against a person who was in
possession of the goods, but who may have obtained them
legitimately.

(*c*) It could be brought by any person interested in the
safety of the goods.

(*d*) The appeal would not succeed where the alleged thief
had not been captured by the appellor, or where the goods
had not been found on him.

(*e*) Recovery of the goods followed on a successful appeal.

(*f*) The appeal had become obsolescent by the fifteenth
century.

8. The action alleging unlawful detention. This action
alleged unlawful detention of chattels and a refusal by defendant to surrender them on demand. The action of detinue (*see*
13 below) was based on a similar set of allegations.

9. Requisite of direct harm. In trespass to goods the harm
must be direct and not consequential. The harm may take a
variety of forms, *e.g.*: beating animals: *Slater* v. *Swann* (1730)
2 Stra.872; chasing cattle: *Farmer* v. *Hunt* (1610) 1 Brownl.
220; cutting down and removing trees: *Heyden* v. *Smith* (1610)
2 Brownl.329. There is no trespass to goods where the interference is indirect: *Covell* v. *Laming* (1808) 1 Camp.497.

10. Deficiencies of the writ of trespass in relation to chattels.
The essence of trespass was a wrongful action *vi et armis*.
Damages only were available. Recovery of goods did not
follow upon a successful action in trespass. The action could
not be brought against X, where X had unlawfully received
the goods from Y, who had obtained lawful possession of them.
The action failed to cover any loss incurred by the return of
damaged goods by defendant. Nor was the action available

in a case of injury due to non-feasance—"not doing is no trespass."

11. Development of trespass and associated actions. *Replevin, detinue sur trover, action on the case sur trover*, developed, with the result that wrongs which were outside the scope of the original writ of trespass and which involved interference with an owner's rights became actionable. The basis of the modern tort of trespass to goods remains, however, an interference with possession.

CONVERSION

12. The modern tort of conversion. Conversion is the wrongful act committed by a person who deals with goods which do not belong to him in such a manner that the title of the lawful owner is thereby denied. The action of *trover* was the remedy for conversion. It is considered at **15** below, together with *detinue* (**13**) and *replevin* (**14**), which were also actions concerned with interference with chattels.

13. Detinue. The remedy of detinue (*see* VII, **5**) was available where X unjustly detained Y's goods. It originated in the twelfth century and developed so that defendant had the alternative choice of surrendering the goods, or paying damages.

(*a*) In the fifteenth century *detinue sur trover* developed. This extended the scope of the remedy, but it was, nevertheless, defective.

    (*i*) Plaintiff could wage his law.
    (*ii*) It was of no avail in the case of goods returned in a damaged condition by defendant.
    (*iii*) A successful plaintiff could not enforce the return of the goods.

(*b*) Action on the case replaced detinue, but after wager of law was abolished in 1833 use of the action revived.

14. Replevin. *See* VII, **8**. Replevin was a remedy for one whose chattels had been unlawfully taken from him.

(*a*) In the Middle Ages it was used to decide questions

arising from wrongful distress, *i.e.* where a distrainee challenged the legality of an act whereby goods were seized from him by way of distress. The procedure following this was that the distrainor raised an "avowry," *i.e.* an admission of the distress supported by reasons for it, such as rent in arrear.

(*b*) Where the question of ownership of the goods was raised, e.g. where the distrainor claimed ownership, it was determined by an interlocutory hearing on the writ of *de proprietate probanda* ("the proof of ownership").

(*c*) In the fourteenth century, replevin was enlarged to include other cases involving the wrongful detention of chattels. But it had no application where the taking was not alleged to have been initially unlawful. Nor did it apply where the chattel had been transferred to a third party.

(*d*) Replevin is governed today by the *County Courts Act*, 1959. It may be sought only where plaintiff has been deprived of possession of chattels by an act of trespass.

15. Trover. *See* VII, **10.** Trover was an action on the case which was brought by P for the recovery of damages against D, who had found P's goods and unlawfully converted them to his (D's) use. The alleged loss and finding became fictitious by the mid-16th century, the use of the fiction enduring until it was abolished by the *Common Law Procedure Act*, 1852.

(*a*) "In form the action is a fiction, in substance a remedy to recover the value of personal chattels wrongly converted by another to his use": *per* Lord Mansfield in *Cooper* v. *Chitty* (1756) 1 Burr.

(*b*) *Trover and detinue.* By the seventeenth century trover had almost supplanted detinue. In the fifteenth century trover had been extended as a supplement to detinue, in a case of damage by defendant's bailee, and in a case of destruction by the possessor of the goods. By the end of the sixteenth century trover had been extended to cover misfeasance and non-feasance. In 1675, in a case in which P claimed that D was wrongfully detaining his goods, P's claim was allowed, and D's refusal to surrender the goods was considered to be a misfeasance: *Sykes* v. *Walls* (1675) 3 Keb. 282. Trover now almost covered detinue.

(*c*) *Trover and trespass.* It was decided in 1662 that a

plaintiff in an action concerning the taking of goods might elect between trespass and trover. The doctrine seemed to be that the unlawful moving of goods constituted not only trespass, but also conversion. That this was not invariably so was demonstrated in *Fouldes* v. *Willoughby* (1841) 8 M. & W. 540. X and two of his horses embarked on Y's boat. Before the journey commenced Y refused to carry the horses and X refused to take them ashore. Y then put the horses ashore and turned them loose. It was held that trover was no remedy, since, although Y's act may have constituted a trespass, it in no way interfered with X's rights of ownership.

(*d*) *Trover and replevin*. By the end of the 18th century trover had become an alternative to replevin.

DECEIT

16. Meaning of the term. The modern tort of deceit arises from a false statement of fact made knowingly or recklessly with the intent that another person shall act on it, with the result that it is acted on by that person who thereby suffers damage.

17. Origin and development. The thirteenth century writ of deceit was used against one who had utilised legal proceedings in order to deceive another, *e.g.* by impersonation.

(*a*) In the fourteenth century actions on the case were brought where defective goods had been warranted as sound.

(*b*) In the same century actions on the case were used so that P, who purchased cattle from D under the impression that they belonged to D, might receive damages when it was established that they really belonged to E.

(*c*) In 1534 Fitzherbert wrote: "This writ lieth properly where one man doth anything in the name of another, by which the other person is damnified and deceived."

(*d*) In *Bailey* v. *Merrell* (1616) 3 Bulstr., there was an important development when it was decided that a cause of action in deceit required fraud *and* consequent damages.

(*e*) In *Pasley* v. *Freeman* (1789) 3 T.R. 51, deceit made its appearance as a separate tort. D had given an assurance to

P that Z was a person to whom goods might be sold on credit with safety. D knew that this representation was false. P gave Z a credit of £2600 for the purchase of cochineal from P. P suffered loss as a result, and it was held that he had an action in tort for deceit.

(*f*) *Deceit and the Statute of Frauds* (1677). This statute required that a promise in the nature of a guarantee had to be written and signed, if it were to be the basis of an action.

(*i*) A method of evading the *Statute of Frauds* seemed obvious after *Pasley* v. *Freeman* (1789). D could assure P, knowing that his statement was untrue, that Z could be trusted and, as a result of this statement and its outcome P might have an action in tort for deceit. In such a case there was merely an oral statement, and not the type of promise with which the Statute was concerned.

(*ii*) The *Statute of Frauds Amendment Act*, 1828, *s.* 6, provided: "No action shall be brought whereby to charge any person upon or by reason of any representation or assurance made or given concerning or relating to the character, conduct, credit, ability, trade, or dealings of any other person, to the intent or purpose that such other person may obtain credit, money or goods upon, unless such representation or assurance be made in writing, signed by the party to be charged therewith."

DEFAMATION

18. Meaning. The essence of defamation is a wrong to a person's reputation. The modern tort arises from the publishing, without lawful justification, of a statement which exposes a person to hatred, ridicule or contempt, or which causes him harm in his office, trade or profession.

19. Libel and slander. A defamatory statement may constitute libel or slander.

(*a*) *Libel* is defamation by means of print, writing or some other permanent form.

(*b*) *Slander* is defamation by means of the spoken word, or a gesture.

(*c*) *The principal differences* between libel and slander are:

(*i*) Libel is always actionable *per se*; slander, subject to some few exceptions (*e.g.* imputation that plaintiff has a contagious venereal disease: *Bloodworth* v. *Gray* (1844) 7 Man & G. 334) is actionable only on proof of special damage.

(*ii*) Slander is not a crime, but a tort; a libel which tends to a breach of the peace is a crime.

DEFAMATION IN THE EARLY LAW

20. The Anglo-Saxon era. The verbal abuse of one person by another was considered, in some cases, to be an offence which merited harsh punishment in the form of the symbolic penalty of cutting out the tongue. This receives mention in the Dooms of Cnut. In other cases the payment of *wite* and *bot* (*see* XVII, **12**) could compensate for a verbal insult.

21. The early local courts. Local courts gave remedies for slanderous statements, often taking the form of a monetary fine and an apology. Thus, fines were imposed for the use of terms such as "whore," "thief," "sorceress," "faithless fellow." The remedies were available not only where the insulting words were uttered to plaintiff, but also where they were addressed by defendant to a third person. The essence of the remedies seems to have been the limitation of possible strife within the community.

22. The king's courts. In the early thirteenth century the king's courts did not provide a remedy for defamation. Statutory intervention in the development of the law of slander did follow later.

23. The church courts. The church courts came to acquire an extensive jurisdiction in cases of defamation, which canon law considered as a spiritual offence.

(*a*) The *diffamatus*, in canon law, was a person of alleged ill-repute who was brought to trial in the church courts merely on the basis of his reputation. But an acquittal implied that those who had falsely put about the allegation were guilty of a crime.

(*b*) Archbishop Langton, in 1222, promulgated excommunication for those who maliciously accused others of a crime so that they were defamed "among good and grave persons."

(*c*) The consistory courts (*see* XII, **28**) had jurisdiction in cases of grave slander, for which they could impose penalties involving a penance.

(d) The common law judges objected to the practice whereby a defendant who had been acquitted by the common law courts then brought proceedings for defamation in the church courts. Edward I enacted that prohibition might result in cases of this nature. In 1285 he enacted, in the *Statute Circumspecte Agatis*, that prohibition would be decreed in the case of a claim for money damages as a result of defamation. But the church courts continued to impose high costs in such actions and to commute severe penances so that defendant seemed to be paying monetary damages voluntarily.

(e) The jurisdiction of the Church courts in defamation was abolished by the *Ecclesiastical Courts Act*, 1855.

THE SLANDER OF MAGNATES—SCANDALUM MAGNATUM

24. Scandalum Magnatum, 1275. *The Statute of Westminster* I, 1275, enacted that a person who published scandalous statements or false information which tended to result in discord between the king and his subjects or the magnates was to be imprisoned until he produced the fabricator of that scandal or information.

(a) The statute was re-enacted in 1378, 1388, 1554, and 1559.

(b) In 1378 the term *magnatus* was construed as referring to prelates, peers, justices and other high officials.

(c) The re-enactments in the sixteenth century added penalties for seditious statements, gave jurisdiction in these matters to the justices of the peace, and introduced very severe punishments—the loss of the right hand for writings which offended against the statute, and the loss of the ears for spoken words which so offended.

(d) In the common law courts the rule grew by which words insufficiently precise to found an action at common law might support an action under the statute.

(e) The offence was abolished under the *Statute Law Revision Act*, 1888.

THE DEVELOPMENT OF LIBEL

25. Origins. The origins of libel may be found in the penalties of the old local courts in cases of insult, and in the offences derived from *scandalum magnatum*. Church law, too, made its contribution. By the seventeenth century the development of the law of libel had become inextricably mixed with political events; thus, enactments of Elizabeth seemed to consider private libel and sedition as offences of almost the same nature.

26. The Star Chamber. *See* XIV, **6.** The Star Chamber enforced rigorously those statutes under which *scandalum magnatum* had originated, and, as a result, it dealt with cases of libel as though that wrong had been a criminal offence.

(*a*) The spread of the printed word was a matter of particular concern to Star Chamber. In the *Case de libellis famosis* (1605), it was ruled that where a defamatory statement had appeared in written form, the proof of the truth of the statement was not material.

(*b*) Coke stated in 1606 that a libel could be prosecuted on indictment and also in the Star Chamber.

(*c*) Star Chamber was able not only to fine an offender, but could award damages to the person who had been injured by the libel—a recognition of libel as a crime and a tort.

27. After Star Chamber. Following the abolition of Star Chamber in 1641, its work was continued for a time by the Council of State under Cromwell. At the Restoration, however, King's Bench took over some of the former Star Chamber jurisdiction, and this led inevitably to the interaction of the developing law of libel and the law of slander.

28. Civil libel. In *King* v. *Lake* (1670) Hardres, 470, Hale, C. B., allowed an action on words considered as being insufficiently clear to form a slander at common law, but which in this case were written. Words which were written ("which contain more malice than if they had been spoken") were actionable *without special damage*.

THE DEVELOPMENT OF SLANDER

29. Action on the case for slander. By the reign of Henry VIII an action on the case for defamatory words could be brought. So, in 1535, a plaintiff was successful in an action in which it was alleged that defendant had spoken of him as a thief. It seemed essential, however, that the defamatory words should impute some criminal act. The reason for this may have been that the common law judges wished to distinguish words which they could consider actionable and words which would be actionable only in the church courts. Thus, to say of plaintiff that he was a heretic imputed an offence (heresy) recognised solely by the church courts; the imputation was not actionable, therefore, in a court of common law. To say of plaintiff that he was a "cunning thief" was to impute an offence which belonged to the jurisdiction of the common law courts; the imputation was, therefore, actionable in those courts.

NOTE: This led to the growth of highly artificial distinctions. In 'Holt v. Astgrigg (1608) Cro.Jac.184, defendant was alleged to have said that plaintiff had struck his cook so that his head had been cleaved, "the one part laying on one shoulder, and another part on the other." It was held that this did not impute an unlawful killing since the statement did not assert that the cook had been killed.

30. Other developments.

(a) Imputations of criminal offences were considered as actional *per se* (*i.e.* without proof of special damage).

(b) Words which damaged a man in his trade or profession (*e.g.* speaking of a doctor as a "drunken idiot") also became actionable *per se* in the seventeenth century. But with these and a few other exceptions it was essential to prove damage in an action for slander.

(c) Mere vulgar abuse was not considered as defamatory.

(d) Publication of the slander to a third party was necessary to the action. It was held, in *The Earl of Northampton's Case* (1612) 12 Rep.132, that the uttering of a defamatory statement might be justified if it merely repeated what another person had stated.

LIBEL AND THE LIBERTY OF THE PRESS

31. Following the Reformation. After printing had been invented in the fifteenth century, the growth of a free press was restricted severely.

(a) The Tudor *Treason Acts* dealt with the printing of matter considered to be treasonable, and the *imprimatur* of a royal licenser was needed before written works were published.

(b) Printing was restricted by patents, monopolies and a restriction on the number of presses and printers.

(c) Under Elizabeth, printing was allowed only in London, Oxford and Cambridge, and only by permission of the Archbishop of Canterbury, the Bishop of London, or the chief justices.

32. The seventeenth century. Restrictions upon the press continued.

(a) In 1637 the Star Chamber issued an ordinance limiting the number of master printers to twenty.

(b) Under the Stuarts, licences for printing books were required, and the peddling of books was prohibited.

(c) *The Licensing Act,* 1662, gave the control of printing to the government. Those who wrote and printed offensive works could be pilloried, flogged, mutilated, or hanged.

(d) In 1680, Scroggs, C. J., and twelve other judges declared that the publication of any matter concerning the government without royal licence was a common law crime. This was affirmed by Lord Holt in *R.* v. *Tutchin* (1704) 14 St.Tr.1095.

33. The eighteenth century

(a) In *Entick* v. *Carrington* (1765) 19 St.Tr.1030, it was held that the warrants under which an editor's books and papers had been seized were illegal.

(b) In *R.* v. *Almon* (1770) 20 St.Tr.803, it was held that the publisher of a libel was criminally liable for his servant's wrongful acts, unless he could establish that he had not assented to those acts. It was declared, also, that the judge alone was to determine the criminality of a libel.

(c) In *Fox's Libel Act*, 1792, "an Act to remove doubts respecting the functions of juries in cases of libel", the jury was empowered to state whether a publication constituted a seditious libel.

34. The Nineteenth century.

From 1792–1832, the so-called "period of reaction," the freedom of publishing was restrained, *e.g.* by the enactment in 1819 allowing courts, in the case of conviction of a publisher of a seditious libel, to seize copies of the libel. From the *Reform Act*, 1832, the freedom of the press became established.

(a) The *Parliamentary Papers Act*, 1840, "an Act to give summary protection to persons employed in the publication of Parliamentary papers" gave absolute privilege to reports of either House which were authorised by Parliament. In *Stockdale* v. *Hansard* (1839) 9 A. & E.,1, privilege had been claimed for a libellous statement published by order of the House. It was held that the House could not alter the law of the land by resolution so as to legalise an illegal act, and that the court would not be prevented from inquiring into the validity of privilege by a resolution of the House declaring that privilege. The 1840 Act terminated this controversy.

(b) *Lord Campbell's Libel Act*, 1843, "an Act to Amend the law respecting defamatory words and libel," allowed an apology in mitigation of damages in an action for libel "contained in any public newspaper or other periodical publication" (*s.* 2).

(c) The *Law of Libel Amendment Act*, 1888, stated: "A fair and accurate report in any newspaper of proceedings publicly heard before any court ... shall, if published contemporaneously with such proceedings, be privileged...." (*s.* 3).

PROGRESS TEST 20

1. What was the essence of trespass to land? **(4)**
2. Explain the assize of nuisance. **(5)**
3. What was the writ *quod permittat prosternere*? **(5)**
4. What was the appeal of felony? **(7)**
5. In what sense was the writ of trespass deficient in relation to chattels? **(10)**

6. Explain the remedy of *replevin*. **(14)**

7. How did *trover* come to cover *detinue*? **(15)**

8. What was the origin of *deceit*? **(17)**

9. How was defamation considered by the church courts? **(23)**

10. Explain *scandalum magnatum*. **(24)**

11. What were the origins of libel? **(25)**

12. Explain the significance of (a) the *Earl of Northampton's Case* (1612), (b) *the Licensing Act*, 1662, (c) *Stockdale* v. *Hansard* (1839). **(30, 32, 34)**

PART SIX

THE DEVELOPMENT OF CONTRACT
AND LAND LAW

CHAPTER XXI

THE DEVELOPMENT OF CONTRACT—1

THE MEANING OF CONTRACT

1. Definition. A contract is an agreement which creates obligations between the parties which are enforceable by law.

2. Elements of a valid contract. In the modern, developed law of contract, the following are the essentials of a valid contract:

(*a*) There must be an intention to create legal relations.

(*b*) The parties to the agreement must have legal capacity to contract.

(*c*) The agreement must be of a legal nature and its object must be possible.

(*d*) There must be genuine consent by both parties to the terms of the agreement.

(*e*) The agreement must be under seal, or there must be valuable consideration (*see* XXII).

(*f*) The agreement must be based on an offer and acceptance.

3. Types of contract. The three principal types of contract are:

(*a*) *Contracts of record*, *i.e.* obligations imposed by a court, *e.g.* a recognisance.

(*b*) *Specialty contracts*, *i.e.* contracts under seal, or deed.

(*c*) *Simple or parol contracts*, *i.e.* contracts made orally or in writing, without seal, or inferred from the conduct of the parties.

EARLY HISTORY OF CONTRACT

4. General. The historical sources of contract are to be found in the common law, in equity, and in legislation.

K   275

(a) The courts of common law fashioned the basic rules.

(b) Equity supplied remedies such as specific performance and the injunction.

(c) Legislation concerning contract has been extensive, e.g. *Statute of Frauds,* 1677, *Infants' Relief Act,* 1874, *Sale of Goods Act,* 1893.

5. Contract in the early courts. In the Anglo-Saxon era an agreement in the nature of a contract was enforced only under certain very restricted conditions, and not as a general rule. A widespread observance and enforcement of agreements in the nature of contract presupposes a level and pattern of exchange and trade which did not exist in Anglo-Saxon times. The courts of that era lacked the means to enforce this type of agreement. The king's judges, according to Glanvill, were not usually concerned with "private agreements."

6. Contract in Anglo-Saxon times. An agreement in the nature of a contract could be concluded in a very few cases.

(a) A, the promisor, delivered to B, the promisee, or to C, a third party, a *wed.*

(b) The *wed* was an article of some value and it acted as security for A's carrying out the agreement.

NOTE: *Wed* (derived from the Teutonic *wadjom*) was known after the Conquest as a *gage.* The early *wedding* was, in essence, an agreement for the sale of the right of guardianship over a woman.

(c) This type of contractual agreement was used as the preliminary to a marriage, or in order to bind a defendant to attend court proceedings.

(d) Following the Conquest, the *bohr* (known also as a *pledge*) acted as a personal surety.

(e) The *gage* came to be replaced by a symbolic article or an amount of money.

7. The church and agreement. When an agreement was made in some kind of formal terms it often involved a pledge of faith. Following the Conquest the church set up its right to control agreements which had been made on the basis of an oath (which was always religious in nature).

(*a*) Such agreements, known as *fides facta*, were enforced by the *courts Christian*, and their breach could involve a severe penance.

(*b*) The common law courts objected to this jurisdiction and attempted to end it by prohibitions. In fact, the jurisdiction continued for several centuries.

(*c*) The church courts were concerned with the *laesio fidei* (*breach of faith*). At common law, however, faith alone was not considered as evidence of a claim based on debt. *Ex nudo pacto non oritur actio*—no action can arise from a nude contract. The so-called *nudum pactum* was a "bare agreement" which could not be enforced. (Today, for example, an agreement not under seal, and lacking consideration, might be considered as a *nudum pactum*.)

THE COMMON LAW REMEDIES

8. General. In the thirteenth century, the common law courts had developed writs and appropriate actions in the case of agreements in the nature of contract. The four writs were: *detinue, debt, covenant, account.*

9. Detinue. *See* VII, 5. Detinue was available to recover a chattel. It could apply to the case of money, which was considered in early times as a chattel.

(*a*) It was an inadequate remedy, since defendant, who had agreed to deliver a chattel and had failed to do so, was not compelled to deliver it as the result of this action. He could pay its price to plaintiff.

(*b*) Plaintiff had no remedy if defendant returned the chattel in a damaged state.

(*c*) Defendant could wage his law.

DEBT

10. The writ of debt. *See* VII, **6.** The writ of debt was employed as a method of enforcing many types of claim.

(*a*) *Debt on the record.* Judgment debts could be enforced by the writ. It was also used to collect customary dues and penalties resulting from a breach of by-laws.

(*b*) *Debt on an obligation.* Where defendant's obligation

arose on a deed, properly signed and sealed, he was bound absolutely and the writ was used to enforce that obligation. Defendant was not allowed to wage his law.

(c) *Debt on a contract.* The writ lay, *e.g.* where P had lent money or sold goods to D.

(i) In all cases of debt on a contract, P had conferred some benefit on D, as a result of which D was obliged to pay money to P.

(ii) In the early fourteenth century the phrase *quid pro quo* (something for something) described this.

(iii) In 1338 an action in debt was heard on the following facts: D appointed P to act as his attorney for an annual fee. P carried out his duties, but D failed to pay. D claimed that he had not agreed by deed and, hence, that he was not liable. This was not accepted, since P had conferred a benefit upon D by carrying out his duties. "Here you have his service for his allowance, of which knowledge may be had, and you have *quid pro quo*": *per* Sharshulle, J.

(iv) An exception to *quid pro quo* emerged in the fifteenth century. A seller of goods could sue in debt for the price before the goods were delivered to the buyer. Detinue was available to the buyer before he had paid the price.

11. Deficiencies of debt. The deficiences of this form of action were severe.

(a) The procedural technicalities were burdensome. *See* VII, **20.** A slight error in the writ or the pleadings vitiated plaintiff's chance of success.

(b) Wager of law was available, unless the action arose on a sealed deed.

(c) Wager of law precluded the bringing of the action against defendant's executors.

(d) Production of a deed prevented D's pleading that he had been discharged. (D could plead, however, that the seal was not his—*non est factum.*)

(e) The action was available only in the case of a liquidated sum. It was not available for the recovery of a sum which was neither precise nor fixed. *Quantum meruit* claims could not be made by use of the writ.

COVENANT

12. Use of the writ. The writ *quod conventio teneatur* was
in use by the first half of the thirteenth century and was employed at that time in the case of agreements involving the
protection of lessees. It could be used also for the recovery of
unliquidated damages where defendant had failed to perform
an act. The use of sealed writing was alone considered as
evidence for the covenant. "No plea of covenant can be without deed and every man ought to be judged according to his
deed": Fitzherbert. Secondary evidence was allowed only at
the end of the eighteenth century. This insistence on a seal
led to the later concept that a seal imports consideration.
Wager of law was not possible in covenant.

13. Deficiencies. The principal limitation on the use of the
writ was the necessity for a seal.

(*a*) The action could be brought originally for the recovery
of a debt.

(*b*) Where defendant had undertaken to pay a definite
amount of money to a plaintiff, *debt*, and *not covenant*, had
to be used.

ACCOUNT

14. Use of the writ. *See* VII, 7. Account was used in the
case of agents who had received money for their principals, or
bailiffs, or guardians.

(*a*) The action was extended so that a principal could
recover money paid to defendant for the performance of an
action which had not been carried out.

(*b*) In *Hewer* v. *Bartholomew* (1598) Cro.Eliz.614, account
was made available for the recovery of money which had
been paid in error.

15. Procedure. The procedure was technical and complex.

(*a*) The court first decided whether defendant came
within the scope of account.

(*b*) Plaintiff and defendant were examined in great detail
by auditors as to the transactions and sums of money
claimed.

(*c*) Plaintiff would have to bring a writ of debt to recover the sum of money due, should plaintiff fail to pay after judgment.

16. Deficiencies. The procedure was very slow, and wager of law was possible. The writ was, nevertheless, widely used in medieval times.

THE GENERAL DEFICIENCIES OF COMMON LAW REMEDIES

17. Inadequacy of the remedies. In general, the common law remedies for contract were dilatory, limited in scope, and increasingly out of step with the growth in trade and commerce. In particular:

(*a*) Agreements to convey land were not recognised unless under seal.

(*b*) The remedies failed to provide for *quantum meruit* claims.

(*c*) The remedies failed to provide for claims for goods delivered, unless the sum had been fixed.

18. Chancery and contract. Because of the limited nature of the remedies available at common law, the chancellor received an increasing number of petitions praying for his intervention. As a result new remedies and procedures were provided in chancery, *e.g.* executory agreements were enforced, land was ordered to be conveyed even in the absence of sealed writing, and defendants were heard on oath.

ACTION ON THE CASE

19. Background. Under the impetus of the competing jurisdiction exercised by the chancellor and the church courts (in spite of prohibitions), the common law courts sought an effective remedy for breaches of contractual agreements. The remedy was found by developing the action on the case.

(*a*) In *Waldon* v. *Marshall* (1370), P alleged that D had undertaken to cure P's horse, and that D's careless treatment of the horse had resulted in its death. D pleaded that P was attempting to sue on a promise and that the remedy should have been covenant, but that as there was no deed (*see* **12** above) there was no remedy. Judgment was given for P because he had suffered damage as a result of D's conduct.

(*b*) In the following years judgment was given for plaintiffs in actions against surgeons who had treated their patients negligently, and against farriers who had injured horses while shoeing them.

20. Misfeasance. Where D had undertaken with P to perform an action and had performed it badly, causing injury to P as a result, P could bring an action of *case* for this misfeasance. "So if a smith makes a covenant with me to shoe my horse well and properly, and he shoes him and lames him, I shall have a good action": *per* Newton, in 1436. Where D undertook, for example, to keep a horse and then failed to provide for it, an action could be brought.

21. Non-feasance. Case could not be used as a remedy for non-feasance. In 1503 it was declared that no action on the case could be brought against a carpenter who had undertaken to build a house and had not carried out any part of his undertaking. In such cases covenant was considered the appropriate remedy. "If a covenant is made with me to keep my horse for me or to carry my goods, and nothing more is done, then an action of covenant lies and no other action, since in such cases defendant only fails to keep a promise": *per* Townshend, J., in 1486.

22. Developments in the sixteenth century. In the early part of the sixteenth century an important development took place.

(*a*) In 1505, Frowyk, C. J., stated: "If I sell you my land and covenant to *enfeoff* you [*i.e.* to invest you with that land] and do not, you shall have a good action on the case, and this is adjudged."

(*b*) In 1506, Fineux, C. J., stated: "If one makes a covenant to build me a house by a certain day, and he does nothing about it, I shall have *action sur mon cas* [action on my case] as much as if he had been guilty of a misfeasance; for I am damaged by this."

(*c*) Thus the distinction between misfeasance and

nonfeasance was no longer important and the form of action developed in these circumstances was known as *assumpsit*—the appropriate writ declared that defendant had taken upon himself (*assumpsit per se*) to perform some action.

(*d*) *Assumpsit* became an action which was available to P where D had promised P to perform an action and had not carried it out at all, or had carried it out badly.

(*e*) In *Jordan's Case* (1528) assumpsit was held to be an appropriate action arising out of defendant's breach of promise.

INDEBITATUS ASSUMPSIT

23. Assumpsit, debt and detinue. *Assumpsit* soon mounted in favour with litigants. Debt and detinue involved wager of law; *assumpsit* did not involve this, and plaintiff could sue not only defendant, but defendant's executors. Hence *assumpsit* eventually replaced debt.

24. Slade's Case (1602) 4 Co.Rep.926. Plaintiff, John Slade, declared that he had bargained and sold wheat and corn growing at Rack Park, to the defendant, Humphrey Morley, and that Morley had failed to pay on the date fixed by the parties.

(*a*) Plaintiff sued, not in debt, but on an *assumpsit*.

(*b*) The jury found that there had been a bargain and sale, but did not find that defendant had made an express promise to pay at the time.

(*c*) The case was adjourned into the Exchequer Chamber for consideration by all the common law judges, and then to Serjeants' Inn. Coke presented Slade's case, Bacon presented Morley's case.

(*d*) It was resolved that plaintiff could recover, the resolution stating, in effect:

(*i*) That *indebitatus assumpsit* [*i.e.*, a type of *assumpsit* in which plaintiff declares that the defendant was already indebted and had undertaken to pay a certain sum of money] was, at the choice of plaintiff, an alternative to debt.

(*ii*) That a recovery in *assumpsit* barred an action of debt.

(*iii*) That the very existence of a debt sufficed for the court to presume an undertaking to pay it. "*Every contract executory imports in itself an assumpsit.*"

(e) The results of this case were of great significance. Case was now an alternative to debt. *Special assumpsit* (i.e. based on an express undertaking) was differentiated from *indebitatus assumpsit* (i.e. presumed from a previous debt). The stage had now been set for the enforcement of implied contracts.

FURTHER DEVELOPMENTS

25. Claim on a quantum meruit. (*Quantum meruit* = as much as he had earned.) Assume that P had undertaken to make a pair of shoes for D, but that there had been no express agreement as to price. P could not bring an action in debt (*see* VII, **6**) and *special assumpsit* was not appropriate in the absence of an express stipulation. In the seventeenth century *assumpsit* was used to imply an undertaking to pay for services performed.

(a) In *Warbrooke* v. *Griffin* (1609) 2 Brownl. 254, it was held that an innkeeper could sue for services rendered to guests. "It is an implied promise ... of the part of the guest that he will pay all the duties and charges which he caused in the house."

(b) In *Nicholls* v. *Moore* (1661) 1 Sid. 36, it was held that a carrier "like a tailor" was liable for negligence, although no price for his services had been fixed.

26. Quasi-Contract. In the seventeenth century actions of *assumpsit* were employed where a contract did not exist, *but could be implied*.

(a) In *Tomkyns* v. *Barnet* (1693) Skin.411, the action of *indebitatus assumpsit* was used where plaintiff had paid money to defendant in error.

(b) In *Martin* v. *Sitwell* (1691) 1 Show.156, plaintiff recovered a premium paid on a policy which was void because he had no insurable interest.

(c) In *City of London Corporation* v. *Gorry* (1677) 2 Lev. 174, the action was used to recover dues from defendant, although there had been no express promise to pay them.

(d) In these cases defendants' liabilities had not arisen out of consent, but were considered as examples of an *obligatio quasi ex contractu* (an obligation arising as if from a contract). Cases of this nature were classified as *quasi-contract.*

PROGRESS TEST 21

1. Under what circumstances was an agreement in the nature of a contract enforced in the Anglo-Saxon courts? **(5, 6)**

2. Explain (a) *wed*, (b) *fides facta*. **(6, 7)**

3. What were the writs available in the thirteenth century in cases of agreements in the nature of a contract? **(8)**

4. Explain the nature of *debt on a contract*. **(10)**

5. What were the deficiencies of *debt*? **(11)**

6. In what circumstances was *covenant* used? **(12)**

7. What type of procedure was employed in *account*? **(15)**

8. What important developments took place in the early sixteenth century concerning the development of *assumpsit*? **(22)**

9. Explain the significance of *Slade's Case* (1602). **(24)**

10. What was the importance of (a) *Warbrooke* v. *Griffin* (1609), (b) *Tomkyns* v. *Barnet* (1693)? **(25, 26)**

CHAPTER XXII

THE DEVELOPMENT OF CONTRACT—2

CONSIDERATION

1. Definition. "A valuable consideration in the sense of the
law may consist either in some right, interest, profit or benefit
accruing to one party, or some forebearance, detriment, loss or
responsibility given, suffered, or undertaken by the other" : *per*
Lush, J., in *Currie* v. *Misa* (1875) L.R.10 Ex.153. "Consideration means something which is of value in the eye of the law,
moving from the plaintiff: it may be some detriment to the
plaintiff or some benefit to the defendant" : *per* Patteson, J., in
Thomas v. *Thomas* (1842) 2 Q.B.851.

2. Executory and executed consideration. *Executory consideration* consists of a promise to confer a benefit, or to suffer
a detriment at some time in the future. *Executed consideration*
is that which has been wholly performed when the contract is
entered into by one or both parties.

3. Rules of consideration. The general rules are:

(*a*) Every simple contract must be supported by consideration.

(*b*) Consideration must be legal.

(*c*) Consideration must not be past.

(*d*) Consideration must move from the promisee.

(*e*) Consideration must be something that the promisee is
not already legally bound to do.

(*f*) Consideration need not be adequate, but it must be of
some value.

4. Source of the doctrine. The following suggestions have
been made concerning the origin of consideration.

(*a*) The doctrine may have originated in the jurisdiction
of the chancellor, who may have developed it from the
Roman concept of *causa*.

(b) It may have originated in the doctrine of *quid pro quo* (*see* XXI, **10**).

5. Assumpsit and consideration. The action of assumpsit (*see* XXI) raised the question: *would the courts of law accept a gratuitous promise as binding?*

(a) By the mid-sixteenth century it had been decided that some element of consideration was necessary, *i.e.* in order to succeed in the action, plaintiff should have given some consideration for the promise made by defendant.

(b) In *Wichals* v. *Johns* (1599) Cro. Eliz. 703, Popham, C. J., stated: "There is a mutual promise the one to the other, so that if plaintiff fails to discharge his promise defendant may have his action against him; and a promise against a promise is a good consideration."

CONSIDERATION AS MERELY EVIDENCE

6. Lord Mansfield's dictum. In the eighteenth century Lord Mansfield challenged the significance of the doctrine of consideration.

(a) In *Pillans* v. *Van Mierop* (1765) 3 Burr.1663, it was held that a written undertaking to honour a bill of exchange was binding on the party who had given the undertaking, although there was no consideration for it. *Per* Lord Mansfield: "I take it that the ancient notion about the want of consideration was for the sake of evidence only. . . . In commercial cases among merchants, the want of consideration is not an objection."

(b) Thus, the decision was to the effect that consideration *was no more than evidence that the parties intended to be bound*; it was not necessary to a contract, therefore, if their intention could be established by any other means.

7. The overruling of Lord Mansfield's view. Lord Mansfield's view was overruled in *Rann* v. *Hughes* (1778) 7 T.R.350. In that case an administratrix had personally undertaken and promised to pay money due from an estate. It was held that there was no consideration for the promise and, hence, the undertaking would not be enforced. *Per* Skynner, L.C.B.: "The law of this country supplies no means, nor affords any remedy, to compel the performance of an agreement made without sufficient consideration. . . . If they [the contracts] be merely written and not specialties, they are parol, and a consideration must be proved."

MORAL OBLIGATION AND MOTIVE AS CONSIDERATION

8. Lord Mansfield's view. Mansfield attempted to establish that a moral obligation was a sufficient consideration.

(a) In *Hawkes* v. *Saunders* (1782) 1 Cowper, 289, an executrix who had promised to pay a legacy was held liable upon that promise. *Per* Lord Mansfield: "Where a man is under a legal or equitable duty to pay, the law implies a promise, though none was ever actually made. *A fortiori* a legal or equitable duty is a sufficient consideration for an actual promise. . . . The ties of conscience upon an upright mind are a sufficient consideration."

(b) In *Lee* v. *Muggeridge* (1813) 5 Taunton, 36, a woman had promised that her executors would settle a debt which had been incurred as the result of a loan to her son-in-law. No consideration had been given for the promise. It was *held* that the executors were liable, since the moral obligation to honour the promise sufficed as consideration. *Per* Gibbs, J.: "It cannot, I think, be disputed now that, wherever there is a moral obligation to pay a debt or perform a duty, a promise to perform that duty or pay that debt will be supported by the previous moral obligation."

9. Rejection of Lord Mansfield's view. In *Eastwood* v. *Kenyon* (1840) 11 Ald. & El.438, Lord Mansfield's view was rejected. Plaintiff had incurred expenses in the education and maintenance of a girl to whom he was guardian. He borrowed money to enable him to do this, and the girl, when she became of age, promised to repay the loan. She later married defendant who also made a promise to repay. Plaintiff, relying on *Lee* v. *Muggeridge*, sued defendant on his promise. It was *held* that plaintiff could not recover. There was no consideration to support defendant's promise and the mere moral obligation was not sufficient. *Per* Denman, C. J., "[To accept a moral obligation as a sufficient consideration] would annihilate the necessity for any consideration at all, inasmuch as the mere fact of giving a promise creates a moral obligation to perform it."

10. Motive and consideration. In *Thomas* v. *Thomas* (1842) 2 Q.B.851, P's husband, before his death, declared that he wished his wife, P, to have the use of a particular house. After his death, D, his executor, agreed to allow P to occupy the house in consideration of her husband's wishes and payment of £1 p.a. towards the ground rent. Although the court accepted that the £1 p.a. was valuable consideration and the agreement was, therefore, binding, they rejected the wishes of the husband as of no relevance in this issue—motives which had contributed to D's promise did not constitute consideration.

THE CLASSIFICATION OF CONSIDERATION

11. General classification. Consideration is classified as executory and executed (*see* 2 above). *Past consideration* consists of an act, or a forebearance to act, sufficient in itself to support a contract, but neither done nor exercised in pursuance of a contract, yet subsequently giving rise to a promise. The modern doctrine is that past consideration is not sufficient for a contract. (There are some exceptions to this general rule: *e.g.*, under the *Bills of Exchange Act*, 1882, *s.* 27, by which consideration for a bill can be constituted by any consideration which suffices to support a simple contract, or by any antecedent debt or liability.)

12. Roscorla v. Thomas (1842) 3 Q.B.234. The doctrine of past consideration was established in this case. Plaintiff had bought a horse from defendant and after the sale defendant had promised that the horse was sound and free from vice. It proved to be vicious and ferocious. It was *held* that defendant's promise was made following the sale and was not supported by any fresh consideration. Since plaintiff could show only past consideration, his action failed.

13. Services performed at the request of defendant. The precise differences between past and executed consideration were discussed by the courts.

(*a*) The problem was: *could assumpsit be brought where*

plaintiff had performed a service for defendant without an
agreement as to payment, and defendant had later promised
payment?

(b) *Lampleigh* v. *Braithwait* (1615) 80 E.R.255. Defendant, D, had feloniously killed X and had asked P, the plaintiff, to do all that he could in order to obtain a pardon from the
King. P rode hard between London and Newmarket, at his
own expense, and D afterwards promised to pay him £100 to
meet his expense. D failed to pay and P sued in *assumpsit*.
D argued that the consideration was past. It was *held* that
P's services had been obtained by D's previous request, and
P was given judgment. "It was agreed that a mere voluntary
courtesy will not have a consideration to uphold an *Assumpsit*. But if that courtesy were moved by a suit or request of
the party that gives the *Assumpsit*, it will bind, for the
promise, though it follows, yet it is not naked, but couples
itself with the suit before." Thus D's request, together with
his promise, constituted an executed consideration.

THE ADEQUACY OF CONSIDERATION

14. The courts and adequacy of consideration. Not every act
or promise will constitute consideration, but the courts will not
enquire into the adequacy of consideration.

(a) The consideration should be capable of assessment in
terms of economic value. In *White* v. *Bluett* (1853) 23 L.J.
Ex. 36, plaintiff alleged that defendant had failed to pay a
promissory note given to his father in his lifetime. Defendant
claimed that his father had released him from the note in
return for a promise to cease complaining about his having
been disinherited. It was *held* that the promise to cease
complaining was not adequate consideration to support release from the note.

(b) The amount of money which constitutes the consideration is of no concern to the court, although obviously inadequate consideration might be taken into account in an
action founded on alleged fraud or duress. In *Sturlyn* v.
Albany (1587) Cro.Eliz.67, it was stated: "When a thing is
to be done by the plaintiff, be it never so small, this is sufficient consideration to ground an action." *See* also *Thomas* v.
Thomas (1842), at **10** above, where a promise to pay £1 p.a.
was held to be good consideration.

(c) A promise to forebear, even where the promise is implicit, is sufficient consideration. In *Alliance Bank* v. *Broom* (1864) 2 Dr. & Sm.289, X owed a large sum to his bankers and, as a result of their demands, he promised security to cover his debt. He did not provide the security and was sued on the promise. X agreed that there was no consideration for his promise. The bank was given judgment. *Per* Kindersley, V. C.: "When plaintiffs demanded payment of their debt and in consequence of that application defendant agreed to give security, although there was no promise on the part of plaintiffs to abstain for any certain time from suing for the debt, the effect was that the plaintiffs did in fact give, and the defendant received, the benefit of some degree of forebearance."

15. Plaintiff bound by an existing contractual duty. Where plaintiff promises to carry out, or carries out, a duty which rests on him as the result of an existing contract between plaintiff and defendant, there is no consideration.

(a) In *Stilk* v. *Myrick* (1809) 2 Camp. 317, two seamen deserted during a voyage. The captain could not replace them and he agreed with the remaining crew that if they completed the voyage they would receive their wages plus the wages of the deserters. It was *held* that the promise of the captain was not binding since there was no consideration. The crew were bound by their original contract to do everything possible to complete the voyage.

(b) In *Hartley* v. *Ponsonby* (1857) 7 E. & B.872, some members of a ship's crew deserted and the captain promised an additional £40 to each of the remaining seamen in order to complete the voyage. It was later found that there would be danger in sailing the ship with a reduced crew. It was *held* that the crew's original agreement did not oblige them to sail an unseaworthy ship, and their promise to sail with reduced numbers was consideration for the captain's promise.

16. Promise to pay less than the amount due. Assume that X owes Y £100, and that he repays, or promises to repay Y £75 in return for Y's promise to forgo the £25. Is Y liable on his promise? The general rule is that Y is not liable, since X has provided no consideration.

(a) In *Pinnel's Case* (1602) 5 Co. Rep.117a, Pinnel sued Cole in Debt for the sum of £8. 10s. which was due on a bond on November 11th, 1600. Cole pleaded that, at the request of Pinnel, he had paid him £5. 2s. 6d. on October 1st, and that Pinnel had accepted the sum in full satisfaction of the debt. Pinnel was given judgment on a technical fault arising out of the pleadings, but the court declared that it would have given Cole judgment, because the part payment had been made on a day earlier than that stated in the bond. "Payment of a lesser sum on the day in satisfaction of a greater cannot be any satisfaction for the whole, because it appears to the Judges that by no possibility can a lesser sum be a satisfaction to the plaintiff for a greater sum. But the gift of a horse, hawk, or robe, etc. in satisfaction is good. For it shall be intended that a horse, hawk, or robe, etc. might be more beneficial to plaintiff than the money in respect of some circumstance, or otherwise the plaintiff would not have accepted of it in satisfaction. . . ."

(b) In *Foakes* v. *Beer* (1884) 9 App.Cas.605 the facts were: B had obtained judgment against F for £2,090, and F had asked for time to pay this. They agreed in writing that B would not take any proceedings on the judgment if F paid immediately the sum of £500, and the remainder of the sum in instalments. The agreement did not refer to the interest on the judgment debt. After F had paid the entire debt, B claimed an additional £360 as interest. F refused to pay and pleaded the agreement, but B claimed that it was not supported by any consideration. Judgment was given for B, since payment of the smaller sum was not consideration for the promise to accept this sum in satisfaction of the debt plus interest. (*See*, concerning this problem, the modern case of *Central London Property Trust, Ltd.* v. *High Trees House, Ltd.* [1947] K.B. 130.)

PROGRESS TEST 22

1. What suggestions have been made concerning the origin of the doctrine of consideration? **(4)**

2. What was the significance of *Pillans* v. *Van Mierop* (1765)? **(6)**

3. Outline the development of Lord Mansfield's attempt to establish moral obligation as a sufficient consideration. **(8, 9)**

4. What was the significance in the development of the doctrine

of consideration of (a) *Lampleigh* v. *Braithwait* (1615), (b) *Roscorla* v. *Thomas* (1842)?   **(12, 13)**

5. Enumerate some of the cases which determined the doctrine that the court will not enquire into the adequacy of consideration. **(14)**

6. What was the importance of *Pinnel's Case* (1602)?   **(16)**

CHAPTER XXIII

THE DEVELOPMENT OF LAND LAW—1

LAND LAW IN LEGAL HISTORY

1. The importance of land. In the primitive and non-industrial forms of society, the main source of the community's wealth is land. Wealth is produced, primarily, by man working on natural resources, the most important of which is land. Thus, he who holds land holds economic power, and the ownership of land becomes the basis of political power. Legal doctrines and institutions spring up in order to deal with matters such as the ownership and conveyancing of land and with disputes arising out of these matters. Hence, in early English law, the development of the law of the land reflects, in considerable measure, the development of society.

2. The importance of land law. From the early land law arose many doctrines which affected other sections of our law. Thus, the early limitations on the free transfer of land led to the invention of the use (*see* X), which in turn led to the trust, upon which was built the fabric of the modern law of trusts. The ownership of land was, for centuries, linked with the right to vote and the right to sit as a member of a jury—both central themes of constitutional law. There are few sections of English law untouched at some point by the doctrines and procedures of the law of real property.

3. Feudal and medieval concepts in land law. Much of the law of land was developed and determined in the context of feudalism (*see* II, 5–7) and the medieval period. In some cases (*e.g.* concerning future interests) the reasoning behind the doctrines is itself medieval in pattern. In particular, the terminology of land law is feudal and medieval in origin. Thus: *tenant, freehold, leasehold, fee simple, entail, incorporeal hereditaments, use, mortgage*—all terms employed in the modern land law—originate in the thought and vocabulary of feudal and medieval England.

4. The principal problems of land law. The following matters are of prime importance in land law:

(*a*) *In what modes may land be held?*—the doctrine of tenures (*see* **5–29** below).

(*b*) *What is the extent of these holdings?*—the doctrine of estates (*see* **30–42** below).

(*c*) *What is meant by "possession" of land?*—the doctrine of *seisin* (*see* XXIV, **1–5**).

(*d*) *How is the title to land transferred?*—the procedure of conveyancing (*see* XXIV, **6–13**).

(*e*) *How is land recovered in an action?*—the forms of action (*see* XXIV, **14–19**).

NOTE: Anglo-Saxon land tenure is considered at I, **14–17**, uses at X, **3–12**, and mortgages and the equity of redemption at X, **13–17**.

TENURES

5. The concept of tenure. Under feudalism as it developed after the Conquest, all land was held of the king. Tenure was considered as existing only as long as the tenant carried out his duties to his lord. Hence:

(*a*) All land is held of some superior lord, *e.g.* the king, a tenant-in-chief, etc.

(*b*) He who *possesses* the land is merely a tenant.

(*c*) The mode of possession is known as *tenure*.

6. Growth of sub-infeudation. *See* II, **6**. Because land was the principal form of wealth the process of sub-infeudation grew rapidly. The process was this:

(*a*) The king granted land to a tenant-in-chief, A.

(*b*) A created a sub-tenancy by transferring part of his holding to B.

(*c*) B created a further tenancy by transferring part of his holding to C.

(*d*) In each case the transferee was a tenant of the transferor.

7. The Statute Quia Emptores, 1290. Edward I and his lords wished, for political reasons, to prevent the growth of sub-infeudation, and in 1290 the Statute *Quia Emptores* was enacted. It took its name from the beginning of its preamble—"Since purchasers. . . ."

(*a*) Every freeman was allowed to alienate the whole or part of his land at his pleasure (except by will) and without the consent of his lord.

(*b*) If part only of the land were alienated the services attached to the land were to be apportioned.

(*c*) Every alienee was to hold the land not of the alienor, but of the lord from whom the alienor had held previously.

(*d*) The crown was not bound by this enactment.

(*e*) The results of the Statute were:

(*i*) Sub-infeudation virtually ceased, and many *seignories* (*i.e.* lordships) became vested in the crown.

(*ii*) Tenants-in-chief (*i.e.* those who held directly from the king) did not benefit from the Statute and they continued to require a licence from the king if they wished to alienate. The licence was given on payment of a fine. In 1327 Edward III allowed his tenants-in-chief to alienate freely without a licence, on payment of a fine. The fines were abolished under the *Tenures Abolition Act*, 1660.

(*iii*) The king continued to create new tenures.

FORMS OF TENURE

8. Variety of forms. The mode in which land was held depended upon the services due from the tenant. These were various, and reflected, in part, the social status of the tenant. In the reign of Edward I tenures existed in the following forms:

(*a*) *Free tenures*: knight service; serjeanties; spiritual tenure; free socage. In the case of free tenures the services involved were considered to be rendered freely.

(*b*) *Unfree tenures or copyholds*: forms of villein tenure. The services rendered were of a servile character.

(*c*) *Customary tenures*: *e.g. gavelkind, borough English.*

KNIGHT SERVICE

9. Origin. Knight service, the main feudal free tenure, originated in the necessity of keeping an armed force. The tenure was based on military services rendered in return for the grant of land.

(a) Originally the tenants, who were the king's tenants-in-chief, *i.e.* the great nobles, were required to serve the king by military service within the realm for 40 days each year if called upon.

(b) They were obliged to provide a fixed number of armed horsemen, usually in multiples of five (probably based upon the unit of ten knights—the *constabularia*).

10. Development. In about 1166, *scutage* (a money payment —*scutagium* = shield money) began to replace the provision of fighting men. It was levied at first on those who held by knight service but who could not themselves fight or provide soldiers, *e.g.* the church landowners. Scutage grew and soon became the accepted mode of levy upon all tenants-in-chief. They, in turn, collected it from their sub-tenants.

THE INCIDENTS OF KNIGHT SERVICE

11. Importance of the incidents. There were many important incidents of knight service, most of them of a burdensome nature. The exaction of these incidents resulted in great unrest, which led directly to the movement for *Magna Carta*. Some of the principal incidents are discussed at **12–19** below.

12. Homage. The homage of the tenant was expressed formally and publicly in the oath taken to serve his lord. "I become your man for the land which I hold of you, and I will bear you faith in life and honour against all men, saving the faith due to the King." Hence, to break allegiance to one's lord was one of the most serious of all known offences.

13. Relief. When a tenant succeeded to land on the death of the former tenant the lord claimed a sum of money, known as a *relief*.

(a) Where the relief was paid on the death of a tenant the heir had immediate possession.

(b) The relief of a knight was fixed by *Magna Carta* at 100s., and of an earl or baron at £100.

(c) Where the land was held directly of the king, an official inquest to decide who was the heir was held by an official *escheator*. The king had a right (*primer seisin*) to enter land in these circumstances and to hold it for a year and a day. Thus, an heir was allowed to enter only after doing homage and paying the appropriate relief.

(*d*) A *mesne lord*, *i.e.* one who held of a superior lord, had a similar right (*simple seisin*) which could be exercised only if the heir did not pay the relief.

14. Suit of court. *See* XII, 5. Tenants had a duty to attend the court held by their lord, and to perform duties concerning the court.

15. Aids. In certain emergencies the tenant was obliged to provide aid for his lord, *e.g.* help in paying scutage and other debts and fines.

(*a*) *Magna Carta, c. 12*, limited aids which could be demanded without the consent of the *commune concilium* to:

    (*i*) ransoming the lord when he was imprisoned;

    (*ii*) helping the lord to provide a dowry for his daughter (*pur file marier*);

    (*iii*) helping the lord with expenses necessary to make his son a knight (*pur fitz chevalier*).

(*b*) In 1275, the *Statute of Westminster I*, fixed the aids of sub-tenants at 20*s*. for a knight's fee, and for £20 value of land held in socage. In 1351 aids of the king's tenants-in-chief were fixed at these amounts.

16. Wardship. Where a male heir was under 21, or a female under 14, the lord was entitled to wardship.

(*a*) He had custody of the lands until the tenant came of age, and was not obliged to account for profits or waste.

(*b*) When the heir or heiress reached the age of majority, they were obliged to "sue out their livery" (*ousterlemain*) and thus obtain delivery of the land.

(*c*) This involved their paying half a year's profits in lieu of all reliefs.

17. Marriage. In the twelfth century the king demanded that he should be consulted by his barons when their daughters wished to marry. Where the baron was dead, the king could give the daughters in marriage and could dispose of their lands.

These measures reflected the king's anxiety concerning alliances of his tenants-in-chief through marriage.

(a) The right of giving female wards in marriage was exercised by the lords and was extended to any daughter who was the presumptive heir of a vassal.

(b) The right was later extended to males by the *Statute of Merton*, 1236.

(c) The lord's offer of a spouse had to take into account the status of the ward.

(d) If a ward refused a match arranged by the lord it resulted in the forfeiture of a sum equal to the so-called "value of the marriage" (*valorem maritagii*), *i.e.* the amount which the suitor was prepared to pay to the lord. If the wards married without the consent of the lord they forfeited double that amount (*duplicem valorem maritagii*).

18. Escheat and forfeiture. Where a tenant committed a felony and was convicted, his land escheated to his lord after the king had held it for a year and a day. This was escheat *propter delictum tenentis*. The lands of one convicted of treason were forfeited to the crown. Escheat *propter defectum sanguinis* took place on failure of legal heirs.

19. Decline of knight service. The onerous nature of these incidents, the growth of scutage and the generally anachronistic nature of this form of tenure led to its abolition under the *Military Tenures Abolition Act*, 1660. The Act abolished the incidents of knight service and declared that lands held by military tenure were to be held under free and common socage.

SERJEANTY

20. Origin. Tenancy by serjeanty may have originated in personal services rendered to the king.

(a) The tenant was bound to carry out a personal service, *e.g.* carrying the royal banner, acting as chamberlain, etc.

(b) This was the appropriate form of tenure in the case of the king's household officers, *e.g.* his steward, marshal, constable.

(c) Mesne lords made grants of serjeanty to those who performed similar services for their households.

21. Grand and petty serjeanty. *Grand serjeanty* was the term applied to tenure enjoyed by the great nobles. *Petty serjeanty* was applied to tenure which involved rendering only a minor service to the lord. These incidents of petty serjeanty were not affected by the 1660 Act.

22. Decline of serjeanty. As the affairs of the royal household became more complex, the necessity for the duties and services required from the holders by serjeanty diminished. Grand serjeanty was converted into a type of socage, but some of the incidents were preserved.

SPIRITUAL TENURE

23. Frankalmoin (= free alms). This tenure had its origins in the Anglo-Saxon era. Lands were granted to the church in return for prayers and masses for the souls of the grantor and his family. It did not involve an oath of fealty. Under the *Constitutions of Clarendon*, 1164, *c.* 9, it was enacted that in disputes between laymen and clerks as to whether land was held in frankalmoin, the chief justice was to decide the matter with the aid of recognition by "twelve lawful men." Frankalmoin became obsolete.

24. Divine service. Tenure in this mode obliged the tenant to say a mass at regular intervals. Fealty was demanded. The tenure was abolished in 1660.

FREE SOCAGE

25. Origin. Socage was a residual tenure, *i.e.* tenure which was neither military, nor spiritual, nor servile. Its name is derived from the *socmen* who sought the protection of a lord. It was created by appropriate words of grant, together with *livery of seisin (see* XXIV).

26. Details of the tenure.

(*a*) Fealty was demanded. Escheats and aids were also involved. Relief was limited in the fourteenth century to one year's rent. Wardship did not apply.

(*b*) Guardianship of an infant socage tenant fell upon the

nearest relative who was unable to inherit. *The Statute of Marlborough*, 1267, enacted that the guardian was liable to an action for account brought by the ward, and that he was forbidden to sell the ward in marriage.

(c) Tenure involved either a fixed rent in money, or some semi-servile service, *e.g.* responsibility for ploughing the lord's fields on one or more days during the year.

(d) Freedom of the tenure from the more onerous incidents of knight service increased its popularity.

27. Other forms of socage tenure. Two other forms of socage tenure were:

(a) *Burgage.* Tenure in burgage applied to land in certain ancient boroughs held by the burgesses for fixed rents or services. One custom which applied to this tenure was known as *borough English* (applying to Surrey, Sussex, and the non-French localities of Nottingham) under which the land descended to the youngest son.

(b) *Gavelkind.* (*Gafolcund* = yielding rent). The inhabitants of Kent received various favours from the Conqueror, and *gavelkind* applied to socage land there. The tenure involved fealty and suit of court.

(i) The land could be alienated by a tenant (by *feoffment*) at the age of 15.

(ii) The land was not liable to escheat for felony.

(iii) The land could be devised.

(iv) In a case of intestacy the land descended to all the sons equally.

(v) A husband surviving his wife was entitled, until remarriage, to a life estate in one half of her land.

UNFREE TENURE

28. Privileged villein tenure. Unfree tenures could be in the hands of tenants who were free or unfree. The unfree tenants were known as villeins. Such tenures could not be the basis of real actions and were not recognised in the king's courts until the fifteenth century.

(a) *Privileged villein tenure* involved duties, usually of an agricultural or domestic character, which were servile in nature. These services were fixed in character and time.

(*b*) *Pure villein tenure* involved services rendered by the tenant which were uncertain in character and time.

29. Development of unfree tenure. The development of unfree tenure, or copyhold, came during the fifteenth century, when copyhold was recognised by the courts. Thus, trespass became available to the copyholder as a remedy. In the next century the Star Chamber acted so as to prevent the extortion of arbitrary penalties from copyholders by their lords. The right to enfranchise copyhold tenure (*i.e.* by obtaining a grant of the freehold interest from the lord) was extended under the *Copyhold Act*, 1894, so that enfranchisement could be made (by the Minister of Agriculture) without the consent of either party. Copyhold tenure was abolished in 1922.

ESTATES

30. The doctrine of estates. *Tenure* applies to the *conditions* under which land was held. *Estate* applies to the *length of time* for which the tenant was entitled to hold the land. "All estates are but times of their continuances" (Bacon). It was established early in the development of land law that:

(*a*) Estates varied according to their duration.
(*b*) Estates could be freehold, or less than freehold.
(*c*) Several persons could own estates in the same land simultaneously.

31. Classification of estates. The common law classification of estates was as follows:

(*a*) *Freehold estates* (*i.e.* estates whose duration is not known):

(*i*) Estate in fee simple.
(*ii*) Estate in fee tail.
(*iii*) Estate for life.
(*iv*) Estate *pur autre vie*.

(*b*) *Less than freehold estates* (*i.e.* where the duration is certain), *e.g.*:

(*i*) Leaseholds for a fixed term of years.
(*ii*) Tenancies from year to year.

FREEHOLD ESTATES

32. Estate in fee simple. The fee simple is the largest estate in terms of duration.

(a) *Fee* (*feodum* = a fief) indicates that the estate is inheritable.

(b) *Simple* indicates that the estate is inheritable by the heirs of the owner with no conditions as to tail (*see* **33** below).

(c) So, a grant "to X and his heirs" indicates that the estate will endure for as long as the person who is entitled to it at any point in time leaves an heir.

(d) In *Shelley's Case* (1581) 1 Rep. 88b, it was declared that: "It is a rule of law where the ancestor by any gift or conveyance takes an estate of freehold, and in the same gift or conveyance an estate is limited either mediately or immediately to his heirs in fee or tail that always in such cases 'the heirs' are words of limitation of the estate and not words of purchase."

(i) Thus, where a freehold was granted "to X for life remainder to his heirs (or the heirs of his body)" the word "heirs" was construed as a term of limitation, and X took an estate in fee simple.

(ii) The rule was abolished under the *Law of Property Act, 1925, s.* 131.

33. Estate in fee tail. (*Taillé* = cut). The estate tail is inheritable only by the specific descendants of the original grantee.

(a) An estate was granted "to X and the heirs of his body.' This gave X a fee simple conditional on the birth of children to him.

(b) *The Statute De Donis Conditionalibus*, 1285, which is contained in the *Statute of Westminster II*, abrogated this rule, and from that time a phrase as in (a) above created a *fee tail*.

(c) The fee tail descended, on the death of the tenant in tail, to his lineal heirs. It would cease to exist if the issue of the original tenant in tail were to die out.

(d) The Statute enabled an heir to use a *writ of formedon* against a grantee from the tenant in tail. This was known as the *writ in the descender*. A reversioner, where issue had failed, was able to use a *writ in the reverter*.

(e) Although *De Donis* had enacted that a fine (which was part of the collusive action of fines and recoveries (*see* XXIV, 11)) used to bar an entail (*i.e.* converting it to a fee simple) would be void, this was later altered in 1540. After that date a fine could be used to bind issue in tail. The estate known as a *base fee* was created—this was a fee simple which would end when the issue of the original tenant in tail died out.

(f) *De Donis* had no application to leaseholds or copyholds.

(g) In 1833 fines and recoveries were abolished under the *Fines and Recoveries Act*.

NOTE: The grant "to X and the heirs of his body" may have had its origin in the old *maritagium* (marriage portion) intended to provide for a family.

34. Life estate. This was an estate which the grantee holds for his life, *e.g.* "to X during his life."

(a) In the twelfth century this was the largest interest in land and was used in the creation of a feudal grant by a lord to his tenant.

(b) It did not, at first, bestow on the grantee the power to alienate, since unfettered alienation might have resulted in the land passing to an enemy of the lord.

(c) *Quia Emptores* (*see* 7 above) removed many restraints on alienation, and gradually the inheritable fee (*i.e.* the fee simple) came to be an estate greater than the life interest.

(d) The *Settled Lands Acts*, 1882–90, allowed a life tenant to alienate the entire fee simple.

(e) Under modern law the life interest is an equitable interest.

35. Life interest pur autre vie. (For another's life). The interest *pur autre vie* was created where there was a limitation "to X for the life of Y." In such a case X is the *tenant pur autre vie*, and Y is the *cestui que vie*.

(a) If a person who is entitled to an estate for his own life assigns his interest to another, that other person becomes the *tenant pur autre vie*.

(b) The *tenant pur autre vie* could alienate during his

lifetime, and following his death the alienee could hold for the life of the *cestui que vie*.

LEASEHOLDS

36. Origins of the leasehold. The leasehold originated in an agreement between the owner of land and a *termor, i.e.* a tenant holding land for a term of years. The term, and the conditions of holding, were definite. In many cases the agreement, which took the form of a covenant, was used in cases where money had been loaned and security was provided. In such cases the lease ended when the loan was repaid.

37. Nature of the leasehold. A lease created for a "term of years absolute" is a lease which should last for a stated and fixed period, although it may be determined before the stated end of the period, *e.g.* by service of notice to quit. "Term of years" also includes a term for less than a year, for one year, or from year to year.

(a) By the fifteenth century a lessee was able to recover possession of the land from strangers (*see* XXIV, **16–19**).

(b) Leases were classified as *chattels real*. See XXIV, **19**(b).

(c) Under the common law, in the case of a lease which did not take effect under the *Statute of Uses*, a lessee did not acquire an estate in the land unless he entered into possession. Until he had entered, his right to take possession was known as *interesse termini* ("interest of a term"). This doctrine was abolished under the *Law of Property Act*, 1925, s. 149(1).

FUTURE ESTATES IN LAND

38. Meaning of a future estate. Where an estate is limited so that it is to come into existence at some future time it is referred to as a *future estate*. Thus, a grant "To X for life and then to the first of his sons to attain 21," creates estates which are to take effect at a time in the future. The estate *in expectancy* took effect on the cessation of the estate *in possession*.

39. Reversions and remainders. The common law classified future estates as reversions and remainders.

(a) *A reversion.* A reversion was created where land was granted by an owner for an estate which was less than his. "A reversion is where the residue of the estate always doth continue in him that made the particular estate" (Coke). Thus, if X, who owns the fee simple in Blackacre, grants Blackacre to Y for life, X has a reversion, since, upon Y's death, the land will revert to X.

(b) *A remainder.* "A remnant of an estate in lands or tenements, expectant upon a particular estate created together with the same at one time" (Coke). So, in a grant "To X for life, and then to Y in fee simple," X is entitled to actual possession, his estate being known as the *particular estate,* and Y's estate is known as a *remainder,* Y being known as the *remainderman.*

(i) *Vested remainders* are those ready to come into possession immediately the particular estate is determined. The common law recognised this type of remainder only at the end of the fourteenth century.

(ii) *Contingent remainders* were limited so that they depended on an event which might never have happened until after the particular estate had been determined. Thus, in a grant "To X for life, and then to Y if he has attained 21," Y would be unable to take if he had not attained 21, at the time of X's death.

40. The common law limitations on remainders.

Continuity of *seisin* (*see* XXIV) was essential in the eyes of the common law, and no conveyance could be tolerated which would result in any interruption of the tenancy of the estate. The following strict rules were formulated:

(a) The limitation of a remainder was void unless limited after a particular estate of freehold. So "To X for life on attaining his majority" would have been void.

(b) The limitation of a remainder after a fee simple was void. "A fee may not be mounted on a fee."

(c) A contingent remainder was void where it was so limited that it would take effect by cutting short the particular estate. The remainder could take effect only upon the *natural determination* of the particular estate.

(d) A contingent remainder had to be limited so that it would vest during the existence of the particular estate, or immediately upon the determination of that estate. So, a grant "To X for life and, two years after the death of X, to Y for life" would have been void.

41. Executory interests. The common law remainder rules did not apply in the case of *legal executory interests*, which were created:

(*a*) Where a grant by deed was made after the *Statute of Uses*, 1535.

(*b*) Where a grant by will was made after the *Statute of Wills*, 1540, by a use or by direct grant to the beneficiaries.

NOTE: The exception to this was the rule in *Purefoy* v. *Rogers* (1671) 2 Wms.Saund.380, whereby a limitation would be construed and treated as a remainder, and *not* as an executory interest, if that were possible as at the time of the grant.

42. Equitable future interests. Following the *Statute of Uses*, a grant "Unto X and his heirs to the use of Y for life, remainder to the use of Z for life" created a double use which gave the beneficiaries equitable interests. The common law remainder rules, and the rule in *Purefoy* v. *Rogers* had no application.

NOTE: (*i*) The rule in *Purefoy* v. *Rogers* was abrogated under the *Contingency Remainders Act*, 1877.

(*ii*) Under the modern law, after 1925, all future freehold interests are equitable, and the remainder rules no longer apply to them.

PROGRESS TEST 23

1. Explain the concept of tenure. **(5)**

2. What was the effect of *Quia Emptores*, 1290? **(7)**

3. Enumerate the principal forms of tenure in the reign of Edward I. **(8)**

4. Explain the origin of knight service. **(9)**

5. Enumerate the principal incidents of knight service. **(12–18)**

6. Explain (*a*) *primer seisin*, (*b*) *ousterlemain*. **(13, 16)**

7. Explain (*a*) *valorem maritagii*, (*b*) *escheat propter delictum tenentis*. **(17, 18)**

8. How did serjeanty originate, and why did it decline? **(20, 22)**

9. Explain (*a*) *frankalmoin*, (*b*) *borough English*, (*c*) *gavelkind*. **(23, 27)**

10. What was the common law classification of estates? **(31)**

11. What was the significance of (a) *Shelley's Case* (1581), (b) *De Donis Conditionalibus*, 1285?   **(32, 33)**

12. What was the origin of the leasehold?   **(36)**

13. What were the common law limitations on remainders? **(40)**

CHAPTER XXIV

THE DEVELOPMENT OF LAND LAW—2

SEISIN

1. Its meaning. *Seisin* was a feudal concept which arose out of the relationship of a tenant to his land. In early law the courts were concerned more with the protection of *possession* of land than with the protection of *ownership*. In an era when title to land was often unwritten, possession was proved more easily than ownership.

(*a*) Possession (*i.e.* physical occupation of land) was referred to as *seisin*.

(*b*) An estate in freehold involved a *right to seisin*; but the owner of such an estate might not necessarily be seised of the land.

2. Its importance. The concept of *seisin* was fundamental to much of the medieval land law.

(*a*) *Proof of seisin was required* in actions for the recovery of land (*see* **15** below).

(*b*) *The feudal services were enforced* only against the person seised of the land.

(*c*) *Abeyance of seisin* was forbidden, *i.e.* the tenancy was to continue without interruption.

(*d*) *Public delivery of seisin* in the case of the transfer of a freehold estate was essential.

3. Position of the disseisee. The person who was disseised lost all his beneficial rights to the land.

(*a*) He lost the right to alienate the land (until the *Real Property Act*, 1845).

(*b*) His widow had no right to dower (*i.e.* "that portion of lands or tenements which the wife hath for term of her life of the lands or tenements of her husband after his decease for the sustenance of herself and the nurture and education of her children": Coke. The right was usually to one-third of the husband's freehold lands.)

(c) His lord was not entitled to wardship if he (the disseisee) died leaving an infant heir.

(d) Under the principle *seisina facit stipitem* (*seisin* makes the stock of descent) he was considered to have left nothing to be inherited by an heir if he died intestate. His heir succeeded to no more than a right of action.

(e) He had no more than a right of entry.

4. Position of the disseisor. He was entitled to exercise the rights of an owner.

(a) He could make a so-called *tortious feoffment*, by which he conveyed the fee simple. This conveyance was effective until succesfully challenged in an action.

(b) He could exercise rights appendant to the land.

(c) After the *Wills Act*, 1540, he could devise the land.

(d) His heir succeeded if he died intestate, and his wife could claim dower.

5. Seisin in law and in deed. *Seisin in law* referred to the *seisin* possessed by an heir whose ancestor had died intestate and seised of the land, where no person had taken actual possession. *Seisin in deed* referred to actual possession of the freehold.

CONVEYANCING

6. Early restrictions on the conveyancing of land. Conveyancing refers to the modes in which interests in land are created and transferred. It was essential that a lord should know (and approve) of a transfer of land. Hence the power to dispose of land freely was restricted considerably.

(a) The freehold estate could not be devised. Transfer of land by will was not in accordance with the practice of public transfer (*see* (c) below).

(b) Transferees could not free themselves from the burdensome feudal incidents.

(c) A conveyance had to be made so that it took effect at once. Under no circumstances could *seisin* be in abeyance.

Hence the forms of interests in land which could be created by conveyance were very few.

(d) A conveyance had to be made in public with appropriate formalities (see **9** below).

7. The creation of the trust. See X, 3–12. By putting lands into trust certain disadvantages of common law tenure were avoided.

(a) *It became possible to devise lands.*

(b) *Settlements of land were made easier.* The trust allowed the creation of equitable estates which were employed so that an owner of land could decide the order in which interests were to take effect.

(c) *Conveyances of land were made easier.* The transfer of a use required few formalities.

(d) *Forfeiture and escheat could be avoided.*

(e) *The Mortmain Statutes could be evaded.* Under these Statutes the licence of the king and the lord was required in order to grant land to a corporation. Without a licence the land was forfeited. The employment of the trust, whereby land was held to the use of a corporation, evaded this enactment.

(f) *Certain feudal incidents could be avoided.* The death of a *cestui que use* (see X, **4**) did not create any right to feudal dues, *e.g.* wardship. These dues arose from tenure, and the trust was not considered as a subject of tenure, since it arose from a "moral obligation."

CONVEYANCING OF FREEHOLD INTERESTS

8. Modes of conveyancing. Freehold interests could be conveyed in two ways:

(a) By act of the parties (see **9** below).

(b) By entry on the court rolls of the common law courts (see **11** below).

9. Conveyance of the freehold by act of the parties. The usual method was by *feoffment of fee with livery of seisin.*

(a) The grantor (X) and the grantee (Y) stood within sight of the land to be conveyed (*livery in law*). X made a symbolic delivery of the property by handing to Y a turf or a tree branch. X then spoke the appropriate *words of donation* (*i.e.* words which stated the nature of the interest which was being conveyed). Coke gives an example of such words: "I give you yonder land to you and your heirs, and go enter into the same, and take possession thereof accordingly." Y's *seisin* was not complete until he had entered upon the property.

(*b*) The grantor (X) and the grantee (Y) stood upon the land to be conveyed (*livery in deed*) and X invited Y to enter, declaring that the turf or tree branch or other object was delivered to Y as a token of seisin of the land.

(*c*) Under the *Real Property Act*, 1845, feoffments of land (*i.e.* conveyance by overt and public delivery of possession) had to be made by deed.

(*d*) *The Law of Property Act*, 1925, *s*. 51(1), abolished conveyance of all lands and interests by livery or livery and seisin, or by feoffment, or by bargain and sale (*see* **10** below).

10. Bargain and sale; lease and release. These modes of conveyance became popular after the Statute of Uses (*see* X, **9**).

(*a*) X, the vendor, entered into a contract to sell land to Y, and received the purchase price—X had *bargained and sold* a fee simple to Y. X made no feoffment, but was considered seised to the use of Y.

(*b*) Under the *Statute of Uses* Y would obtain the legal estate. Hence, this method would have provided a means of conveying a legal estate without an overt and public declaration.

(*c*) The *Statute of Enrolments*, 1535, prohibited the passing of an estate of inheritance or freehold, or the creation of a use, by bargain and sale, unless the bargain and sale had been made by deed and enrolled in a Court of Record.

(*d*) The *Statute of Enrolments* did *not* apply to leaseholds. The following transaction, known as *lease and release*, and ascribed to Serjeant Francis Moore, in the reign of James I, came to be employed. Its employment was accepted in *Lutwich* v. *Mitton* (1621) Cro.Jac.604. This was the procedure:

(*i*) X bargained and sold the land to Y for one year (*i.e.* as a leasehold property).

(*ii*) X was seised to the use of Y on payment of the price.

(*iii*) The legal estate passed to Y (by the *Statute of Uses*), but the reversion remained in X.

(*iv*) On the following day X extinguished his reversion by a deed of release. As a result, Y's leasehold became a fee simple.

NOTE: In 1841 a release alone was substituted for lease and release. Under the *Real Property Act*, 1845, a deed of grant replaced the release.

11. Conveyance by entry on the court rolls of the common law courts. Entry of a conveyance on the court rolls was binding upon the parties. The main modes of entry were the *fine* and the *recovery*.

(*a*) *The fine (finalis concordia).* A writ was issued, followed by permission from the court to compromise the action (*licentia concordandi*). The agreement of the parties was recorded in the *pedes finium* (*see* V, **16**(*b*)) which included details of the property.

(*b*) *The recovery.* This was another collusive action. A writ of right was issued, following which the grantor asked the court for permission to *imparl*. An *imparlance* was a discussion between plaintiff and defendant in order to arrive at a settlement. The grantor did not return to court after the fictitious imparlance, and judgment in default was given against him and in favour of the grantee.

NOTE: (*i*) Transfer of the property in the case of fine and recovery involved a later overt *livery of seisin*, unless the grantee was already in possession.

(*ii*) Fines and recoveries were abolished in 1833.

THE CONVEYANCING OF LEASEHOLDS AND COPYHOLDS

12. Leaseholds. Under the *Statute of Frauds*, 1667, ss. 1, 2, it was enacted that leases (which formerly could be granted by word of mouth) had to be in writing.

(*a*) The Statute enacted that the writing was to be signed by the parties making the lease, or by their authorised agents. If not in writing, the agreement would operate only as a lease at will.

(*b*) There was an exception in the case of a lease not exceeding a term of three years in which the rent reserved was at least two-thirds of the full annual value.

(*c*) Under the *Real Property Act*, 1845, leases required to be in writing under the *Statute of Frauds* were considered void for the purpose of the creation or conveyance of a legal estate unless made by deed.

13. Copyholds.

The alienation by copyholders of their estates by feoffment was forbidden, since they were merely tenants at will. Because they were not seised of their estates they were forbidden to employ a conveyance based on the *Statute of Uses*.

(*a*) By custom of the manor a copyholder could transfer his estate by *surrendering* it to the lord of the manor. The lord then granted it (by *admittance* entered in the court rolls) to the person who was named in the surrender.

(*b*) The surrender could be made in or out of court to the lord in person, or to his steward, or bailiff.

(*c*) The surrenderor remained the tenant until the surrenderee was admitted.

(*d*) At a later date the vendor of a copyhold entered into a covenant to surrender to the use of the purchaser. This created an equitable estate by which the purchaser could obtain a vesting order if there was a failure to perform the covenant.

ACTIONS FOR THE RECOVERY OF LAND

14. The recovery of freeholds.

The principal actions for the recovery of freeholds were:

(*a*) The Writ of Right (*see* VI, **15**).
(*b*) The Possessory Assizes (*see* VI, **17–20**).
(*c*) The Writ of Entry (*see* VI, **21–23**).
(*d*) The Action of Ejectment (*see* VII, **3**).

15. Seisin and the actions for recovery.

Seisin was the basis of the right of a tenant to an action. He was obliged to prove that his *seisin*, or his right to *seisin*, had suffered some interference. The possessory assizes were concerned with the *restoration of seisin*. The writ of entry was concerned with *disseisin*.

The object of these actions was the protection of *seisin*, rather than the determination of questions of ownership.

ACTIONS FOR THE RECOVERY OF LEASES

16. Action of Covenant. Where a covenant had been made between lessor and lessee, there was an action of covenant against the lessor and his heirs. A successful action led to the recovery of the property.

17. Quare Ejecit infra Terminum, *c*. 1235. This writ gave the lessee protection against the lessor, his heirs, *and against the assignees of the lessor.*

18. Further developments.

(*a*) *Quare Clausum fregit, c.* 1245, gave the lessee an action for damages against a third party who had ejected him. He could not recover the land by use of this action.

(*b*) *Statute of Gloucester*, 1278, allowed a lessee to intervene in a collusive action brought against the lessor which could have resulted in the forfeiture of the estate.

(*c*) *De Ejectione Firmae, c.* 1310, allowed an action for damages (and later for the recovery of the land) against a person who had disturbed the possession of a lessee.

19. Availability of real actions to freeholders only. A leaseholder was considered to be possessed of the land, not *seised* of it. Consequently, if he were to be dispossessed the actions available to him were the *personal actions*. The *real actions* were available to freeholders only—they were *seised* of the land. Because of this:

(*a*) The term *real property* was confined to immovable property which could be recovered by a real action, *i.e.* freehold interests.

(*b*) The term *chattels real* was applied to leaseholds. "Chattels real are such as concern or savour of the realty; as terms for years of land . . . these are called real chattels, as being interests issuing out of or annexed to real estates; of which they have one quality, *viz.* immobility, which denominates them real, but want the other, *viz.* a sufficient legal indeterminate duration, and this want it is that constitutes them chattels": Blackstone.

(c) Thus, these historical distinctions based on the appropriate actions available, resulted in freehold interests being classified as *real property*, while leasehold interests are classified as a species of *personal property*.

PROGRESS TEST 24

1. What was the meaning of *seisin*?   **(1)**
2. Why was the idea of *seisin* of importance to medieval land law?   **(2)**
3. Explain (a) *seisina facit stipitem*, (b) *tortious feoffment*, (c) *seisin in law*.   **(3, 4, 5)**
4. Why were there restrictions on the conveyancing of land?   **(6)**
5. What were the advantages of putting lands into trust?   **(7)**
6. Explain (a) *livery in law*, (b) *livery in deed*.   **(9)**
7. Outline the procedure of lease and release.   **(10)**
8. Explain fines and recoveries.   **(11)**
9. Enumerate the principal actions which were available for the recovery of freeholds.   **(14)**
10. Explain the origin of the term *chattels real*.   **(19)**

TABLE SHOWING SOVEREIGNS AND DATES OF ACCESSION

House	Name	Year of accession
Norman	William I	1066
	William II	1087
	Henry I	1100
	Stephen	1135
Plantagenet	Henry II	1154
	Richard I	1189
	John	1199
	Henry III	1216
	Edward I	1272
	Edward II	1307
	Edward III	1327
	Richard II	1377
Lancaster	Henry IV	1399
	Henry V	1413
	Henry VI	1422
York	Edward IV	1461
	Edward V	1483
	Richard III	1483
Tudor	Henry VII	1485
	Henry VIII	1509
	Edward VI	1547
	Jane	1553
	Mary	1553
	Elizabeth I	1558
Stuart	James I	1603
	Charles I	1625
	The Commonwealth	*1649*
	The Protectorate	*1653*

House	Name	Year of accession
Stuart	Charles II	1660
	James II	1685
	William & Mary	1689–94
	William III	1694–1702
	Anne	1702
Hanover	George I	1714
	George II	1727
	George III	1760
	George IV	1820
	William IV	1830
	Victoria	1837
Saxe-Coburg	Edward VII	1901
Windsor	George V	1910
	Edward VIII	1936
	George VI	1936
	Elizabeth II	1952

APPENDIX II

BIBLIOGRAPHY

Reference Books

Holdsworth: *A History of English Law* (Methuen and Sweet & Maxwell).

Pollock and Maitland: *A History of English Law before the time of Edward I* (C.U.P.).

Source books.

Kiralfy: *Source Book of English Law* (Sweet & Maxwell).

Fifoot: *History and Sources of the Common Law, Tort and Contract* (Stevens).

Stubbs: *Select Charters* (O.U.P.).

Holdsworth: *Sources and Literature of English Law* (Clarendon Press).

Elton: *The Tudor Constitution, Documents and Commentary* (C.U.P.).

Kenyon: *The Stuart Constitution, Documents and Commentary* (C.U.P.).

Williams: *The 18th Century Constitution, Documents and Commentary* (C.U.P.).

Constitutional history.

Taswell-Langmead: *Constitutional History* (Sweet & Maxwell).

Adams: *Constitutional History of England* (Jonathan Cape).

Maitland: *Constitutional History of England* (C.U.P.).

General legal history.

Potter: *Historical Introduction to English Law and its Institutions* (Sweet & Maxwell).

Kiralfy: *Potter's Outlines of English Legal History* (Sweet & Maxwell).

Plucknett: *A Concise History of the Common Law* (Butterworth).

Radcliffe and Cross: *The English Legal System* (Butterworth).

Jenks: *A Short History of English Law* (Methuen).

Other topics.

Harding: *A Social History of English Law* (Penguin).
Maitland: *Forms of Action at Common Law* (C.U.P.).
Maitland: *Domesday Book and Beyond* (C.U.P.).
Allen: *Law in the Making* (O.U.P.).
Simpson: *An Introduction to the History of the Land Law* (Clarendon
  Press).

EXAMINATION TECHNIQUE

1. The general purpose of examinations in legal history. Public examinations in legal history are usually designed so as to test a student's understanding of the broad principles of the development of the law. A successful candidate in a first examination of this nature will have demonstrated his grasp of these principles and his ability to illustrate them with examples. The first examinations in legal history are *not* designed to test a student's memory concerning the *minutiae* of ancient practices and procedures. An awareness of the significance of *novel disseisin* counts for more than a knowledge of its detailed procedures. The place of the ordeal in the development of criminal procedure is of more importance than the priestly rites which accompanied it. Detail may often illuminate a bald statement of principle; mere detail, however, unrelated to a knowledge of principles is of little value.

2. Types of question. Questions on English legal history which are set in first examinations tend to be of two principal types:

(*a*) *The type demanding a purely factual answer, e.g.*

(*i*) Give an account of the jurisdiction and constitution of the Hundred Courts.

(*ii*) What was the scope and content of the *Judicature Acts*, 1873-75?

(*iii*) Why was the *Statute of Uses* enacted? How far was it successful in achieving its objects?

(*iv*) Trace the origins and development of King's Bench.

(*b*) *The type requiring a discussion, e.g.*

(*i*) "England had little cause to grieve for the passing of Star Chamber." Discuss.

(*ii*) How far would you agree with the aphorism: "Equity came to fulfil the law"?

(*iii*) Estimate the importance in English legal history of the king's peace.

(*iv*) How did the use of fictions by the courts aid the development of the common law?

3. The factual question. The answer required is one characterised by relevance, precision and understanding. Facts must be marshalled correctly and with attention to their significance.

Irrelevancies, side-issues, and dissertations beyond the scope of the question must be avoided. Thus, in 2(*a*) (*iii*) above, an examiner would expect from a candidate a clear understanding of the reasons why lands were put in use, why the king objected to this procedure, what he sought to limit by the enactment, what aspects of conveyancing by the device of the use failed to be caught by the Statute, etc.

4. The discussion question. Answers to this type of question must be characterised by a logical discussion based on a foundation of fact. The discussion should arise naturally out of the facts. Where there is assertion or speculation supporting facts must be given. The discussion should be relevant, clear, confined within the terms of the question, and designed to illustrate a knowledge of principles. Thus, 2 (*b*) (*ii*) above calls for a discussion on the origins and general development of equity. How and why did it arise? What was its initial relationship with common law? Has it ever sought to replace rather than supplement common law? Does its separate identity and development vitiate in any sense the meaning of the aphorism?

5. Technique in the examination room. The student's written examination in English legal history should be the culmination of a planned sequence of study and revision. Pre-examination revision must be planned and must be considered as essential as the initial learning of facts. In the examination room the following matters should be kept in mind carefully:

(*a*) The instructions must be read with great care.

(*b*) The time allowed for the examination (usually 2–3 hours) must be allocated to the answering of the exact number of questions required. To leave only a few minutes for the answering of the final question is to risk the loss of valuable marks.

(*c*) Plan each answer. A preliminary sketch of the answer is well worth the time spent on it. Dates, principles, matters of particular significance, must be called to mind and marshalled effectively.

(*d*) A few minutes should be left in order to look through the written answer so as to correct any errors of expression, of fact, etc.

Sample Question: Give an account of the General Eyre.
Suggested Answer:

A general eyre consisted of a detailed investigation by the king's itinerant justices into the affairs of the counties of the realm. Henry I had sent justices of the *Curia Regis* to travel through his realm in order to collect the royal revenues and to hear civil and criminal pleas. The itinerant justices became known as *Justices of the Eyre* (the term *eyre* meant "a hearing") and their functions were of a judicial, administrative, and supervisory nature. The session of the general eyre was held in the county towns and was a regular feature of the thirteenth century.

Before the visit of the justices took place, the sheriff was commanded to prepare an account of all the "doings, misdoings and non-doings" in the county since the time of the last eyre. The justices presented a series of interrogatories (the so-called *capitula itineris*) which covered administrative as well as judicial matters. Franchises had to be proved and claimed, account had to be given of the apprehension of suspected criminals, and coroners, together with other representatives of the hundreds and vills had to answer for the affairs of their communities.

Default was punished by fines, which were often heavy. Since one of the purposes of the eyre was the collection of money for the crown, fines were imposed on communities and individuals even for minor infringements of a royal right.

The Justices in Eyre also exercised an equitable jurisdiction as representatives of the king. In this role they were able to hear petitions without the issue of a formal writ. This jurisdiction was often exercised in the case of very poor litigants.

The general eyres became very unpopular. They were looked upon as providing the king with an opportunity of extorting money, in the form of amercements (money fines). So unpopular did the sessions of the eyre become, that in 1221 the inhabitants of the vills in Cornwall took to the woods during the visit of the justices, preferring to be punished for not attending the eyre rather than having to account to the justices in the fashion demanded by the eyre. All freeholders were required to attend an eyre, and this became a burden on the county.

Henry III was obliged to promise that eyres would be held only once in every seven years. As Parliament became more significant, the king looked to it for revenue, and the income derived from the eyre became of diminishing importance. "Compounding the eyre" by payment of money prior to the eyre became common. In the reign of Edward III the eyres were held infrequently, and the last eyre took place about 1340, in the reign of Richard II.

APPENDIX IV

SPECIMEN TEST PAPERS

Instructions:

1. Answer any *five* questions in each of the three papers.
2. The time allowed for each paper is *three hours*.
3. The test papers should be worked under examination conditions, *i.e.* without the use of any aids, such as textbooks or notes.

NOTE:

All the questions are taken from the University of London examinations. The year in which a question was set is indicated at the end of the question.

TEST PAPER 1

1. "A general proposition of some value may be advanced with respect to the agencies by which law is brought into harmony with society. These instrumentalities seem to me to be three in number, Legal Fictions, Equity and Legislation. Their historical order is that in which I have placed them". (Sir Henry Maine). Consider whether this proposition fits the facts of English legal history.   [1966]

2. What kinds of right might a lord have in respect of land held of him in knight service? How far was the development of English land law affected by the existence of those rights?   [1966]

3. Describe the law of contract in England before the rise of *assumpsit*.   [1965]

4. Trace the origin of (*a*) nuisance and (*b*) account.   [1964]

5. Describe the origin and jurisdiction of the Court of Star Chamber.   [1962]

6. "It is still too often said that English law can only be understood historically. Now English law may be bad, but is it really as bad as that?" (Plucknett). Discuss this statement in relation to *either* the modern judicial system *or* the modern law of property.   [1967]

7. How was the need for legislation met in the Anglo-Saxon age?   [1962]

323

8. For what purposes were lands put into uses? Explain the historical relationship between the use and the modern trust.

[1965]

9. Describe and assess the work and importance of *two* of the following:

(*i*) Glanvill;
(*ii*) Littleton;
(*iii*) Nottingham;
(*iv*) Hardwicke.   [1964]

TEST PAPER 2

1. What modes of proof were used in Anglo-Saxon times? How long did they survive?   [1962]

2. Explain the reasons for the enactment in 1535 of the *Statute of Uses* and the *Statute of Enrolments*.   [1964]

3. To what extent, and why, did criminal law and procedure develop in isolation from the other branches of the common law?   [1965]

4. "The modern law of contract bears the scars of its history." Do you agree?   [1966]

5. What were the defects of the common law of larceny? What was the explanation of these defects, and how were they remedied?   [1966]

6. What views have been advanced as to the origins of the jury? Discuss the change in the character and functions of the trial jury in English law.   [1964]

7. Explain the scope and limitations of the petty assizes. [1964]

8. How far do you think that the jurisdictional boundaries between courts were a factor in the substantive development of the common law?   [1965]

9. Describe the working, and assess the historical importance, of the action of debt.   [1967]

TEST PAPER 3

1. How and why did the writs of entry develop, and how did they work? In what sense can they be called "possessory"? [1965]

2. During most of our history there were no legal text-books in the modern sense. Why not? What took their place? [1967]

3. Explain the origins and importance of the division of crimes into felonies and misdemeanours.   [1964]

4. Trace the history of *either* defamation *or* the tort of negligence.   [1967]

5. Trace the history of the doctrine of consideration.   [1964]

6. Describe the mercantile courts and assess their contribution to the English legal system. [1964]

7. Outline the history of the Court of Admiralty and explain what contribution it made to English law. [1965]

8. "Equity gave new institutions, new remedies and new procedures." Explain and illustrate. [1964]

9. What were the disadvantages of the old system of forms of action? How far were these eliminated by the legislation of the 19th century? [1961]

INDEX